The Cybersecurity Playbook for Modern Enterprises

An end-to-end guide to preventing data breaches and cyber attacks

Jeremy Wittkop

Packt

BIRMINGHAM—MUMBAI

The Cybersecurity Playbook for Modern Enterprises

Group Product Manager: Vijin Boricha
Publishing Product Manager: Prachi Sawant
Senior Editor: Sangeeta Purkayastha
Content Development Editor: Nihar Kapadia
Technical Editor: Rajat Sharma
Copy Editor: Safis Editing
Project Coordinator: Shagun Saini
Proofreader: Safis Editing
Indexer: Manju Arasan
Production Designer: Roshan Kawale
Marketing Coordinator: Hemangi Lotlikar

First published: March 2022
Production reference: 1010222

Published by Packt Publishing Ltd.
Livery Place
35 Livery Street
Birmingham
B3 2PB, UK.

ISBN 978-1-80324-863-9

www.packt.com

To my wife, LeSean, for being my loving partner throughout our joint life journey. To every young person considering a career in cybersecurity. You will be on the front lines of the battle to defend our way of life for future generations.

– Jeremy Wittkop

Contributors

About the author

Jeremy Wittkop has spent the last decade architecting, implementing, and managing information protection programs for over a decade with a focus on helping multinational organizations comply with a changing regulatory landscape and protecting their most sensitive intellectual property. As InteliSecure's former chief technology officer, Jeremy was a foundational architect for InteliSecure's internationally recognized data protection, cloud security, and user and entity behavior analytics services. Jeremy is a trusted information protection thought-leader and a published author, blogger, public speaker, and advisor to clients as well as public and private equity investors.

Thank you to my wife, who always makes time in our busy lives to allow me to pursue my dreams. Also, thank you to my friend and technical editor, Cosmo, who is always there to make me laugh when I feel like frowning. A special thanks to the Packt team, you have been a pleasure to work with throughout.

About the reviewer

Cosmo Romero has worked in high-tech since 1998 and in cybersecurity since 2003. Cosmo has a bachelor's degree in high-tech management and has professional experience in networking, system administration, and cybersecurity. Today, Cosmo helps organizations adopt technology and services to secure data (Information Security) and manage the risk posed by trusted insiders (Insider Threat Management).

I would love to thank my family, friends, and mentors (you know who you are) for supporting me in reviewing this important work. Just know I could have never become me if it were not for all of you, so thank you! I love you all, everyone!

Table of Contents

3

Anatomy of an Attack

Section 2 – Building an Effective Program

4

Protecting People, Information, and Systems with Timeless Best Practices

5
Protecting against Common Attacks by Partnering with End Users

6
Information Security for a Changing World

Section 3 – Solutions to Common Problems

7

Difficulty Securing the Modern Enterprise (with Solutions!)

8

Harnessing Automation Opportunities

9

Cybersecurity at Home

Answers

Index

Other Books You May Enjoy

Preface

The world is becoming increasingly digitized. Businesses rely on information technology to allow them to compete in the modern economy. However, each innovation brings new threats and vulnerabilities that threaten our livelihoods, our identities, and the global economy. The threats we face have never been greater than they are today.

At the same time, we are facing a historic shortage of information security professionals who will help keep us safe. In the long term, we must attract more people to our field to help secure our environments and protect the most vulnerable among us. In the short term, we must build processes that maximize the people we have and the technologies available to us to defend against capable adversaries who seek to compromise our systems and steal our valuable information.

I wrote this book to share the knowledge I've gained over the last decade I've spent helping organizations defend against cyber threats. Too often, we get caught up in technology and tactics and forget to look at the big picture of what we are trying to accomplish. We see breaches in the headlines, but we fail to understand what went wrong and identify the lessons we can learn to enable a more secure future.

I am disheartened by stories I hear of people who want to get into cybersecurity but find it difficult to get started. We are desperate for talent in our discipline, and it is critical for us to make cybersecurity more accessible. It is my hope that those who read this book will be attracted to cybersecurity as a profession and will acquire the tools necessary to understand the space holistically.

Information is among the most valuable commodities in the world today. Our ability to protect it will determine the opportunities available to future generations.

Who this book is for

This book is for people who are considering a career in cybersecurity and need to understand the landscape. It is also for people who are in a single cybersecurity discipline who would like to expand their understanding to advance their careers. Finally, this book is for those who are skilled in cybersecurity but find it difficult to relate the concepts to non-technical people.

What this book covers

Chapter 1, Protecting People, Information, and Systems – a Growing Problem, introduces you to the modern cybersecurity landscape and provides examples of the problems we are facing.

Chapter 2, The Human Side of Cybersecurity, introduces the roles humans play in cybersecurity, on both the attacker and the defender sides. Cybersecurity is about people attacking people. While cybersecurity is new, the dynamics are as old as humanity itself.

Chapter 3, Anatomy of an Attack, introduces different attack types and how they typically happen. We will explore common techniques and what the attacker must accomplish to be successful.

Chapter 4, Protecting People, Information, and Systems with Timeless Best Practices, discusses how while many measures and countermeasures change with technology, some best practices are timeless and effective. We will explore these timeless best practices, which are rarely implemented effectively and could limit the damage caused by the majority of breaches.

Chapter 5, Protecting against Common Attacks by Partnering with End Users, discusses how people often think of security as the domain of a small team inside an environment. The best security programs partner with end users as the first and last lines of defense.

Chapter 6, Information Security for a Changing World, discusses how the pace of change is both faster than it has ever been and the slowest it will ever be. Change is the only constant, and it is accelerating. Future-proofing a security program requires a conceptual understanding of objectives that transcends technology.

Chapter 7, Difficulty Securing the Modern Enterprise (With Solutions!), looks at how there are a number of current challenges in the cybersecurity space with no easy answers. This chapter will talk about those challenges and provide recommendations for how you can solve them.

Chapter 8, Harnessing Automation Opportunities, discusses automation and how automation will not solve all of the problems associated with cybersecurity today. However, effective programs will find ways to use automation where appropriate to make people more effective.

Chapter 9, Cybersecurity at Home, looks at how, as the world is not just more dangerous for businesses, cybersecurity knowledge can also protect those who matter most to us at home.

To get the most out of this book

There are no prerequisites to reading this book other than an open mind, a positive attitude, and a thirst for knowledge.

Download the color images

We also provide a PDF file that has color images of the screenshots and diagrams used in this book. You can download it here: `https://static.packt-cdn.com/downloads/9781803248639_ColorImages.pdf`.

Get in touch

Feedback from our readers is always welcome.

General feedback: If you have questions about any aspect of this book, email us at `customercare@packtpub.com` and mention the book title in the subject of your message.

Errata: Although we have taken every care to ensure the accuracy of our content, mistakes do happen. If you have found a mistake in this book, we would be grateful if you would report this to us. Please visit `www.packtpub.com/support/errata` and fill in the form.

Piracy: If you come across any illegal copies of our works in any form on the internet, we would be grateful if you would provide us with the location address or website name. Please contact us at `copyright@packt.com` with a link to the material.

If you are interested in becoming an author: If there is a topic that you have expertise in and you are interested in either writing or contributing to a book, please visit `authors.packtpub.com`.

Share Your Thoughts

Once you've read , we'd love to hear your thoughts! Scan the QR code below to go straight to the Amazon review page for this book and share your feedback.

`https://packt.link/r/1803248637`

Your review is important to us and the tech community and will help us make sure we're delivering excellent quality content.

Section 1 – Modern Security Challenges

The world is changing at an ever-increasing pace. The flywheel of technological innovation is spinning at such a rate that traditional change management is obsolete and change leadership has become the norm. Each new technology that affects the modern workplace presents new challenges for the teams chartered with securing the organization's most important systems and information.

Few people understand the breadth of the global cybercrime community and the actors who play a role. Understanding how attacks happen and why is critical to building the proper defenses to secure a modern enterprise.

This part of the book comprises the following chapters:

1 Protecting People, Information, and Systems – a Growing Problem

Few people understand the sophistication of the global cybercrime community and the actors who play a role, understanding how attacks happen and why it is critical to build the proper defenses to secure the modern enterprise. The world is changing at an ever-increasing pace. The flywheel of technology innovation is spinning at such a rate that traditional change management is obsolete, and change leadership has become the norm. Each new technology that enhances the modern workplace presents new challenges for the teams chartered with securing the most important systems and information. It is impossible to predict the future, but by understanding timeless best practices, threats, and modern architectural techniques, it is possible to build a security posture that is flexible and resilient enough to meet current and future threats. Doing so is difficult and requires a deep strategic understanding of what you are trying to accomplish.

In this chapter, we will explore why cybercrime is appealing to criminals and the impact of cybercrime on the global community, introduce the core tenants of information security, and discuss the cybersecurity talent shortage. Throughout this chapter and the remainder of the book, we will explore example cases that provide real-world illustrations of the topics we will cover. At the end of each chapter, there are a few open-ended questions you should be able to answer in your own words after reading the chapter. After reading this chapter, you should be able to communicate these concepts to others and illustrate the main ideas with real-world examples.

In this chapter, we will cover the following topics:

- Why cybercrime is here to stay–a profitable business model
- The macro-economic cost of cybercrime
- The role of governments and regulation
- The foundational elements of security
- The cybersecurity talent shortage

Why cybercrime is here to stay - a profitable business model

In the year 2017, if cybercrime was a country, it would have the 13th highest GDP in the world, between South Korea and Australia. In 2021, according to a recent *Cybercrime Magazine* article, "*If it were measured as a country, then cybercrime — which is predicted to inflict damages totaling* $6 trillion USD *globally in 2021 — would be the world's third-largest economy after the U.S. and China.*" (Morgan, Cybercrime to Cost the World $10.5 Trillion Annually by 2025, 2020). The same article predicts that the number will grow to $10.5 trillion by 2025. Part of the reason for this growth is that cybercrime is an attractive proposition for attackers.

Cybercrime is a very profitable business with few risks. Think of a bank robber. Prior to the invention of the internet, if someone wanted to rob a bank, they would need to be in the same physical location as the bank and plan to physically enter the bank and demand money and get away from the bank with the money without being apprehended by the authorities. If someone were to undertake such a robbery and were not successful, there is a significant likelihood that they would be arrested, wounded, or killed. Cybercriminals can attempt to rob thousands of banks around the globe with little fear of repercussions. If their attack is unsuccessful, they can simply move on and target another bank. Compare the risks and effort involved with the example case given as follows:

Example Case: The GozNym Gang and the $100 Million Heist

In 2016, the GozNym gang, using a piece of malicious software known as a banking trojan by the same name, stole $100 million from individual bank accounts, mostly in the United States and Europe. The GozNym banking trojan was a piece of malicious software the gang could install that would wait for a user to log onto a bank account, and then transmit their credentials to a GozNym server. Once they had the credentials, "*certain members of the GozNym crew then used the stolen credentials to access the victim's bank account, to steal money from it, and launder the funds via US and foreign bank accounts controlled by the gang.*" (Vijayan, 2019)

This case was one of the few where the criminals were pursued across borders, and most were brought to justice. The numbers in this case are staggering. As a criminal endeavor, what other means outside of cybercrime could a criminal gang use to steal $100 million per year? Cybercrime is profitable and has a relatively low risk because a clever piece of software can victimize thousands of people with little effort on the part of the attacker. Adding to the allure for cybercriminals, in all but the largest cases, is that it is difficult to get the international cooperation necessary to identify the members of a criminal enterprise, find those people, and extradite them to another country for prosecution. In many cases, it is an open secret that criminal gangs are operating, and there is little political will to stop them. It is worth noting that this criminal gang chose to use traditional currency and bank accounts, which made them much easier to track. Criminal gangs using ransomware and cryptocurrency for payment are far less traceable. While their exploits are generally less lucrative, their risk of being caught is also far lower.

The Romanian city of Râmnicu Vâlcea is a well-known hotspot for cybercriminals. In this city, the cybercriminals are very wealthy and are unafraid to flaunt their wealth, since there is very little fear that they will be arrested and brought to justice. Cybercrime and the internet, along with anonymous cryptocurrencies and few global authorities with the power to pursue international criminals across jurisdictions, create the perfect conditions for the growth of cybercrime. While steps could be taken to curb the rise of cybercrime, in the current environment, it is incumbent on people and organizations to protect themselves.

Most people do not realize cybercriminals benefit from an entire underground economy hosted on the dark web. The dark web is not a place but is essentially a secretive network. Think of it as the dark side of the internet. Just like the regular internet, the dark web is a collection of websites. Unlike the internet, these websites are not indexed by most search engines and require a special browser known as **The Onion Router (TOR)**. The TOR browser is designed to make internet traffic anonymous, which is a key element for criminals in cyberspace to remain hidden. Most destinations on the dark web are not accessible to anyone who is browsing like they are on the traditional internet. The dark web is more akin to a collection of forums that have moderators and require invitations to gain access. The best example in the physical world is to think of the dark web as a network of speakeasies. Each has its own password and verifies the identities and intentions of its attendees, but once a person is accepted into a few and becomes a known entity in the underworld, they would have an easier time gaining access to other establishments.

The dark web itself serves two major purposes for cybercriminals. First, it provides access to marketplaces where stolen information can be bought and sold. Criminals may hack into a database such as Yahoo, for example, and steal millions of email addresses and passwords. The attacker may have no use for that information, so they can go to the dark web and offer it for sale. Other criminals can buy the information and use it for different purposes, such as launching a campaign against the list of email addresses to fool the user into clicking on a link or delivering a virus. Alternatively, attackers could use the email address and password combinations in popular sites to see whether the victim reuses their password so they can gain access to high-value sites to steal something of value. This underground economy provides an efficient marketplace where those who have the skills to steal data can profit from their work.

Second, the dark web offers marketplaces for criminals to purchase exploit kits containing phishing lures and malicious software or contract with other criminals for expertise they may not have. For example, if you wanted to deliver a ransomware attack, you could purchase the ransomware itself from one group, complete with documentation, instructions, and even technical support, and purchase a sophisticated phishing lure from another criminal and a list of potential victims from a third. TOR networks and botnets can be used to launch attacks to make their origins more difficult to trace. In fact, all you need to launch a relatively sophisticated and low-risk cyber-attack in the modern world is access to the dark web, a Bitcoin wallet, and a questionable moral compass.

Bitcoin and other cryptocurrencies make cybercrime more profitable and less dangerous. Whether you like or dislike cryptocurrency, there is little debate that its existence and the corresponding rise in the scale and profitability of cybercrime is no coincidence. Bitcoin is the most popular cryptocurrency. Cryptocurrencies operate on a technology known as blockchain. Blockchain is a distributed transaction ledger that allows the anonymous transfer of stored value between parties. For example, if you were to hold someone for ransom and asked them to pay you in United States dollars, somewhere there would be a record of that transaction, and with enough effort, the owner of the account, the kidnapper, would be identified. When ransoms are paid in Bitcoin, it is impossible to trace who the actual recipient of the money is or how they spent the money they received.

These factors lower the barriers to entry for cybercriminals to get into a profitable business. Never in human history has crime had higher rewards with lower risk. In fact, in some places throughout the world, there is a technically skilled population whose best economic prospects are to become criminals.

There is also a significant imbalance between the proceeds of cybercrime and the cost of cybercrime, which means the attackers are more motivated than the defenders. For every dollar cybercrime costs an economy, it generates $3 for the attacker. It stands to reason those attacks would continue to proliferate until balance is reached. If I could purchase something from you for $1 and sell it for $3, I would make as many purchases from you as I could. The equation for cybercrime is similar. While these macro-economic forces are unlikely to change in the short term, there are measures we can take to increase the costs and risks of cybercrime to make these attacks less appealing to criminals. Currently, it is far too easy for attackers to infect systems. People and organizations fail to follow simple best practices that make it significantly more difficult for attackers to be successful. Those best practices are explained in detail in *Chapter 4, Protecting People, Information, and Systems with Timeless Best Practices.*

Many people ask why cybercrime is growing and attacks are increasing in terms of scale, complexity, and frequency. The simple answer is that cybercrime is good business. If a person does not take moral issue with cybercrime, the economic opportunity is attractive, and the risk is lower than other criminal opportunities. In fact, economically speaking, cybercrime is the most lucrative profession available to many people around the world. However, there is another side to the equation. While criminals can benefit from crime, the damage to individual victims and economies is serious.

The macro-economic cost of cybercrime

The impacts of cybercrime on the global economy are significant. The impact of ransomware on infrastructure has been highlighted by the 2021 Colonial Pipeline ransomware attack, which is detailed in *Chapter 3*, *Anatomy of an Attack*. Colonial Pipeline supplied gasoline for large portions of the United States. With the pipeline offline, several states experienced gas shortages and gas prices rose significantly. The Equifax breach involved the personal information of millions of people, which contributes to the ongoing identity theft problem in industrialized nations. The American Semiconductor case, which began in 2011 and did not reach resolution until 2019, involved an existential threat to an American company that barely survived as a shell of its former self.

Each of these instances highlights the importance of cybersecurity in the modern world. Every organization, and even every person, has an interest and a responsibility in protecting their sensitive information.

While there are many direct and ancillary economic impacts of cybercrime, here are three major categories we should highlight. First, there is a global cost to identity theft. The implications for economies are significant, but behind the numbers are thousands of stories of individuals and families who have been hurt. Second, intellectual property forms the bedrock of Western economies. It could be said that all industrialized nations depend on intellectual property for prosperity; Western economies rely on personal property rights to power the economy. Finally, it is easy to lose sight of the damage done to individual companies and the employees who rely on them for their livelihood. When we look at the three major impacts of cybercrime, it is clear the damages can be devastating.

The global cost of identity theft

Identity theft has become a major problem globally. This problem impacts not only individuals but also entire economies. **Personally Identifiable Information** (**PII**) is information about an individual that can identify them from others and also could be used to impersonate them. National identifiers such as social security numbers, social insurance numbers, or other government-issued identifiers are commonly associated with PII, but other factors, such as names, phone numbers, and addresses, in combination can also be damaging. There is a well-established marketplace to buy stolen personal information on the dark web.

According to a CNBC article, "*identity fraud cost Americans a total of about $56 billion*" (Leonhardt, 2021) in 2020. Children are often victims and identity fraud costs generally fall directly on the consumer. As a result, a group of identity protection providers has emerged to help customers protect their identity, and if it is stolen, to pay legal fees to repair the damage. When companies lose large amounts of PII, the remedy is often to provide identity protection services for the impacted consumers.

Simply restoring an identity is not enough though. Many Western economies are consumer-driven, and if consumers are losing money to identity theft, they are not spending that money elsewhere in the economy. Therefore, the money lost to identity theft can be seen as economic leakage, causing downstream harm to businesses and individuals that are not victims of identity theft. In the United States, more than 1 in 100 people were victims of identity theft in 2020. The *data privacy regulations* discussed later in this chapter are the direct response from governments to this growing problem.

Intellectual property and Western economies

Most industrialized nations are built on the idea of personal property rights. Many times, those rights are dependent on the protection of intellectual property rights. It could be said, then, that the foundation of the global economy, with notable exceptions such as China, is the exclusivity of information and the ability for a person or a company to benefit economically from their ideas and discoveries. Theft of intellectual property threatens that foundation and if it cannot be protected, makes it less likely companies will invest in creating new inventions, and therefore the economy will not grow as quickly as it otherwise could.

To prevent this from happening, Western economies have developed intellectual property protections that encourage discovery and offer exclusive rights for a set period of time for the person or entity that made the discovery or created the work. Intellectual property comes in many forms, with varying time limits as well as degrees of protection. In some cases, an organization could protect intellectual property in different ways. For example, a secret recipe could be protected by a patent, which would give it strong legal protections for a set period of time, after which it would go into the public domain, and anyone could see the recipe and use it for themselves. Alternatively, the company could choose to classify it as a trade secret, which has limited legal protection but no requirement for disclosure. As a result, most companies who make recipes, outside the pharmaceutical industry, use trade secrets. However, using trade secrets requires a higher level of protection to keep it a secret. Protecting intellectual property appropriately requires an understanding of the property type and the legal protections offered. Let's have a look at them.

Copyrights

Copyrights are designed to protect works such as books, movies, and music. In the United States, a copyright must be registered with the Library of Congress for legal action to be taken, but copyright is granted as soon as a work is fixed in a tangible form, meaning committed to a hard drive, a piece of paper, or otherwise taken from an idea stage to a stage where it exists in the physical world.

Copyright grants five exclusive rights to an owner, which can then be licensed to others for the owner to earn income from their idea. Those five rights are the right to reproduce the work, publish the work, perform the work, display the work, or make derivatives from the work. Copyrights are normally long lasting, designed to last more than the lifetime of the person who created the work, but eventually, works do go into the public domain where others can use the work without paying the owner. Since copyrights are designed to protect the rights of the owner of a public work, there are few information security implications for protecting copyrights.

Patents

Patents are designed to give the owner an exclusive right to an invention for a relatively short period of time. After that time, the invention goes into the public domain and anyone can use it. The easiest example to understand is with medication. To incentivize pharmaceutical companies to invest capital in researching treatments and drugs, they are granted a period of time, generally between 10 and 20 years, where they are the only company that can sell that treatment or drug, and, within reason, they can charge whatever price they would like for it. When that time expires, other companies can access the formula and produce generic versions of the drug. When the patent for Tylenol expired, for example, anyone could use the formula to make generic acetaminophen, which is the same chemical formula as Tylenol; they just couldn't call it Tylenol because the brand name was protected by a trademark.

In the United States, patents must be filed with the United States Patent and Trademark Office, which is a lengthy process. There is a period of time between when something is being discovered and tested and when it is filed for patent protection, and during that time, that idea or invention is very sensitive and should be protected. Most countries around the world that offer patent protection have a similar patent office that allows inventors to register their inventions and apply for patent protection. Also, most countries that recognize patents will also enforce patents originating in other countries to encourage trade.

Trade secrets

Trade secrets offer limited legal protection but have the advantage of never going into the public domain. In the beginning, trade secrets were protected only to the extent that the organization could keep them a secret. In 2016, the Defend Trade Secrets Act was passed in the United States, which provided a forum for victims of trade secret theft to bring lawsuits against those who have stolen or otherwise misappropriated their trade secrets if the secrets were intended to be used in interstate or international commerce. In the Act, a trade secret is defined as "*all forms and types of financial, business, scientific, technical, economic, or engineering information, including patterns, plans, compilations, program devices, formulas, designs, prototypes, methods, techniques, processes, procedures, programs, or codes, whether tangible or intangible, and whether or how stored, compiled, or memorialized physically, electronically, graphically, photographically, or in writing.*" (American Bar Association, 2016). There is a major caveat though, in the fact that the victim must prove they took reasonable measures to keep the information secret.

Therefore, if a company is a victim of trade secret theft and would like to bring a case, they must show what security measures they had in place to defend the secret. As a result, protecting trade secrets has become one of the most important parts of an information security program with respect to intellectual property protection. Since this is a young law, there is little precedent with respect to what qualifies as a reasonable measure. The most high-profile case so far concerns Uber and Waymo.

Example Case: Uber versus Waymo

In January 2016, a Google engineer named Anthony Levandowski left Google's self-driving car division, known as Waymo, to start his own self-driving truck business, named Otto. In August of the same year, Otto was acquired by Uber. Shortly thereafter, Waymo filed a lawsuit against Uber for trade secret theft. In 2018, 5 days into the lawsuit's trial phase, a surprise settlement was reached for approximately $250 million in Uber stock. Mr. Levandowski was eventually forced to declare bankruptcy and was sentenced to 18 months in prison for trade secret theft.

The story is not as simple as an employee leaving for another firm and taking information with him. It appears that the hiring of Mr. Levandowski was planned by then Uber CEO Travis Kalanick. "'*I wanted to hire Anthony [Levandowski], and he wanted to start a company,' Kalanick said on Tuesday. 'So, I tried to come up with a situation where he could feel like he started a company, and I could feel like I hired him.*'"(Larson, 2018). The question then became, was Uber part of Mr. Levandowski's plot to steal trade secrets from Waymo? Did Travis Kalanick have advanced knowledge of the theft? The case was among the highest-profile trade secret theft cases in history.

This is a classic insider threat case. Anthony Levandowski was a very talented and well-respected engineer. He was trusted by his friends and colleagues at Google, who he ultimately betrayed. When he was hired, it is unlikely he intended to cause harm to Google. At some point, his motivation changed and he became a malicious insider. The civil lawsuit between Waymo and Uber was settled, and the criminal case against Mr. Levandowski ended in a plea agreement, so we may never know exactly how Google knew he stole documents on his way out. According to an article about the case published on *The Verge*'s website, "*Levandowski stole 14,000 documents from Google containing proprietary information about its self-driving cars and downloaded them on to his personal laptop.*" (Hawkins, 2019). While the article doesn't explicitly state what evidence Google had to support its claim, the fact they knew the number of documents and the method of exfiltration tells us two important things. First, they had a system in place to monitor transfers from a repository where sensitive information was hosted, likely in the cloud, and second, they had their system configured to identify the difference between sensitive information and commodity information. In short, Google had an effective information protection program. If they didn't, Uber would likely be using the information to gain a competitive advantage over Google, and Mr. Levandowski would be a very rich, free man.

Defending trade secrets is difficult, but it is important. Many organizations dedicate significant capital to research and development. If the output of that research is not properly protected, an organization can fail to realize the full value of their discoveries. While Google had to spend money to defend their trade secrets in court, ultimately, they were successful in gaining both financial and injunctive relief and are free to compete in the marketplace without a primary competitor having the ability to compete against them unfairly. Now that you are aware of how trade secrets function, let's move on to trademarks.

Trademarks

Trademarks are a type of intellectual property designed to allow the provider of a good or service to distinguish that good or service from others. The intention of a trademark is to avoid customer confusion. The protection prevents someone from creating a product to compete with a well-known brand and making the name of the product and the look of the packaging so similar that the customer cannot tell the difference. Trademarks are designed to be as widely publicized as possible, so there is little need for an information security program to focus on protecting them.

Now that you have had a brief introduction to intellectual property, we should move on to the impact of cybercrime. Throughout the book, there are example cases that are designed to highlight specific concepts related to the topics we are covering. It is easy to look into the details of a case and forget about the real people behind the cases.

Micro-level impacts and responses to cybercrime

In addition to the macro-economic implications, the stories behind the headlines involve real companies and real people who are being hurt. We will examine some select high-profile example cases throughout the book to discover what happened, how similar attacks could be prevented, and just how damaging the attack was for those involved. It should be noted that many of these cases have been studied enough where root causes have been identified. While there are lessons to glean from others, I caution you against simply trying to build detection and prevention mechanisms for these specific attacks. Many security systems have tried such approaches in the past, with poor results. Trying to guess how an attacker will attack you and building an alarm to identify that specific attack pattern is ineffective. It is far more effective to identify what should happen inside your environment and build systems and processes to detect and respond to anomalies.

Each of the cases is an example of the devastating impacts of cybercrime for someone. As you read the cases, please try not to focus only on what happened technically and how these types of incidents can be prevented tactically; try to also consider the impact of the incident on the victim, the company, and the attacker. In some cases, the case seems to end well for the attacker. In many cases, it does not.

The impacts of cybercrime can be devastating, but the benefit to the attacker still outweighs the cost to individual companies. In many cases, the macro-economic damage far outweighs the direct cost to the company that failed to protect information, especially when dealing with PII. As a result, governments have introduced regulations in an effort to compel companies to protect information that has been entrusted to them.

The role of governments and regulation

In response to escalating costs associated with personal data theft and the identity theft that follows, governments and industries around the world have passed regulations to compel companies to take their security programs seriously. While meaning well in their intentions, new regulations have led to a disjointed patchwork of requirements global organizations must comply with, which can be counterproductive. However, regulations will need to balance the equation between the costs of cybercrime and the benefits to attackers if they hope to stem the tide of cyber-attacks and the growing impact cybercrime is having on the global economy.

Industry regulation

Historically, information protection regulations were created on a per-industry basis. For example, in 2004, the world's largest credit card companies' council, known as the **Payment Card Industry** (**PCI**) Council, released the first **Payment Card Industry Data Security Standard** (**PCI-DSS**). This guidance was applicable to anyone who sought to store, process, or transmit payment card data and set certain requirements based on the number of transactions a company was involved in during a given year. In 1996, the United States passed the **Health Insurance Portability and Accountability Act** (**HIPAA**), which included privacy regulations for health-related data.

Industry regulations are often prescriptive and specific when defining what types of information should be protected and how. For example, PCI-DSS has 6 control objectives that organize 12 specific requirements for anyone storing, processing, or transmitting credit card information. Because the scope of data to be protected is so narrow, giving specific guidance to companies is feasible.

As time has passed, additional industry-specific regulations have given way to broader data privacy regulations passed by governments who were interested in curbing the economic effect of identity theft. Additionally, many of the regulations are designed to establish the rights of people to exert control over data used to identify them and define the responsibilities of the organizations that collect their data.

The growing need for data privacy regulation

The invention of computers and digital storage changed the nature of data collection and control over information. The digital age has made copying data and sharing it with others easier than ever before. As technology changed and outsourcing specific functions became more prevalent, individuals lost control over who had access to information that could cause them harm. There were a few rules related to how data could be handled and who it could be shared with. Furthermore, there was little transparency when a person provided their information about how it would be used and who it would be used by. Over the years, countless data breaches caused harm to individuals. In many cases, the organization that was breached had information belonging to individuals who had never provided their information directly. In response, governments began to pass regulations designed to establish data subject rights and severe penalties for those who violate them. The European Union's **General Data Privacy Regulation** (**GDPR**) has been the most impactful and well-known data privacy regulation.

GDPR

In 2016, the European Union sought to broaden regulations related to personal data and passed GDPR, which went into effect in 2018.

GDPR is made up of 11 chapters and 99 articles. It covers a wide variety of topics and seeks to establish data privacy as a basic right for European citizens and to give control to data subjects over how their data is used and processed. The 99 articles and 11 chapters of GDPR are detailed on the following website: `https://ec.europa.eu/info/law/law-topic/data-protection/data-protection-eu_en`.

Originally, much of the conversation about GDPR was about the harsh penalties that are laid out in the legislation. Companies can be fined up to 4% of their global revenue for violations of GDPR. However, the supervisory authorities have been mostly collaborative with companies who are trying to comply and protect data subjects' personal data and associated rights. Willful negligence or a failure to exercise due care with personal data can be punished severely.

Parts of GDPR are groundbreaking and have forced companies to adopt new best practices. For example, GDPR sets limits on how long data can be retained and forces companies to map how personal data flows throughout their organizations. Both are best practices for all types of sensitive data, but prior to GDPR, few companies understood their data well enough to comply with these provisions.

Unlike PCI-DSS, GDPR must cover a broad spectrum of companies and data types, so the requirements are far less specific. Also, the regulation was written to establish rights and responsibilities, so as technology changes, the methods of protecting information can change without amending the legislation.

Example Case: British Airways

British Airways suffered a data breach in 2018 that affected 400,000 customers. The **Information Commissioner's Office (ICO)** is the GDPR supervisory authority in Great Britain and therefore is assigned to British Airways. After the breach was made known, the ICO investigated the factors that led up to the breach of sensitive information. The ICO determined British Airways had security weaknesses in systems processing personal information that they knew about and failed to address. In addition, the ICO determined that more people were affected than necessary based on British Airways' failure to discover and remediate the issue in a timely manner. After the investigation, the ICO said, "*Their [British Airways'] failure to act was unacceptable and affected hundreds of thousands of people, which may have caused some anxiety and distress as a result. That's why we have issued BA with a £20m fine – our biggest to date.*" (Page, 2020)

The source of the breach was a known vulnerability in a third-party piece of JavaScript known as Modernizr, which British Airways used as part of its payment processing site. A hacking group was able to exploit the vulnerability to redirect personal and payment information to a website they owned, which caused criminals to gain access to crucial customer information. In many cases, companies claim they are the victim of an advanced attack when a breach occurs, but that was clearly not the case in this instance. According to a *Wired* article, "*The vulnerability in Modernizr is a well-known one, and BA had not updated it since 2012 – long after problems were known to exist.*" (Stokel-Walker, 2019). Even after the breach, the ICO found British Airways had failed to take adequate steps to secure their website.

The fine was significant because it was determined that British Airways was not only a victim of a cyber-attack, but they also failed to exercise due care to protect customer information, and as a result, consumers were harmed. This was the exact situation GDPR was developed to address. The legislation provides a method for supervisory authorities to compel companies to take the protection of PII seriously.

While the fine was record-breaking, it was reduced after an appeal by British Airways citing the COVID-19 pandemic and the damage it caused to their business. The original recommended fine was £183 million. Part of the reason for the reduction between the proposed amount and the settlement amount was in recognition of the improvements that British Airways made to prevent similar events from happening in the future.

For many years, organizations have ignored security best practices and put individuals' information at risk. Because of the pace of cyber-attacks, the brand damage is often short lived, and the cost of securing information could outweigh the benefits. The implementation and enforcement of GDPR has ensured securing personal information belonging to consumers is good business and not securing information appropriately carries severe consequences.

While GDPR is the best-known privacy regulation, there are several others around the world with similar goals that are also enforced. One of the challenges for multinational enterprises is keeping up with all the global regulations they are subject to and the changes to each.

Next, we will look at a law older than GDPR that is being updated to place a greater emphasis on individual rights to data.

Act on the Protection of Personal Information (APPI)

The next consequential legislation, Japan's **Act on the Protection of Personal Information** (**APPI**), predates GDPR. However, since the passage of GDPR, APPI has been updated to establish the rights of data subjects and the responsibilities of companies to protect personal information.

Japan's APPI predates GDPR and was originally passed on May 30, 2003. It has been amended several times, but the most recent amendment, passed in 2020, comes into effect in April 2022. The **International Association of Privacy Professionals** (**IAPP**) often writes about changes to international privacy regulations. You can find an article on the recent changes to APPI at the following link: `https://iapp.org/news/a/japan-enacts-the-act-on-the-protection-of-personal-information/`.

There is commonality between the objectives of APPI and the objectives of GDPR, but the rules are different. As a result, companies operating in Europe and Japan must build their security programs to meet the requirements of both jurisdictions.

California Consumer Privacy Act (CCPA)

It is difficult to operate globally and comply with different regulations between countries and regions. However, in the United States, the situation is much worse. In the absence of national data privacy regulations, many states have begun passing their own patchwork regulations. The most comprehensive and well-known is the **California Consumer Privacy Act** (**CCPA**), but there are separate pieces of legislation across many states that further complicate compliance efforts. CCPA was largely based on GDPR. However, it has fewer articles and has expanded the definition of personal information to include information that can be used in machine learning datasets. There is a good summary of CCPA provided by Thomson Reuters Westlaw at the following link: `https://govt.westlaw.com/calregs/Browse/Home/California/CaliforniaCodeofRegulations?guid=IEB210D8CA2114665A08AF8443F0245AD&originationContext=documenttoc&transitionType=Default&contextData=(sc.Default)`.

When studying regulations around the world, some common themes emerge:

- Data subjects own the data that identifies them. People who store, process, or transmit it are granted the license to do so only through consent and they do not own the information.
- Companies who collect information cannot sell or share that information without the consent of the data subjects.
- Data subjects should know exactly how data about them is being used.

There are many companies, such as advertising companies that curate lists and social media companies that trade *free* services for information about individuals that they can profit from, that are under direct attack through this type of legislation.

There are several other privacy regulations passed by individual countries, such as PIPEDA in Canada and Australia's Privacy Act. Most new regulations deal with personal information and many of the objectives are similar. However, the responsibilities a company has under each law can be contradictory. Multinational enterprises struggle with a regulatory tapestry that grows in complexity with each passing year.

There is no doubt that identity theft is a major problem globally. However, the patchwork of regulations around the world makes it difficult for short-staffed security teams to comply with the regulations. Furthermore, security begins where compliance ends, and if security teams are spending all their time on compliance initiatives, there is little time remaining for those teams to focus on their primary mission.

While data privacy regulations are growing in popularity, data sovereignty regulations also exist. The primary difference between data privacy and data sovereignty is that data privacy is designed to control who can access information, whereas data sovereignty primarily regulates international data transfers.

Data sovereignty regulations

Many regulations are designed to control the flow of data between countries. In most cases, data can be transferred under certain circumstances. The stated purpose is to ensure private data is not transferred to countries where the government can infringe upon privacy rights. Countries such as China and the United States, where the government has the power to compel companies to share information about individuals without their consent, are often primary targets of data sovereignty rules. There are differing opinions about the right to privacy among countries around the world. As a result, many countries seek to limit the flow of information across borders. However, these regulations often create complexity in the modern world. Information does not respect terrestrial borders, and cloud services are designed to optimize performance, not to operate in specific jurisdictions. As a result, the unintended consequence is to make it more difficult for companies headquartered in countries with restrictive data sovereignty rules to be competitive globally. Few new regulations include data sovereignty elements, but many restrictive data sovereignty rules still exist.

Another area where governments have regulated business affairs that relates to information security is the idea of workers' councils. Workers' councils are designed to represent the interest of employees and balance power between labor and companies. While these councils serve many functions, among them is reviewing a company's plans for employee monitoring and electronic surveillance.

Workers' councils

In several countries, such as Germany, Switzerland, and the Netherlands, workers are granted rights and representation that allow them input into how employees are monitored in the workplace. These workers' councils often hold significant power and must be consulted before a company can implement security controls that monitor employee communications and behavior. The rules and objectives differ between jurisdictions, but the councils are in place to prevent employers from using electronic surveillance in an oppressive manner.

However, to protect information and comply with relevant regulations, organizations must implement forms of electronic monitoring. As a result, these conversations become an important element of a security program. The types of issues raised by workers' councils are often related to whether the systems can monitor worker productivity, invade their privacy with respect to personal communications, or present the opportunity for human bias to influence the security program. Security professionals operating in these areas must listen to the workers' councils and become skilled in explaining what the intention of their controls is and how they will protect workers' rights throughout implementation and operation of their controls.

These types of regulations allow governments to exert influence on how data is collected, stored, processed, or transmitted. They have been implemented to correct an imbalance or to compel organizations to secure information properly. Simply complying with regulations does not constitute an effective security program. Compliance regulations set rules for what an organization can and cannot do. Security is the art and science of protecting people, information, and systems.

The foundational elements of security

Many people look at information security as a highly technical field and allow themselves to be distracted by technical jargon or complex attack tactics. Security is quite simple. Many of the concepts that apply to security have corollaries in the physical world. Throughout human history, people have been protecting assets of value. Knowing what you are trying to protect is the first step. The foundation of security is protecting people, information, and systems. While strategies, tactics, and technologies can be technical and confusing, the basic underlying principles are easy to understand. Albert Einstein once said, "*If you can't explain something simply, you don't understand it well enough.*" I challenge all security leaders to learn to explain their strategies and tactics in simple terms. In order to do so, we need to go back to the basics.

People

There is a major misconception that information security is all about technology. Technology plays a role, but ultimately, every security breach starts with a person, and the vast majority of attackers launch their attack against an individual person as well. The real story of security is one of people attacking people and it is as old as humanity itself. From the beginning of time, as soon as one group of humans amassed something of value, it became necessary to protect it from other humans who would take it from them if they could. As we organized into tribes, societies, and ultimately nations, the concentration of wealth grew.

The internet has connected the world and changed it forever. For many centuries, access to knowledge was a source of wealth. In the modern world, anyone with an internet connection and a device can access any information they desire. This connectivity has offered great benefits to society and the global economy. However, with great power comes great responsibility. Since information can now move more freely than ever before and can be replicated across systems in microseconds, it can be stolen or otherwise exploited just as quickly. However, people don't adjust their habits as quickly as technology accelerates.

People are fallible by nature. Most exploits are delivered through the applications people are most familiar with and trusting of, such as email. Many attacks are designed to trick people into doing something they would not normally do. All these types of attacks are collectively known as social engineering. Social engineering is simply an attempt to convince someone to do something that is not in their interest for the benefit of the attacker. We will discuss social engineering types in detail in *Chapter 5, Protecting against Common Attacks by Partnering with End Users*.

Since people are often the weakest link and the last line of defense, educating and supporting people is the first pillar of an effective information security program. Additionally, looking for behavior patterns is an effective way to identify attacks early and mitigate their impact on a person or organization.

The unfortunate truth is not all security challenges related to people are accidental on the part of the trusted insider. There are three categories of human-based insider threats to an organization. First is the well-meaning employee, who accidentally puts information or systems at risk. This can be due to seeking the most expedient way to accomplish their job function, a failure to adhere to best practices, such as reusing passwords between personal and corporate accounts, or negligence in terms of their responsibilities in handling sensitive information. The second is the compromised account. This threat is based on an attacker gaining access to an employee's credentials in some way and using those credentials to masquerade as the employee. There are many ways accounts can be compromised, and if there is a program in place to identify signs of a compromised account early, there are effective ways to mitigate the risk. However, if an attacker can compromise an account and remain undetected, they can cause massive amounts of damage in a relatively short period of time. Finally, there are malicious insiders. These are people you have provided access to who intend to do harm to the organization. It is important to note that most insiders don't start as malicious; they become that way based on changing circumstances.

It is important to understand the categories of insider threats and respond to them appropriately. If you treat a malicious insider as a well-meaning employee, you will give them time and insight that will allow them to do more harm to the organization. If you treat a well-meaning employee like a malicious insider, you will alienate them at best. The objective should be to identify the type of insider you are dealing with and respond appropriately.

Information

The term information security indicates that the point is to protect information, but many programs inexplicably deprioritize the information-specific controls in their security programs. Many security practitioners have become enamored with technology and tactics and forget about what is most important. People is the first pillar of security because it is people who are attacking systems to steal information, and it is often people that are being exploited by attackers to get into the environment. Information is a close second, because that is the target and that is the valuable item the program should be trying to defend.

There is a well-known information security concept known as the **Confidentiality, Integrity, and Availability** (**CIA**) triad. Data breaches are attacks against the confidentiality of data. Although less common, attacks where someone is trying to modify a record, such as if you were to hack into your bank and lower your credit card balance, are an attack against integrity. Ransomware is an attack against availability. The key point to remember is what matters is the confidentiality, integrity, and availability of information. As a result, an effective program understands what information is important, where it resides, and how it should be protected.

With respect to understanding information and how it flows inside an organization, there are three aspects to consider. First is the content. What is the information we have that we should protect? How do we define it? What makes it sensitive? Second is the community. Who is authorized to interact with the information? Who should not interact with the information? Are those that are allowed to interact with the information allowed to share it with others? If so, whom? The third is the channel. When information is moving, how should it move? What are the authorized repositories for the information? Putting these three elements together allows you to understand the authorized behavior of information and the acceptable use of sensitive information by people in your organization. Once you have identified who in the organization will be handling sensitive information, you can support those people with additional training on what their responsibilities are and how that information should be handled and used. Since you have defined the authorized behavior of the information, you now can implement technologies to detect unauthorized movement of data and unauthorized interactions between information and people.

The other key element of information is understanding its life cycle. The first aspect is to understand how information comes into the environment. Is it created by our organization as is often the case with intellectual property? If so, who creates it and what is its journey from the idea stage through legal protection in the form of a patent or copyright? If it is a trade secret, protecting it becomes even more important because there are few internationally recognized legal protections for trade secrets. In other cases, such as PII, the organization does not create the information, rather it is entrusted with the information by a data subject or a customer. In that case, it is important for the organization to understand the mechanisms it uses to collect information. What are the ways a customer could provide their information to us? Do we have safeguards to ensure sensitive information isn't inadvertently provided through other channels? Once the customer provides their information to us, where do we store it? Storage is the second stage of the information life cycle.

Storage refers to where and how information is stored inside and even outside your environment. Some organizations outsource the storage and processing of information to third parties. This type of arrangement has become popular with credit card information, especially for smaller organizations that do not have the proper resources to comply with the rigors of the PCI-DSS. Other organizations use cloud storage offerings such as **Software as a Service** (**SaaS**) or **Infrastructure as a Service** (**IaaS**) platforms. While these solutions are often seen as an extension of the organization's environment, there is also a shared security model that must be understood by the organization, so it is clear what responsibilities they have and what responsibilities the service provider has in the arrangement. In every arrangement, controlling what information is stored in which location and who has access to that information is the responsibility of the organization. Those responsibilities cannot be transferred to the cloud provider. It is also likely that different security tools and controls will be necessary to secure cloud environments. Since the organization does not own the infrastructure, many of the traditional tools used to secure information on-premises will be impossible to deploy, ineffective, or both.

The third stage of the life cycle is transmission. Most information will be transmitted at some point throughout its life cycle internally, externally, or both. While sensitive information is in transit, it can be vulnerable as not all transmission methods are created equally in terms of security. It is important that individuals and organizations understand the risk posed with each transmission method against the need for efficiency of the transmission. Generally, more secure transmission methods are more onerous for the users involved in the transmission. For example, sending an email with an attachment is very expedient, but it isn't the most secure transmission method. This is likely acceptable for most email exchanges containing commodity information. If the information should be protected but the communication is still necessary, such as when my doctor's office sends me health information, a secure message is likely an acceptable solution. This requires me to log in to view the encrypted message and is more secure than a traditional email. When more sensitive information is being shared, a secure share with multifactor authentication is likely more appropriate. This method will require the recipient to take multiple steps to access the information but will be a much more secure transmission method. These are just a few examples. There are countless methods of transmission to choose from. Choosing the right transmission method requires an analysis of the sensitivity of the information, the need for expediency and a seamless end user experience, and the frequency of transmission. It is important that a thoughtful analysis is conducted and methods are selected for each sensitive information type. By being intentional about authorized transmission methods, the organization can put more meaningful controls in place to identify deviations from acceptable practices.

The final stage of the information life cycle is data destruction. At some point, retention requirements only stipulated a minimum amount of time information should be retained. As a result, most organizations simply didn't delete anything. This led to a scenario where over-retention was often the largest source of residual information risk in an organization. Europe's GDPR seeks to put maximum limits on data retention. GDPR states that data subject information must only be retained if it provides business value, consent to the information is not withdrawn by the data subject, or retention is required by law. GDPR stipulates that organizations destroy data that no longer has business value. As a result, organizations must plan when they collect PII from European citizens why they need the data, how long they need it, and how it will be destroyed when it no longer has business value. While this regulation is only required by GDPR for European citizens' PII, it is in the organization's best interest to apply this discipline throughout their information protection program.

Systems

The ability to secure systems has been impacted significantly by the rapid adoption of cloud-based technologies. Systems security falls into three major categories: securing on-premises workloads, securing cloud workloads, and securing endpoints. Each of these categories poses its own challenges based on the access and responsibility of the organization to provide security. Each category also has specific technology solutions designed to help an organization fulfill its responsibilities given the level of control it has over each environment.

Example Case: Citibank and Lennon Ray Brown

Lennon Ray Brown was a trusted Citibank employee who had privileged access to Citibank systems. In December 2013, Mr. Brown had a discussion with his supervisor about his performance. Reports vary with respect to whether the discussion was a scheduled performance review or simply a discussion about Mr. Brown's performance at Citibank. Regardless, Mr. Brown did not like the conversation. In response, "*Brown caused the transmission of a program, information, code and command, causing damage without authorization to a protected computer.*" (Department of Justice–Northern District of Texas, 2016) Mr. Brown had knowledge of the network and completed his actions with malicious intent.

"*Brown knowingly transmitted a code and command to 10 core Citibank Global Control Center routers, and by transmitting that code, erased the running configuration files in nine of the routers, resulting in a loss of connectivity to approximately 90% of all Citibank networks across North America.*" (Department of Justice–Northern District of Texas, 2016) After he took down most of the Citibank network, Mr. Brown went home. It is not immediately clear why the last router did not go down, taking the entire network down with it, but Mr. Brown's intention was to damage the systems he had access to.

Ultimately, Lennon Ray Brown was sentenced to 21 months in prison and ordered to pay restitution of $77,000. Mr. Brown did not make good choices, but the case highlights the fact that any trusted insider could become malicious based on circumstances that may not be foreseen. It is important to apply the concept of least privilege and the separation of duties to ensure a single rogue employee cannot cause catastrophic damage. Monitoring privileged employees is also important. Monitoring employees may not prevent them from doing something damaging but may dissuade them from doing so knowing they will be held accountable if they do. As the saying goes, *good fences make good neighbors*. To be clear, there is no evidence Citibank did anything wrong in this case. The fact that a case was made and justice was served indicates that Citibank had the proper monitoring of privileged users in place. However, the key lesson is you cannot always anticipate where an insider threat may come from. If Citibank thought Lennon Ray Brown was likely to do something like this, they would have never hired him. *Malicious insiders don't often start out malicious, they become that way.*

This case also highlights the fact that insider threats don't always leave an organization with data. Many common perceptions revolve around the theft of intellectual property, as was highlighted in the Uber versus Waymo example case. However, sometimes malicious insiders target systems and intend to cause damage to avenge a perceived slight, rather than targeting privileged information for personal or financial gain.

Protecting systems is very important. Most organizations put protections in place to prevent intrusions from outside the organization. The preceding example case highlights the additional challenges posed by insider threats. When protecting systems, there are two major categories of systems that need to be protected, on-premises workloads and cloud workloads.

Securing on-premises workloads

On-premises workloads are easier to secure than their cloud counterparts because all aspects of securing them are well understood by the security team. Also, the workloads are under the full control of the organization. From physical security to network security and through the application stack, solutions and best practices for security exist.

The traditional on-premises layered security approach starts at the perimeter and flows through the network, endpoints under the control of the organization, applications, and ultimately to critical information. This approach is antiquated for most modern organizations. For most practitioners who are familiar with the recent changes in the IT reference architecture for organizations, a major challenge is immediately apparent. Organizations no longer own their perimeter since there is no meaningful perimeter between on-premises workloads and cloud-based workloads. Organizations also no longer own their networks since remote work was beginning to be normalized before the COVID-19 pandemic in 2020 but has now become the standard mode of operation. While some companies may have staff return to the office full time after the pandemic is over, many will continue to provide flexible work arrangements, remote work arrangements, and hybrid work models to their employees.

As a result, it should be assumed that any controls dependent on a user being connected to the corporate network are partially effective at best. Also, with the rise of easily accessible SaaS solutions, most organizations allow access to workloads from employees' personal devices, either explicitly or by default because they lack the ability to stop employees from logging in from non-corporate devices. While **Cloud Access Security Broker** (**CASB**) solutions offer controls to only allow connections from corporate devices with up-to-date security software and settings that comply with the corporate endpoint security posture standards, most organizations have not deployed that level of control.

Additionally, applications are no longer exclusively on-premises and neither is information. This means that this entire model, while useful for building the on-premises portion of an information security program, is no longer a comprehensive framework for information security. In the modern world, cloud security must also be considered as part of systems security, and congruent capabilities for both should be deployed so people, information, and systems are protected comprehensively regardless of the source location or destination location of the connection.

In addition to the layers in the traditional model, much of the traditional monitoring and response capabilities have been focused on on-premises workloads. Both **System Incident and Event Management** (**SIEM**) technology solutions and **Security Orchestration, Automation, and Response** (**SOAR**) technology solutions have been built on log aggregation. Both solutions are designed to aggregate information and, in some cases, allow organizations to take action across multiple technologies. Cloud-native solutions and **Managed Detection and Response** (**MDR**) capabilities are beginning to replace legacy on-premises systems, but many similar monitoring and response capabilities for cloud workloads remain delivered by disparate systems. Due to how different securing on-premises workloads is from securing cloud workloads, many organizations keep those disciplines separate. Doing so presents both efficiency and efficacy challenges to an organization. While it is necessary for tactics and technologies to differ across on-premises workloads and cloud workloads, the overarching capabilities and objectives should be congruent.

Securing cloud workloads

Many organizations struggle to properly secure cloud workloads because they lack a fundamental understanding of the shared security model. The shared security model shows what organizations are independently responsible for and what their cloud platform vendors are responsible for with respect to security. Understanding the shared security model requires a basic understanding of the basic flavors of cloud services.

SaaS includes thousands of offerings that allow applications to be consumed as a service, rather than deployed on servers. SaaS platforms were the first to be adopted and have the largest market share of any of the cloud platforms. Microsoft Office 365, Box.com, and the **Customer Relationship Management** (**CRM**) portion of Salesforce.com are popular examples of SaaS applications. In a SaaS environment, the vendor takes on most of the responsibility for security because the consumer has limited capabilities to secure their own SaaS environment.

IaaS includes a smaller number of offerings, the most well known of which are **Amazon Web Services** (**AWS**), Microsoft Azure, and **Google Cloud Platform** (**GCP**). IaaS offerings offer many styles of computing power that can be rented monthly or provisioned in a way where you are billed for what you use, like an electricity utility. Since you are given significant control over this environment, you are responsible for far more of the security stack than you would be for a SaaS platform.

Platform as a Service (**PaaS**) confuses many people because it sits somewhere in between SaaS and IaaS. To further confuse the matter, most of the popular PaaS offerings are offered on platforms that also have SaaS or IaaS elements. For example, Salesforce is a SaaS offering, but the underlying Force.com platform is a PaaS offering that offers a suite of tools and capabilities to develop custom applications that can go far beyond CRM. Also, there is a marketplace where developers who have developed applications on the Force.com platform can sell their applications to other Salesforce customers as add-ons. Popular add-ons to Salesforce include commission tracking software, **Sarbanes-Oxley** (**SOX**) compliance software, and even ticketing systems. Also, AWS has several offerings that could be considered PaaS offerings. Their generic compute workloads, such as **Elastic Compute Cloud** (**EC2**), are clearly IaaS offerings, but offerings such as Lambda and Elastic Beanstalk, also offered by AWS, are clearly PaaS offerings.

Distinguishing PaaS from IaaS has significant security implications as will be demonstrated by the shared security model. What is the difference between PaaS and IaaS? IaaS provides underlying infrastructure and operating systems only, while PaaS also provides a development environment to allow developers to focus on coding and not on deploying and managing the software necessary to create the environment. It is the middleware between the operating system and the application that is being developed that distinguishes PaaS offerings.

Due to the differences in the models, it stands to reason that the provider would be responsible for different aspects of security in each. Conversely, the consumer of the services always has some responsibility as well. While awareness is growing, there was an early misconception in the wave of cloud computing adoption that when an organization moved to the cloud, security was solely the cloud provider's responsibility. Some elements of a security program, such as physical security and network security, become the cloud provider's responsibility in all cases. Some elements of security, such as governing access to the environment and securing the data inside the environment, are always the responsibility of the consumer. Gartner and others have published statistics that state most cloud data breaches are likely to be the customer's fault. This has been proven true. There are a few cases where cloud providers failed in their responsibilities, but many where the customer failed to meet theirs. Some of the failures are due to poorly deployed and configured controls. Others are due to a lack of understanding of who was responsible for each security layer. There are many versions of a shared security model that can be found, but the following is mine. Regardless of which model you refer to, it is important to understand your responsibilities:

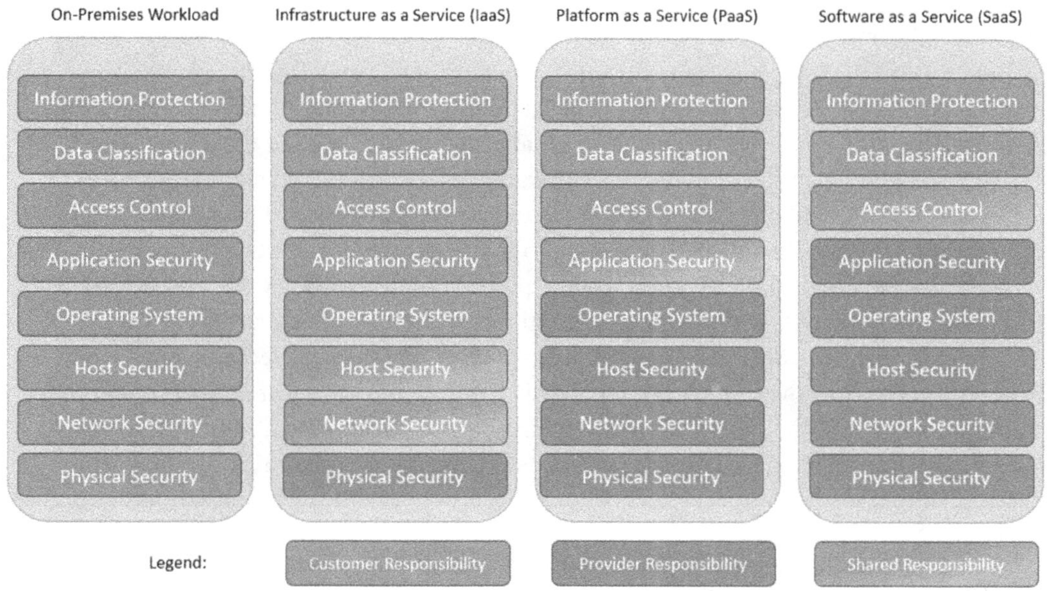

Figure 1.1 – Shared security model for various cloud computing environments

In response to the growing adoption of cloud computing, security solutions have been developed to help customers meet their responsibilities. Traditional on-premises tools could not be deployed in a SaaS environment, for example, so new tools had to be developed and deployed. Since SaaS solutions were the first to be widely adopted, CASBs were developed to help customers meet their specific responsibilities in SaaS models. However, as many organizations embraced IaaS solutions, they tried to apply their CASB solutions to their IaaS environments. While CASB solutions will integrate with the **Application Programming Interfaces** (**APIs**) of popular IaaS environments, they were developed to help with information protection, data classification, and access control, the customer's responsibilities in the SaaS model. They were not developed to address application security, operating system configuration and patching, host security, or network security. As a result, many organizations have significant gaps in their security posture. In *Chapter 6, Information Security for a Changing World*, we will explore the cloud security landscape in detail and revisit the shared security model.

Next, let's move on to securing endpoints.

Securing endpoints

Securing end computing devices or endpoints is a part of security that has received significant attention and investment over the last decade. Originally, antivirus technology, such as McAfee and Symantec, would detect malicious software based on signatures. Essentially, when a new type of malicious software was identified, the team at McAfee or Symantec would build a profile of that malicious code and look for it on machines where the endpoint was installed. There are two major problems with this approach. First, there is a period of time between when a piece of malicious software is developed and a signature is created. Malicious software in this period is called a zero-day threat. Traditional approaches offer no protection against zero-day threats. Second, and a more common problem, was over the years, the number of different types of malicious software packages has grown to the extent where matching against an increasing number of signatures becomes inefficient, and the antivirus software was consuming an increasing percentage of the host resources, which were needed to perform the intended function of the device.

Starting in 2011, next-generation endpoint protection platforms began to emerge. These platforms, such as CrowdStrike, Carbon Black, and Cylance, deployed techniques such as machine learning, advanced response capabilities, and scanning for indicators of compromise rather than simply looking for virus signatures. These more feature-rich endpoint protection platforms have significantly increased the security of corporate endpoints when compared to their predecessors.

However, an increasing amount of information and workloads that belong to an organization is being accessed by endpoints they do not own or control. **Bring Your Own Device** (**BYOD**) has become popular for mobile devices in most organizations because cloud computing makes data accessible from anywhere and most employees don't want to carry a separate phone for personal and corporate use. While **Mobile Device Management** (**MDM**) solutions exist, they are not as feature rich as endpoint protection platforms, and they are not widely deployed to employees' personally owned devices. As a result, securing endpoints in the modern world has become a more difficult challenge.

The cybersecurity talent shortage

To add to the problem, there is an extreme shortage of cybersecurity professionals to help organizations defend themselves. According to a 2019 *Cybercrime Magazine* article, "*there will be 3.5 million unfilled cybersecurity jobs globally by 2021, up from one million positions in 2014.*" (Morgan, Cybersecurity Talent Crunch To Create 3.5 Million Unfilled Jobs Globally by 2021, 2019). To add to the challenge, even when an organization hires a cybersecurity analyst, they don't stay in their role for long. According to the National Cybersecurity Training Academy, "*The typical tenure for an IT Security Specialist is less than 1 year.*" (National Cybersecurity Training Center, 2021). If we are to meet the cybersecurity challenges of the future, we need to attract and train talent to fill these positions at an unprecedented level.

While the talent shortage remains a major problem, cybersecurity challenges are becoming a board-level conversation for most organizations. The news cycle continues to raise awareness of cyber threats. However, while major attacks against large companies grab headlines, little is done to communicate the scope and breadth of the problem to the average person. For every data breach or ransomware attack that makes headlines, hundreds go unnoticed. Worse yet, many attacks by truly sophisticated attackers may never be detected. The future of information security as a discipline is dependent on the ability to attract and retain new cybersecurity professionals. It is important for current professionals to be ambassadors to the next generation. There are few career paths with more opportunities or better job prospects. If you are considering a career in cybersecurity, please join us. We need you.

Summary

The challenges facing modern security teams are immense and rapidly evolving. As many security practitioners lament, the security team must be right 100% of the time and an attacker only has to get lucky once. While attackers can and do get lucky from time to time, assuming attackers are attacking organizations or individuals blindly is a misunderstanding of the current threat landscape. In most public cases, attackers are not getting lucky. They are launching their attacks using well-researched tactics against the weakest parts of an organization's security posture. Many times, the source of the breach is an employee who was not supported properly by training and technology and made a mistake, or a system that was left vulnerable long after a patch for a security vulnerability was available. It is true that no matter how well a security program is built and managed, it will not be impenetrable. However, there are many best practices and strategies available that will limit the likelihood and impact of an attack.

After reading this chapter, you now understand why cybercrime is attractive to criminals and the impacts it has on the global economy. You've learned about costs associated with identity theft and the different types of intellectual property, and how the proper protections for a piece of intellectual property vary based on the type of intellectual property and the associated legal protections. You have learned about how governments are responding to cybersecurity challenges around the world across data privacy, data sovereignty, and workers' councils. Finally, you learned about the foundational elements of security and the cybersecurity talent shortage that is making it so difficult for organizations to secure their environments. This knowledge will help form the basis of your understanding of cybersecurity and provide you with a framework to understand and articulate security concepts.

In the next chapter, we will specifically cover the human side of cybersecurity. Cybersecurity is fundamentally a people problem where people are attacking people. Understanding the people behind the attacks and the tactics is a critical element to establishing a cybersecurity foundation.

Check your understanding

1. What makes cybercrime attractive for criminals?
2. Why is cybercrime damaging to companies and the larger economy?
3. What are global jurisdictions doing to convince organizations to harden their defenses?
4. Choose a case from the chapter and describe what happened in your own words.
5. What are the three foundational elements of cybersecurity?

Further reading

- Banta, R. (2021, August 30). State of California Department of Justice. Retrieved from California Consumer Privacy Act (CCPA): `https://oag.ca.gov/privacy/ccpa`
- Department of Justice–Northern District of Texas. (2016, July 25). Former Citibank Employee Sentenced to 21 Months in Federal Prison for Causing Intentional Damage to a Protected Computer. Retrieved from United States' Attorney's Office Northern District of Texas: `https://www.justice.gov/usao-ndtx/pr/former-citibank-employee-sentenced-21-months-federal-prison-causing-intentional-damage`

- Hawkins, A. (2019, August 27). Ex-Google and Uber engineer Anthony Levandowski charged with trade secret theft. Retrieved from The Verge: `https://www.theverge.com/2019/8/27/20835368/google-uber-engineer-trade-theft-secrets-anthony-levandowski-charged`
- IAPP. (2020, June 09). Japan enacts Amendments to the Act on the Protection of Personal Information. Retrieved from IAPP: `https://iapp.org/news/a/japan-enacts-the-act-on-the-protection-of-personal-information/`
- Intersoft Consulting. (2021, August 30). General Data Protection Regulation. Retrieved from Intersoft Consulting: `https://gdpr-info.eu/`
- Larson, S. (2018, February 10). What we learned in the Waymo v. Uber case. Retrieved from CNN Business: `https://money.cnn.com/2018/02/10/technology/waymo-uber-what-we-learned/index.html`
- Leonhardt, M. (2021, March 23). Consumers lost $56 billion to identity fraud last year—here's what to look out for. Retrieved from CNBC: `https://www.cnbc.com/2021/03/23/consumers-lost-56-billion-dollars-to-identity-fraud-last-year.html`
- Morgan, S. (2019, October 24). Cybersecurity Talent Crunch To Create 3.5 Million Unfilled Jobs Globally by 2021. Retrieved from Cybercrime Magazine: `https://cybersecurityventures.com/jobs/`
- Morgan, S. (2020, November 13). Cybercrime to Cost the World $10.5 Trillion Annually by 2025. Retrieved from Cybercrime Magazine: `https://cybersecurityventures.com/hackerpocalypse-cybercrime-report-2016/`
- National Cybersecurity Training Center. (2021, September 01). CyberSecurity, IT, and Network Security Salaries. Retrieved from National Cybersecurity Training Center
- Northrop Grumman. (2013, April 8). Developing a Framework To Improve Critical Infrastructure Cybersecurity. Retrieved from NIST: `https://www.nist.gov/system/files/documents/2017/06/02/040813_northrop_grumman_response_part2.pdf`
- Page, C. (2020, October 16). U.K. Privacy Watchdog Hits British Airways With Record-Breaking £20 Million GDPR Fine. Retrieved from Forbes: `https://www.forbes.com/sites/carlypage/2020/10/16/ico-hits-british-airways-with-record-breaking-fine-for-2018-data-breach/?sh=2871f5481ac0`

- Sebastian, C. (2018, March 23). Chinese trade secret theft nearly killed my company. Retrieved from CNN Business: `https://money.cnn.com/2018/03/23/technology/business/american-semiconductor-china-trade/index.html`
- Stokel-Walker, C. (2019, August 07). A simple fix could have saved British Airways from its £183m fine. Retrieved from Wired: `https://www.wired.co.uk/article/british-airways-data-breach-gdpr-fine`
- Thomson Reuters Westlaw. (2021, August 30). Chapter 20. California Consumer Privacy Act Regulations. Retrieved from California Code of Regulations: `https://govt.westlaw.com/calregs/Browse/Home/California/CaliforniaCodeofRegulations?guid=IEB210D8CA2114665A08AF8443F0245AD&originationContext=documenttoc&transitionType=Default&contextData=(sc.Default)`
- Vijayan, J. (2019, May 16). US Charges Members of GozNym Cybercrime Gang. Retrieved from Dark Reading: `https://www.darkreading.com/attacks-breaches/us-charges-members-of-goznym-cybercrime-gang`

2
The Human Side of Cybersecurity

It is important to understand the human side of cybersecurity. Too often, people get caught up in the technology related to cybersecurity and lose sight of an important fact – all attacks involve people attacking people. Both attackers and defenders use technology to do their work, but the underpinnings of most successful attacks seek to exploit a human before they exploit a system.

In this chapter, we will cover social engineering techniques, types of malicious software that are used to compromise an environment, and the types of insider threats an organization will face. While tactics and technologies change for both attackers and defenders, the motivations of human beings are more predictable. Understanding the people behind the breaches creates a more solid information security foundation as opposed to chasing the latest technology.

By the end of this chapter, you will be able to identify social engineering attacks, types of malicious software and their purpose, and types of insider threats and know what to do about them. We will start off with a discussion about the people on the attacker's side.

In this chapter, we will cover the following topics:

- People exploiting people
- The three types of insider threat

People exploiting people

It is a sad fact that cybercriminals are in the business of exploiting people. They exploit their victims' hopes and dreams or willingness to help to install malicious software on their machines or gain access to their credentials. Then they exploit that access to steal identities or financial information or hold their victims for ransom. While technology is involved in every step, the story of cybersecurity is a human story. Cybercriminals are no different from other criminals; they use shady tactics to exploit people for their own gain. Cybersecurity, then, is the art and science of protecting people from harm.

The first element of the human story that is cybersecurity is understanding the tactics from the attacker's perspective. When people set out to exploit others in cyberspace, the following categories of techniques are most popular:

- Social engineering techniques
- Stealing credentials
- Malicious software

When describing social engineering, most people will intuitively understand what it is, even if they are not familiar with the term.

Social engineering techniques

Social engineering is the collective name for tactics designed to persuade someone to do something they wouldn't normally do so the attacker can gain something of value. Sometimes the attacker seeks to gain access to sensitive information they can profit from. Other times, the attacker may want to gain access to a system to install malicious software. Regardless of the end goal, social engineering is often an important step in the attack chain. The following are common social engineering techniques attackers use to advance their cause.

The first and most common form of social engineering is known as **phishing**.

Phishing

Phishing is the most common social engineering technique because it is easy to launch large-scale attacks. Phishing specifically refers to email attacks that are designed to trick an end user into clicking on a link or opening an attachment. Often, link-based phishing attacks are designed to harvest a password. For example, if an attacker sends you a phishing lure that looks like a Chase banking alert and you click on it, the link will likely take you to a page that looks like a Chase login page. If you enter your login credentials, the attacker now knows you bank at Chase and has your username and password. They now have access to your bank account. If you don't bank at Chase, you either wouldn't click the link or wouldn't enter a password. Attackers are smart, and they try to find ways to increase their likelihood of success. For example, in a scenario where they are targeting XYZ company, they may register the `XYZSecurity.com` domain name. That way, when they send their messages, it looks more legitimate and may fool a user into clicking on the link and entering their credentials to *log in*.

Attachment-based phishing messages are designed to get you to click on a malicious attachment, which will then install malicious software on your machine. This is a common vector for ransomware attacks. Often, these attachments are designed to pique your curiosity. For example, sometimes a PDF file will be attached to a message that looks like someone in finance sent it to the whole company by mistake. The attachment may be named something such as *Next Year's Salaries and Bonuses*. There is a good chance that someone will want to see what is in that attachment.

These examples are not comprehensive. For example, there are phishing messages that contain links where the URL will install malicious software or attachments that are malicious but do not install malicious software. **Business Email Compromise** (**BEC**) attacks contain no payload at all. The purpose of the phishing message is to convince someone to do something such as wiring money to a fraudulent bank account.

Regardless of the payload and the tactics, there are some common elements of a phishing attack. First, attackers know that if a target user takes their time to examine a message, they will be able to find elements of the message that give them pause. For example, hovering over a link may expose the real URL or looking closely at the sender email address may show the sender isn't who they appear to be. As a result, attackers try to create urgency in their messages. They are trying to make their victim feel the need to act quickly and if they don't, something bad will happen or they will miss out on an opportunity. The second element is the lure. Criminals know that if people are in a hurry and they can make something look close to legitimate, people will likely click on it. An example of this technique is to include a coupon to a popular service that is *expiring soon.* The intention is to make the user think they will be missing out on something of value if they don't act quickly. Since companies use similar tactics to create urgency in buying behavior, the urgency raises fewer red flags. In general, if someone is trying to motivate you to act quickly, whether an attacker or a legitimate business, it should give you pause. There are several ways to support users and stop them from falling victim to phishing attacks. We will cover methods for teaching end users how to identify phishing attacks in *Chapter 5, Protecting against Common Attacks by Partnering with End Users*. Sometimes people will ask about **smishing**. Smishing is simply phishing over text message. While there is a different name for it, it is the same as phishing, simply using a different medium.

According to a *Security Boulevard* article, "*85% of all organizations have been hit by phishing attacks*" (Meharchandani, 2020) in 2020. Security awareness training can be helpful against generic phishing attacks, but a successful program will not yield a 0% click rate. In fact, most companies would be satisfied with a click rate of less than 10%. Without compensating controls designed to support users, 1 in 10 phishing attacks will be successful. Those statistics make it easy to understand why there are so many breaches and ransomware infections. The numbers are not on the security practitioner's side.

While phishing is generally designed to be broadly distributed, and therefore easier to defend against, there is a specifically targeted form of phishing, known as spear phishing, which is more targeted, specific, and difficult to defend against.

Spear phishing

While phishing campaigns are generally targeted at broad groups of intended victims and are generic, spear-phishing campaigns are targeted attacks aimed at one specific person. Unlike phishing campaigns, spear-phishing campaigns do not need a high click rate to be successful. Popular corporate targets include CEOs and CFOs. Spear-phishing campaigns, then, are much better researched and designed to fool a specific person. For example, a spear-phishing campaign may be targeted at the CEO of a company. The person launching the attack likely knows the names and interests of all the CEO's family members thanks to social media. The attacker has likely also purchased information about the CEO's family members on the dark web. They may even have gained access to their email account. Now they can send a message to the CEO pretending to be a member of their family, in a manner that is convincing because the attacker knows how that person interacts on social media and maybe even over email. This highlights one of the many ways that social media can help attackers conduct reconnaissance. Spear phishing is much more difficult to detect and prevent because it is an attack uniquely designed to exploit a specific person. In many cases, people who are likely to be attacked in sophisticated ways should be supported by additional technology to help them not fall victim to such attacks.

According to the same *Security Boulevard* article cited earlier, "*97% of users are unable to recognize a sophisticated phishing email*" and "*95% of all successful attacks targeting enterprise networks are caused by successful spear phishing.*" (Meharchandani, 2020). While generic phishing attacks are more common and less successful, spear-phishing attacks are a dangerous threat. Generic phishing attacks only need a small fraction of users to click to deem their exploits successful, and they may not know precisely what they are targeting. Spear-phishing attacks are often launched by more sophisticated attackers targeting a small group of users in a specific organization, often for a specific purpose. These attacks are more likely to be successful, less likely to be detected since they affect a smaller group of people, and more likely to be catastrophic if successful.

The good news is most companies can predict which people would be targeted by a spear-phishing attack if their organization were targeted. Putting additional protections around those people will help protect them from potential spear-phishing attacks. Because of the prevalence of LinkedIn, it is not difficult to find the names of people in leadership and who have roles that would indicate they may have elevated privileges, for example, IT administrators. Most companies have a public domain name as well, and there are only a few combinations of first and last names that are used by companies to build email addresses. Put all of that together and most attackers can send targeted emails to specific people in specific roles. As a result, protecting from spear phishing requires some thought or technology that can help identify who is attacked most frequently to put additional safeguards around those accounts.

Next, we will discuss a tactic that is generally deployed in the physical world, known as **baiting**.

Baiting

Baiting is a technique designed to exploit people's natural curiosity. The idea of baiting is to leave something, normally a physical device such as a USB storage device, in plain view. Sometimes it is generic and other times it is marked in a way that is designed to make someone curious. Regardless, the intention of the attacker is for someone to plug the device into a machine to see what is on it. As soon as they do, their machine will become infected. If they are connected to a network, they will spread the infection to other machines. In other cases, the payload may be a backdoor, which is a specific type of malicious software that allows an attacker to access the target system remotely. Baiting can also occur with fake ads or giveaways that redirect users to a website that installs malicious software.

The next session will cover a tactic that is social engineering masquerading as malicious software known as scareware.

Scareware

Scareware is another tactic that was popular for some time. Scareware pops up ads and banners designed to scare a user into thinking they've been infected. An antidote is then offered to remove the infection. In some cases, the **antidote** is the real malicious software that the user just installed with their administrator privileges. In other cases, the antidote is offered in exchange for money. The key difference between scareware and other forms of malicious software that makes scareware a social engineering technique is that scareware by itself does not have the access it needs to perform its intended function. Its purpose is to trick the end user into taking an action that leads to further compromise.

Scareware is designed to play upon fear. The next tactic we will discuss, tailgating, is designed to appeal to a person's helpful nature.

Tailgating

Tailgating is a method of gaining unauthorized physical access to a secure facility. The classic example is someone going to a secure facility with a stack of boxes of pizza or doughnuts. They will ask someone to hold the door for them. Seeking to be helpful, the unsuspecting victim will hold the door for the attacker, not wanting to be rude and make them put everything down to get their badge. This type of exploit plays on a person's desire to be polite and helpful. Once the attacker has physical access, there are several techniques they can use that would not have been possible without physical access to the facility.

Gaining physical access often opens the door for subsequent attacks. One attack is known as shoulder surfing.

Shoulder surfing

Shoulder surfing is popular at places where large numbers of people are working on their computers, such as coffee shops or the gate area of an airport. The idea of shoulder surfing is for the attacker to walk behind someone on their computer to gain access to information they shouldn't have. For example, if a person is working on a spreadsheet that contains personal information or financial information, the attacker could gain access to that information. There are even examples of shoulder surfing where the attackers rent a building across from a specific office building and use cameras to take pictures of screens.

Not all social engineering techniques are designed to exploit systems directly. In some cases, such as pretexting, the technique is designed to gather information that will increase the likelihood of success of subsequent attacks. It is important to understand that most attacks are chains of events, not single techniques. Most attacks will use multiple techniques. Most begin with one or more forms of social engineering.

Pretexting

Pretexting is a reconnaissance technique designed to gain information about a target. The easiest example is the surveys on social media that you will see people answering. If someone posts something such as *Your rock star name is the street you grew up on and your mother's maiden name!* and someone posts a reply, the attacker now knows the answer to two common identity verification questions. You will see variations of this scheme all over social media. Some of these surveys may be innocuous, but many of them would allow the person posting them to build a database of identity verification questions that would allow them to compromise accounts belonging to the people who responded.

Now that we understand social engineering techniques, we can examine their intended outcomes. In most cases, the intended result is either the theft of credentials or the installation of malicious software. We will begin with stolen credentials.

Stealing credentials

When credentials are stolen, bad actors can use them to gain unauthorized access to systems and data. Later in the chapter, we will explore what attackers do with stolen credentials and review an example case that shows the damage that can be caused.

In addition to social engineering, credentials are stolen through data breaches. If attackers can access databases containing usernames and passwords, they can steal that information and not only use it to access that service but also, in many cases, use the same combination to access several other services. An attack where sets of credentials are used to try to access several services in an automated fashion is called a **credential-stuffing** attack. Once the original attacker is finished exploiting the information, they will often sell it on dark web marketplaces for others to exploit. Many people hear that they should not reuse passwords and they should change their passwords frequently. If one account is compromised and you reuse the same credentials on several sites, the damage can be catastrophic. Many people will ask, "*If I can't reuse my passwords, how will I remember them all?*" This is a fair question.

Password managers are part of the answer. They store all your passwords, encrypt them, and allow you to unlock them with a master password. A master password should be long, complex, memorable, and not used for any other account. Your master password should never be written down or shared with anyone. Multifactor authentication is also helpful in ensuring a stolen credential alone will not give attackers access to the account. We will discuss password managers and multifactor authentication in more detail in *Chapter 9, Cybersecurity at Home.*

In 2021, a single repository was leaked by a user of a popular hacker forum. Depending on which reports you believe, the list contains either 82 billion or 8.4 billion passwords. Either number indicates multiple passwords per active user (Whitney, 2021). It is important to remember this is a single source on a single forum that likely has more than one password you have used, obtained from data breaches of a service you have an account with. As a result, if you reuse passwords or have a password that has not been changed recently, it is likely someone has that password and it is a matter of time before your account is compromised. Passwords are disposable and should be treated that way. As technology improves, the demand for complexity increases and the shelf life of passwords decreases.

Example Case: Yahoo Data Breach(es)

Most people know Yahoo as the successful personal email provider and search engine. Security professionals know Yahoo as the company that leaked billions of usernames and passwords over the course of multiple data breaches over several years. Because Yahoo houses email addresses and passwords for many people, it was an attractive target for attackers. They also developed a reputation for poor security practices, so they were frequently attacked.

In 2019, Yahoo agreed to pay $117.5 million to settle damages from several data breaches between 2012 and 2016. The company also said data breaches involving stolen information occurred between 2013 and 2016. In 2012, there were multiple intrusions where the attackers didn't steal information but gained unauthorized access to systems. In 2013, attackers again breached Yahoo and gained access to information about all 3 billion Yahoo users. It is not known whether the attacks in 2013 were launched by the same bad actors that compromised Yahoo in 2012. The 2013 data breach was among the largest in history and included enough information for attackers to access users' email accounts and calendars. With this access, attackers could now launch attacks against other users while pretending to be a friend or family member. Yahoo's response to the breach and commitment to users was underwhelming. Many Yahoo users, including me, began to question their commitment to cybersecurity. In 2014, attackers breached Yahoo again. This time, they targeted the user database, and 500 million users were affected. In the 2014 breach, attackers successfully stole **Personally Identifiable Information** (**PII**) such as names, addresses, phone numbers, and birthdays along with usernames and passwords. Attackers were now building the types of profiles on these users that could be used to steal identities or gain additional information to craft targeted attacks against victims. To make matters worse, Yahoo failed to disclose some of its incidents, so it is difficult to know with certainty that there weren't more. Even if Yahoo did not intentionally withhold information, their poor security practices at the time call into question whether they would have known if they were attacked by a sophisticated actor.

The Yahoo breaches started to get attention from regulatory authorities. The size and scale of the breaches make estimating the total economic damage impossible. If you have a Yahoo account, your information is likely for sale on the dark web. Whatever passwords you have used for Yahoo should be assumed to be compromised and you should not use them again. The **Securities Exchange Commission** (**SEC**), which regulates financial markets, acted against Yahoo, claiming that their failure to disclose data breaches misled investors. The $117.5 million settlement was separate from the SEC action and went to help victims of the breach with out-of-pocket costs and monitoring. However, it would be difficult for an individual to know whether the damage they suffered was or was not connected to the Yahoo data breach. Verizon acquired Yahoo in 2016 and pledged to spend five times more on security for the Yahoo business unit than Yahoo spent as an independent company. The question is, will people trust the Yahoo brand again? (Stempel, 2019) (McAndrew, 2018) (Matthews, 2019)

The Yahoo case shows how attackers can target a known repository of email address and password information. Since many websites use email addresses as the default username and many users reuse passwords across multiple sites, these types of attacks are often successful. Furthermore, if an attacker controls a person's email account, they could often reset passwords to other services and pass basic multifactor authentication methods. Many multifactor authentication methods offered to consumer accounts allow users to send codes to their email or phone number tied to the account. If an attacker controls the email account, they can defeat the multifactor authentication challenge. These multifactor systems are not performing true multifactor authentication. The three factors of authentication are something you know, such as a password, something you have, such as a physical device, and something you are, which is often a fingerprint or another biometric technique. Multifactor authentication requires more than one of those factors. A text message to a phone may be something you have, but access to an email account is something you know, like a password. Therefore, if the activation code can be sent to an email account, it is stronger than authentication without two steps, but it is not true multifactor authentication.

Next, let's discuss malicious software, which is another common tool attackers use to exploit people.

Malicious software

In many cases, the purpose of social engineering is to install malicious software, also known as **malware**, on a device to provide an advantage to an adversary. Sometimes the purpose is to cause damage to a target system or to spy on the end user. Ransomware is increasing in popularity because it is generating direct revenue for attackers, unlike stealing credentials where the theft itself is only part of the chain necessary for an attacker to monetize their exploits. There are many types of malicious software. Some of the major categories are as follows:

- Viruses
- Worms
- Trojans
- Ransomware
- Spyware

Many people get confused by the differences between similar malicious software types. Let's start with viruses.

Viruses

Computer viruses get their name from their ability to spread from one infected host to another, normally on the same network. They are designed like biological viruses to be as transmissible as possible. Like many biological viruses, the most dangerous among them are the ones that lay dormant and replicate before causing noticeable damage. Computer viruses are designed to either cause damage or steal information. Many years ago, viruses were often used to cause damage for no apparent purpose. Modern viruses are designed to steal data or destroy systems. Different threat actor groups are likely to use different types of malicious software to accomplish their goals. Hacktivists and governments may use viruses to destroy systems. Criminal groups are more likely to use viruses that steal data so they can sell it for a profit or ransomware so they can extort victims directly. A key characteristic of a virus is that it needs activation from a host. As a result, a virus must be paired with a social engineering technique to be effective. While often conflated, worms are different from viruses.

Worms

Worms are like viruses in their aims but are far more sophisticated. A worm can replicate itself and infect other systems on a network without a user doing anything. Worms only need to breach one system on a network and can compromise all other connected systems. Worms can be extremely powerful and are often used by nation-state actors. One of the most famous worms, **Stuxnet**, was used to disrupt Iran's nuclear program. You can read more about Stuxnet in an example case in *Chapter 3*, *Anatomy of an Attack*, detailing the operation. While worms are often more sophisticated and damaging than viruses, there are successful worms available for sale on the dark web. As a result, an unsophisticated attacker with resources can launch this advanced capability against unsuspecting victims. While worms and viruses often seek to exploit systems as soon as they can do so, trojans are a type of malicious software that are designed to remain undetected.

Trojans

Trojans get their name from the story of the trojan horse. A trojan is a piece of malicious software masquerading as a legitimate piece of software. To work properly, a trojan must have two sides. One side is the legitimate software that must function properly for someone to keep it installed. The other side is the malicious side, which allows the attacker some level of access to the machine. An example would be a game that a user could download and install. They would be able to play the game and it would work, but the software would also be providing remote access to an attacker. This type of trojan is commonly called a **Remote Access Trojan** (**RAT**).

Other types of trojans lay dormant until activated by an attacker. An example would be a **Distributed Denial of Service (DDoS)** attack. A DDoS attack occurs when an attacker coordinates many machines that flood a target system with a large volume of illegitimate requests, so it does not have the capacity to service legitimate requests. To successfully launch such an attack, a bad actor must be able to access a large number of machines on command. Trojans offer the ability for attackers to create these types of networks, often referred to as a botnet. Some attackers will use trojans to build a botnet and then sell or lease the network to other bad actors to monetize their attacks. Botnets can be used for many types of attacks, such as credential-stuffing attacks, in addition to DDoS attacks.

Next, let's talk about a malicious software type that often makes headlines, ransomware.

Ransomware

Ransomware can be delivered as a virus or a worm, but it has become popular enough that it warrants its own section. Ransomware is designed to hold files or systems for ransom to demand payment from a victim. Often, it works by encrypting as many files as possible and demanding ransom in exchange for the decryption key. If the ransom is not met within a specific period, the files will be destroyed.

Ransomware has become popular largely because it is profitable and people are paying the ransom. Ransomware groups have even dedicated resources to providing technical support and ensuring that when victims pay the ransom, their files are restored. If the victim believes they are doomed regardless, they are less likely to pay. As a result, ransomware groups guard their reputation carefully. Unlike ransomware, spyware is installed to collect information rather than to extort the victim.

Spyware

Spyware is designed to steal information and monitor activity rather than cause harm to a system or explicitly steal data. An example is a keylogger. A keylogger creates a record of everything you type on a keyboard for the purposes of finding information that could be valuable to an attacker, such as a password or credit card number.

Spyware can also be used for industrial and state-sponsored espionage. Spyware is often covert and designed to use as few resources as possible to remain undetected for as long as possible. Think of spyware as the computer equivalent of a *bug* or listening devices from decades past.

Now that we understand malicious software types, we will discuss the types of insider threats. We will start with the largest population, well-meaning insiders.

The three types of insider threats

Inside an organization, there are three basic human profiles. First, well-meaning insiders are people trusted by the organization to perform a function and are attempting to do so. Either for the sake of expediency or by error, those people can often expose the organization to unnecessary risk. Second, trusted insiders can become compromised through social engineering tactics, such as phishing, and someone outside the organization may be masquerading as them. These compromised accounts can lead to major data breaches and damage. Third, there are malicious insiders. These people are trusted and likely started as well-meaning insiders, but at some point became malicious. In some cases, the employees are bribed by outside actors. In other cases, they are frustrated by real or perceived slights by the organization. Regardless, their knowledge of the environment and privileges makes them very dangerous.

First, we will discuss well-meaning insiders.

Well-meaning insiders

Most users in an organization are simply trying to do their jobs within the confines of acceptable behavior. Supporting well-meaning insiders is an important function of any effective information security program. The first way that well-meaning insiders expose data or systems is by making simple mistakes.

Mistakes leading to exposure

The first category of risk attributable to well-meaning insiders is a simple mistake. One common mistake is sending the right information to the wrong person. For example, you may have a `John.Smith@abccompany.com` and a `John.Smith@xyzcompany.com` in your email address book. Since they have the same exact name until you get to the company name, a person may mistakenly attach ABC company's information to XYZ company's email. Doing so would be considered a data breach, but one that was purely accidental. Another common mistake is sending an Excel spreadsheet where the sensitive data is hidden but not entirely removed, so if the recipient or someone who intercepted the message unhid the rows or tabs, they would be able to access information inappropriately. Tools such as **Data Loss Prevention** (**DLP**) and **secure email gateways** offer capabilities that help prevent these types of mistakes from causing harm to the organization.

Outside simple mistakes, many large-scale data breaches happen because of misconfigurations. In many cases, the person configuring the systems has not been properly trained.

Challenges with new technologies

Another common mistake people make is misconfigurations due to gaps in knowledge around solutions they are managing. In many cases, the adoption of new technologies happens faster than an organization's ability to retrain its staff on these new technologies. In many cases, cloud configurations feel familiar to network administrators but have significant differences, as noted in the following example case related to Alteryx. Issues related to the shared security model are important for cloud administrators to understand. With the skills gap in security, it is important to offer training opportunities for existing team members as technologies change. Unfortunately, many professionals are put into situations where they are asked to perform high-risk functions without the proper training and support.

Example Case: Alteryx

Alteryx is a technology company that builds software to power data science and analytics. Because of the nature of their business, Alteryx has information belonging to most American households. Collection of personal information for the purpose of analytics is one of the practices that the **General Data Protection Regulation (GDPR)** in the European Union and the **California Consumer Privacy Act (CCPA)** seek to regulate. The massive Alteryx data breach is one of the major reasons why regulations such as GDPR and CCPA exist.

Alteryx accidentally exposed information that belonged to 123 million of the estimated 126 million households in America. If you live in America, there is a 97.6% chance that Alteryx made your sensitive information publicly available, but most Americans do not know who Alteryx is or did not provide the information directly to Alteryx. How did Alteryx gather the information before the breach? They purchased it from Experian so they could analyze the information. Most people also did not voluntarily give their information to Experian. Credit monitoring agencies have historically had the ability to collect information about individuals without their consent and then sell it to third parties without notification. When organizations collected and curated information about people in the past, it was common practice for them to resell that information to other parties who may wish to use it, often without the knowledge of the data subject. Cases such as Alteryx have made it popular to allow consumers to make their own choices with respect to who has their information.

The information involved in the Alteryx breach was stored in a popular cloud platform, **Amazon Web Services (AWS)**. AWS is an **Infrastructure as a Service (IaaS)** platform where companies can rent space and processing power. For analytics companies such as Alteryx, renting high-powered computers or server farms on-demand is simpler and more cost effective than building large data centers filled with powerful servers sitting idle most of the time. The problem is, security controls for AWS are different than on-premises systems, and the people who work with AWS must be trained to secure the environment properly. The good thing about the cloud is the data is accessible from anywhere. The bad thing about the cloud is the data is accessible from anywhere. As a result, if it is not secured properly with techniques such as access control, it can be accessible to anyone. That is exactly what happened in the case of Alteryx.

Fortunately, Alteryx's mistake was discovered by a security researcher, not a criminal (that we know of), and quickly corrected. In fact, "*Chris Vickery, the director of cyber risk research at cybersecurity start-up UpGuard, discovered the data Oct. 6 on Amazon Web Services, or AWS*" (Lien, 2017). Mr. Vickery and UpGuard should be applauded for finding this vulnerability and making Alteryx aware of it. However, it is difficult to know for sure if anyone else accessed the information before the vulnerability was reported to Alteryx. Technology is changing quickly. It is critical to ensure employees are trained properly when working with new technologies and safeguards are put in place to ensure an individual mistake cannot cause a large-scale data breach.

If we know that well-meaning insiders can make mistakes that can cause damage to the organization and many people are asked to perform tasks for which they have not been properly trained, we must then establish how we can support these well-meaning insiders.

Supporting your teams

Most employees are trying to do the best job they can. It is the responsibility of leaders and organizations to give them the support they need to be successful. Training and mentorship are important parts of the equation. Employees should be trained thoroughly to perform their functions, expectations should be clearly set, and performance should be objectively measured. Additionally, technology should be deployed to support employees and make sure a single mistake cannot cause harm to the organization. I tell my teams, "*If a single person can cause a failure, it is the leadership and the process that failed, not the person.*"

Too often after breaches, companies will publicly claim the breach was the result of the failure of a single person. Equifax made this claim after their 2017 breach. If a mistake by a single well-meaning person can cause the breach of sensitive information belonging to 148 million people, it is clear to me that the blame for the incident does not belong to the individual who made the mistake. While one person may have neglected to patch a system, there should have been a process in place to catch that mistake before a data breach occurred.

When people make mistakes, it is not because of a lack of intelligence or care in most cases. It is important to ensure that systems are designed to identify security failures and mitigate damage. Often, security programs are focused on stopping external attackers. While that is important, it is also important to ensure information and systems are not put at risk by honest mistakes made by well-intentioned people.

It is important that we do not conflate the term *well-meaning* with the term *harmless*. Well-meaning insiders can cause major problems for an organization.

Well-meaning, but dangerous

Well-meaning insiders, by definition, do not intend to do harm. However, they can cause damage if they are not supported correctly. To compare the cost of data breaches and the frequency of data breaches associated with the categories of insider threats appropriately, we will use the same source for each, the 2021 *Ponemon Cost of a Data Breach* study. This study, released annually by Ponemon and one of their sponsors, along with the Verizon **Data Breach Investigations Report** (**DBIR**), is among the best sources of information related to data breaches. While no study can capture all data breaches, especially since some are completely unknown, these two studies include wide participation from a variety of industries and companies.

According to the 2021 *Ponemon Cost of a Data Breach* report, well-meaning insiders accounted for the lowest frequency of insider threat-related data breaches and the lowest average cost. However, the cost was still an average of $4.11 million per breach and accounted for 6% of all data breaches (Ponemon Institute, 2021). Since there is no adversary in data breaches involving a well-meaning insider and the person who could potentially cause the breach often wants to be part of the solution, helping to support well-meaning insiders can be a low-cost, high-return cybersecurity investment opportunity. We will discuss how to help support well-meaning insiders in *Chapter 5, Protecting against Common Attacks by Partnering with End Users.*

Next, we will discuss the second category of insider threats, which is compromised accounts.

Compromised accounts

The actions taken by compromised accounts are not taken by insiders at all; they are controlled by someone else masquerading as a trusted insider. However, if you are not monitoring trusted insiders, you will not be able to identify and stop an attack using a compromised account. Systems use accounts to identify people. As a result, when an account is compromised through phishing or other means, the actions taken are often undetected. Often, when talking about insider threat programs, people will say, "*We trust our team members and don't need to monitor them.*" However, only one of the three categories of insider threats involves a trusted person causing the organization harm.

Compromised accounts were the most common cause of a data breach in the 2021 *Ponemon Cost of a Data Breach* report, accounting for 1 in 5 of all data breaches in 2020. The average cost of a data breach involving stolen credentials was $4.37 million, and, when combined with phishing-originated data breaches, accounted for 37% of all data breaches (Ponemon Institute, 2021). Simply put, taking measures to protect against phishing and having an effective method to identify and remediate a compromised account are among the most important cybersecurity initiatives that could be undertaken.

Stealing credentials is only the first step in compromising an account. Once an attacker has stolen credentials, what do they do with those credentials? Understanding the pattern helps to identify compromised accounts before irreparable harm is done.

What attackers do with stolen credentials

When an attacker steals credentials, receives stolen credentials from a fellow attacker, or purchases them on the dark web, they often will try to use them across multiple services, not just the services they were stolen from. This is one of the reasons that email addresses and passwords in combination with each other are especially useful. Many services use a person's email address as their username, and many people reuse passwords across multiple accounts. *Do not reuse credentials across multiple accounts. Also, do not use the same password for any personal service that you use for any corporate account.* One of the many reasons you should never reuse credentials is the risk of a credential-stuffing attack. A credential-stuffing attack is where an attacker using a bot network loads email address and password combinations into software and tries those combinations across many popular services. Reused passwords will yield access to multiple services per credential for the attacker. Due to the number of username and password combinations available for sale, attackers can easily compromise many services using this technique, and they can do so very quickly.

Once an attacker is inside a system, the next step is often to try to escalate privileges or move throughout the environment to gain more access to systems and data.

Lateral movement and privilege escalation

Lateral movement refers to an attacker using access gained to one system to move to other systems on a network. Unsegmented or *flat* networks are most susceptible to lateral movement. When security teams talk about segmentation or micro-segmentation, they are often designing countermeasures for lateral movement, among other things. The goal of lateral movement is for the attacker to discover what is accessible on the network in terms of systems and information.

One of the purposes of lateral movement is to increase the opportunity for privilege escalation. In some cases, attackers have all the privileges they need based on the account they compromised. Often, they do not. However, if they can access enough systems, they may find one with a security flaw that allows them to gain elevated access. With that access, they can run commands to exfiltrate data or make changes to systems that they could not make without escalated privileges.

Example Case: Marriott and the Starwood Acquisition

Marriott acquired Starwood Hotels and Resorts Worldwide in 2016 for $13 billion to become the largest hotel chain in the world. This acquisition allowed Marriott to provide unparalleled options and benefits to their rewards program members and brought new members to them from Starwood's rewards program. From a business perspective, it allowed Marriott to consolidate a significant market share of the hotel space and put them in a better position to compete with newer alternatives, such as **Vacation Rentals by Owner** (**VRBO**) and Airbnb. However, Marriott also acquired a hidden problem that would cost them dearly.

In 2018, Marriott announced that one of its reservation systems had been accessed by an unauthorized party. The reservation system in question was the guest reservation system for Starwood brands. It was discovered that the attackers had stolen hundreds of millions of customers' personal information along with credit card numbers and passport information. On September 8, 2018, a Marriott tool discovered anomalous activity that led to the discovery of the breach. Upon further investigation, it was discovered that the attackers had originally breached Starwood in 2014, 2 years before Marriott acquired the company (Fruhlinger, 2020). Two things are immediately apparent when reading this story. First, Marriott did not immediately integrate IT systems, which meant that any problems with the Starwood systems were unlikely to be resolved. Second, Marriott put monitoring tools in place that identified activity that Starwood did not have the capability to identify. Both are lessons learned. It could be argued that Marriott could have prevented some of the damage by integrating their acquisition more quickly. However, they did at least apply their security controls to both environments, which led to the discovery of a breach that had been undetected for 4 years.

As more information became available, it was apparent that multiple elements discussed in this chapter were used to create this breach. It should be noted that most successful data breaches involve multiple techniques used together. At some point, the attackers successfully installed a RAT, which gave them persistent access to the network. Since the systems remained post-acquisition, they had access to the network after Starwood was acquired, which gave them access to additional information belonging to Marriott members who were now booking Starwood properties. The attackers then installed a tool designed to harvest usernames and passwords from the memory of other systems (O'Flaherty, 2019). To do so, they had to escalate their privileges after they gained access. There is evidence that attackers moved laterally throughout the network during their 4-year dwell time. While no one knows the exact cause of the initial infection, RATs are often installed by a successful phishing attempt.

This case is a great example of how the lessons of this chapter are interrelated and will help you understand newsworthy attacks in greater detail. Beyond the common claim that breaches were the result of a sophisticated attack, few people understand how these incidents occur and what can be done to prevent them.

We will discuss the phases of an attack and how lateral movement and privilege escalation relate to the broader attack chain in *Chapter 3, Anatomy of an Attack*. For the purposes of this discussion, it is most important to understand that when an attacker gains access to a system or network with a compromised account, they will use that account to move laterally and escalate permissions. Overly permissive accounts greatly reduce the level of effort necessary for attackers to accomplish their objectives. We will talk about best practices that help limit the damage associated with compromised accounts in *Chapter 4, Protecting People, Information, and Systems with Timeless Best Practices*.

Now that we understand how attackers use credentials and how they move throughout an environment, we will discuss how you can identify those movements and reduce dwell time, or the amount of time an attacker is in your environment before they are detected and removed. The longer the dwell time, the more damage can be done.

Identifying compromised users

Of the three categories of insider threats, compromised accounts are the most difficult to detect and mitigate. Effective detection of compromised accounts requires behavior analysis. Behavior analysis is a technique, normally using machine learning or artificial intelligence, that observes patterns of behavior among employees to establish a baseline of normal behavior. Then, the system detects deviations from that standard pattern. Behavior models range from very simple to very complex.

A simple example is the popular *impossible travel* model. If the same account logs in from San Francisco, California, and Râmnicu Vâlcea, Romania, within 15 minutes of each other, it is obvious that at least one of the logins is illegitimate, because it is impossible for a person to travel between those locations in 15 minutes. Because it is likely that the legitimate user still needs access, the common mitigation technique is to send a two-factor authentication notification to the legitimate user's device and prompt them to change the password when they pass two-factor authentication. While this technique is simple and effective, it requires several security controls to be in place prior to the event. First, multifactor authentication must be deployed to all employees. Second, a system with basic behavior analytics capabilities must be deployed to broker traffic. Third, that solution must have the ability to force step-up authentication when certain conditions are met.

A more complex behavior model is the effort to model what the average employee in a specific role or function does during their day. Then, the system will look for major deviations from that baseline. This technique requires advanced technology capabilities, but it is effective against both compromised accounts and malicious insiders. In either case, trying to anticipate how the bad actor will steal information is nearly impossible, but in every case, the behavior associated with that account will change. If an attacker gains access to a system for the first time, they are likely to explore the access that has been gained. A real user would behave differently because they know the location of the necessary resources. A malicious insider will likely manipulate and move larger quantities of information than a normal user. These deviations from patterns along with known exploitation techniques make human behavior analysis a critical information security function.

Now let's talk about the third category of insider threat, which is the least common but often the most damaging, the malicious insider.

Malicious insiders

Malicious insiders are the third group of insider threats, and the group most often associated with the insider threat category. Malicious insiders are easy to discuss theoretically, but an uncomfortable topic when discussing people who are your friends and co-workers. The reality is that malicious insiders do exist. Malicious insiders turn malicious for different reasons, mostly centering on themes of revenge or personal gain.

According to the 2021 *Ponemon Cost of a Data Breach* report, malicious insiders account for 8% of data breaches, with an average cost of $4.61 million. Also, if a company were to have a catastrophic data breach, it would likely originate with a malicious insider. The fact that malicious insiders exist is an inconvenient truth for most companies. Few people want to consider the fact their friends and co-workers may be actively plotting to damage their livelihood. However, if 8% of all data breaches are caused by malicious insiders, it is important to acknowledge their existence and put programs in place to identify them and mitigate the damage they can cause.

While the number of people in an organization who are malicious at any given time is statistically a very small minority, a single trusted insider with malicious intent can cause massive damage to an organization in a very short period. If you compare a malicious insider with a traditional attacker, the malicious insider has several key advantages. First, they do not have to breach perimeter defenses because they can simply log in and bypass the defenses most organizations focus most of their time and resources putting in place. Second, the malicious insider does not need to spend time or risk getting caught performing reconnaissance because they already know the exact location of the target systems and/or information. Third, malicious insiders are trusted and know they are trusted, and therefore know most of their activity will not be closely monitored.

Using these advantages, malicious insiders can bypass most of the cyber-attack kill chain detailed in *Chapter 3, Anatomy of an Attack*, that most attackers must work through, and the insider can take actions against their objectives more quickly. As a result, malicious insiders are more difficult to detect and stop than external attackers.

When trying to build a program to identify malicious insiders, it is important to understand the factors that lead a person to become malicious.

Becoming malicious

In most cases, trusted insiders do not join a company with the intent to steal information or compromise systems. The *Becton Dickinson case*, detailed in *Chapter 3, Anatomy of an Attack*, is a notable contrary example. In most cases, the insider becomes disenfranchised at some point, as was the case with the story of Lennon Ray Brown in *Chapter 1, Protecting People, Information, and Systems – a Growing Problem*, or they become motivated by potential financial gain as was the case in the Uber versus Waymo case also detailed in *Chapter 1, Protecting People, Information, and Systems – a Growing Problem.*

In either case, it is difficult to predict how or when an insider will become malicious. In every case, however, after the motivating event occurs, the insider's behavior will change. Therefore, the best way to detect an insider threat is to monitor the behavior of every employee with access to sensitive information and systems and detect changes in their behavior or known suspicious behavior patterns. You cannot predict who will become malicious and targeting specific individuals for additional monitoring without cause is a dangerous endeavor both legally and morally. It is better to monitor everyone the same way and follow where the evidence leads. In some cases, it may not be necessary to monitor everyone due to their level of access. For example, if an employee has limited access to systems or data repositories, there may be limited harm they could cause. However, those with significant privileges also present a risk to the organization if they become malicious.

Example Case: American Semiconductor

American Semiconductor is a company based in the United States that makes technology designed to power wind turbines. In 2007, they partnered with Sinnovel, a Chinese manufacturer of wind turbines, to supply the technology necessary for Sinnovel to implement their turbines in China. American Semiconductor became a very successful business. In 2011, things began to go wrong. A CNN business article was able to secure an interview with American Semiconductor CEO Daniel McGahn, who explained what happened next.

CEO Daniel McGahn stated that Sinnovel's strategy was to kill American Semiconductor as a business so they could use the technology without paying for it. Sinnovel owed American Semiconductor $70 million for a shipment it had already received and refused to pay for it. In addition, American Semiconductor had prepared their next shipment of goods, which Sinnovel refused to receive. These events were devastating to American Semiconductor's business, and they began to ask questions about why Sinnovel had suddenly stopped doing business with them and how they would be able to do so without harming their own operations.

Eventually, it was discovered that an employee at an American Semiconductor subsidiary in Austria, Dejan Karabsevic had stolen critical engineering information and provided it to Sinnovel representatives. Eventually, Karabsevic confessed that he had stolen the information from American Semiconductor on behalf of Sinnovel. In July 2011, representatives from Sinnovel met Mr. Karabsevic at a coffee shop and offered him $2 million among other benefits in exchange for stealing proprietary source code for American Semiconductor's wind turbine control software (Sebastian, 2018).

American Semiconductor did survive the attack, but it suffered irreparable harm from the events of 2011. Mr. Karabsevic was sentenced to prison and ordered to pay restitution, but hundreds of people lost their jobs because of his actions.

Aside from the case reading like a spy novel, it is an interesting thought experiment into human psychology. Most people wouldn't steal from their employer, but most people have also not been offered $2 million to download files to removable media and hand them over. If they were, how many would do it? Even if it isn't the majority, it only takes one person being tempted by such an offer to create a sudden insider threat. This case highlights the effects of insider threats and stolen trade secrets well, but it also highlights the need to implement timeless best practices such as the concept of least privilege. The operative question is not whether an employee can be bribed to steal information but whether any employee should have access to enough information to single-handedly compromise all the company's intellectual property. Whether the cause is a stolen account or an employee who was compromised by bribery, many breaches are more damaging than they should be because people are granted more access than they need. Stopping all insider threats may be an impossible task but limiting the damage a malicious insider can do is within the control of most organizations.

Now that we understand how insiders become malicious, we will discuss what can be done to stop them.

Stopping malicious insiders

Detecting malicious insiders is difficult, but stopping them is more difficult. Even when effective detection capabilities are in place, it is critical to act quickly when an insider becomes malicious. Often, the insider is discovered too late, and the information is gone or the damage has been done before the incident response team can act. Such delays cause companies to incur legal expenses to defend themselves or their property. In some cases, such as American Semiconductor, it is impossible to undo the harm that was done to the organization. Stopping malicious insiders means building an effective monitoring program that has the proper resources to identify malicious insiders quickly and has the necessary processes built to respond quickly to any incident.

It is important to remember that controls must be built *before* the insider threat event occurs. This means developing a monitoring program when no one believes there is an insider threat at all. This can be politically unpopular and proves difficult for many organizations. Reviewing example cases and the fallout from the events can be a powerful way to discuss this topic with business leaders. This can happen to you, and you may never know until after it is too late unless you deploy the proper controls now. The CEO in the example case talked about the fact they had deployed security measures that exceeded security best practices. It is clear they did not deploy an **insider threat management solution**. They are not alone. Companies with an effective insider threat management program are in the minority. Companies that ignore insider threats do so at their own peril and are gambling with their company's future.

Summary

In this chapter, we have defined several common social engineering types, several types of malicious software, and the three major categories of insider threats. You have learned how to identify different tactics and technologies so you can build better defenses. You have gained an understanding of different insider threat types so you can support well-meaning insiders, identify and eradicate compromised accounts, and stop malicious insiders before they cause irreparable harm to your organization. We have begun to establish a solid foundation for information security.

In our next chapter, we will detail the anatomy of an attack. We will introduce the stages of an attack and provide example cases where detail is available so we can see exactly how attackers performed reconnaissance, gained access, escalated privileges, and acted on their objectives.

Check your understanding

1. Define well-meaning insiders and describe how security technology can support them.
2. Describe some common social engineering techniques in your own words. Which is the most common?
3. Describe some types of malicious software in your own words.
4. What does lateral movement mean?
5. What are some of the reasons a trusted insider may become malicious?

Further reading

- Fruhlinger, J. (2020, February 12). Marriott data breach FAQ: How did it happen and what was the impact? Retrieved from CSO: `https://www.csoonline.com/article/3441220/marriott-data-breach-faq-how-did-it-happen-and-what-was-the-impact.html`
- Lien, T. (2017, December 22). Alteryx data breach exposed 123 million American households' information. Retrieved from Los Angeles Times: `https://www.latimes.com/business/technology/la-fi-tn-alteryx-data-breach-20171222-story.html`
- Matthews, K. (2019, October 7). Incident Of The Week: Multiple Yahoo Data Breaches Across 4 Years Result in a $117.5 Million Settlement. Retrieved from Cyber Security Hub: `https://www.cshub.com/attacks/articles/incident-of-the-week-multiple-yahoo-data-breaches-across-4-years-result-in-a-1175-million-settlement`
- McAndrew, E. J. (2018, May 11). The Hacked & the Hacker-for-Hire: Lessons from the Yahoo Data Breaches (So Far). The National Law Review.
- Meharchandani, D. (2020, December 7). Staggering Phishing Statistics in 2020. Retrieved from Security Boulevard: `https://securityboulevard.com/2020/12/staggering-phishing-statistics-in-2020/`
- O'Flaherty, K. (2019, March 11). Marriott CEO Reveals New Details About Mega Breach. Retrieved from Forbes: `https://www.forbes.com/sites/kateoflahertyuk/2019/03/11/marriott-ceo-reveals-new-details-about-mega-breach/?sh=214d15b6155c`
- Ponemon Institute. (2021). Cost of a Data Breach Report 2021. Traverse City: Ponemon Institute.

- Sebastian, C. (2018, March 23). Chinese trade secret theft nearly killed my company. Retrieved from CNN Business: `https://money.cnn.com/2018/03/23/technology/business/american-semiconductor-china-trade/index.html`
- Stempel, J. (2019, April 9). Yahoo strikes $117.5 million data breach settlement after earlier accord rejected. Retrieved from Reuters: `https://www.reuters.com/article/us-verizon-yahoo/yahoo-strikes-117-5-million-data-breach-settlement-after-earlier-accord-rejected-idUSKCN1RL1H1`
- Whitney, L. (2021, June 9). Billions of passwords leaked online from past data breaches. Retrieved from Tech Republic: `https://www.techrepublic.com/article/billions-of-passwords-leaked-online-from-past-data-breaches/`

3
Anatomy of an Attack

Many people are familiar with reports of attacks that have happened with some details about the extent of the damage resulting from the attack. Most people, however, aren't familiar with the process of how an attack gets from the reconnaissance phase through to the accomplishment of the attacker's final objective. First, we will cover the types of threat actors that exist. Second, we will look in detail at how different types of attacks unfold based on the objective. Understanding the attack techniques and how they vary by objective can help defenders build more meaningful defenses to specific threats. Finally, we will explore the dark web economy for specialized skills that make it easier for unsophisticated actors to launch sophisticated attacks.

Gaining the skills necessary to identify different threat actor groups and the types of attacks they favor will enable you to identify like adversaries you will encounter and defenses to better protect your organization and yourself. By doing so, you will be able to build better defenses based on your risk assessment and the likely adversaries you will encounter. As you explore different types of attacks and adversaries, you will likely see parallels between the cyber world and the physical world, specifically military concepts for both attackers and defenders. In the Art of War, Sun Tzu said *Know the enemy and know yourself in a hundred battles you will never be in peril. When you are ignorant of the enemy but know yourself, your chances of winning or losing are equal. If ignorant both of your enemy and of yourself, you are certain in every battle to be in peril.* Understanding what your defensive capabilities are and what your attackers' capabilities are is a foundational element for building an effective cyber defense posture.

In this chapter, we will cover the stages of attack and how the stages vary based on the objective. We will specifically discuss extortion schemes such as ransomware, data theft attacks, and attacks designed to disrupt or destroy systems. Finally, we will cover the dark web marketplace, which helps unsophisticated actors launch sophisticated attacks. We will cover the following topics:

- Understanding the risk from targeted attacks
- Stages of an attack
- Extortion
- Stealing information
- System disruption or destruction
- Attackers for hire

Understanding the risk from targeted attacks

As we discussed in *Chapter 2, The Human Side of Cybersecurity*, all cyber attacks are people attacking people. Understanding the people behind the attacks helps defenders prioritize their investments to protect themselves appropriately. It is not economically feasible for a company to defend itself from every potential attack.

The first threat actor group we will explore are organized criminals. The term *organized* is used loosely in this context because these actors range from sophisticated groups with defined hierarchies to informal cooperatives of people who have never met outside of dark web forums. While there are multiple types of threat actors, what unites all threat actors are their motivations and tactics. In the following sections, we will learn about the various types of threat actors and the common tactics they use to attack victims.

Organized crime

Organized criminals in cyberspace are no different from organized criminals in the physical world. They are engaging in illegal behavior to make a profit. This means that they are looking to steal information that can easily be monetized, or they are looking to extort an organization using ransomware. Some organized criminals, especially those targeting financial institutions, are very sophisticated. However, of the threat actor groups, the attacks launched by organized criminals tend to be less specifically targeted and less sophisticated than the attacks launched by other groups.

The first target of organized criminals is information they can sell on the dark web. Historically, this has been financial information such as credit card numbers and **Personally Identifiable Information** (**PII**) that can identify an individual or help facilitate identity theft. In either case, the amount of revenue they can generate is directly related to the amount of information they are able to steal. As a result, these attacks often target large organizations that house the targeted information type. If your organization houses large volumes of these types of information, you'll find the *Stealing information* section of this chapter very important.

The second target of organized criminals that has recently grown in popularity is ransomware. Ransomware is a specific type of malicious software that encrypts information and holds it for ransom, providing the decryption key, and therefore access to the information, in exchange for payment. In 2021, the number of ransomware attacks more than doubled from 2020.

Several factors are driving the increasing popularity of ransomware. First, more victims are paying the ransom. Organized criminals have taken steps to ensure victims who pay the ransom have a good experience in restoring their information. Organized criminals who specialize in ransomware have gone as far as to brand themselves and have created technical support organizations to help victims who are having difficulty with the decryption key. Second, cryptocurrency has made it much easier for criminals to collect payment with less risk of getting caught. With traditional currency payments, the money must be laundered, which requires sophistication, expertise, and capital. With cryptocurrency, laundering the payments is not necessary. Third, people continue to fall victim to phishing schemes. Ransomware is popular because it works. It is not difficult for ransomware groups to infect computers, collect a payment, and restore them. Until the average computer user becomes more cautious, we will continue to see ransomware infections increase.

Organized criminals are more likely than other groups to launch indiscriminate attacks across many potential victims. Organized criminals can be successful in accomplishing their objectives without targeting a single, specific victim. As a result, organized criminals are more likely to use commoditized malicious software or seek to exploit known vulnerabilities. Since organized criminals are either looking for the largest or the softest targets, defenders can deploy basic countermeasures that will make them a less attractive target. Most organizations that fall victim to a cyber attack and are successfully attacked are either very large and specifically targeted, or they failed to follow basic best practices, which made them an attractive target.

Organized criminals operate similarly to legitimate businesses in how they make decisions. They evaluate their operations based on risk and reward as well as profitability. The target that allows them to generate the most revenue with the least effort and the least risk is the most attractive.

An important aspect that is unique to organized criminals is the monetization step of the attack chain. This step is often the step where the operation is discovered. Many companies are notified by law enforcement that is monitoring the dark web when their information has been breached. As a result, there is more known about attacks by criminals than other groups.

The next group, state-sponsored actors, is harder to detect and behaves differently.

State-sponsored actors and military operations

State-sponsored actors are generally the most sophisticated group of adversaries and the most difficult to detect. It is difficult to know how many state-sponsored attacks happen because state-sponsored actors are not motivated to reveal their operations. There is no need to sell information on the dark web and the information they are targeting is known before the operation is launched. The targets are very specific and are rarely targets of opportunity. Most countries have an offensive cyber-warfare capability.

State-sponsored actors are more likely than any other group to research their own exploits and create zero-day threats. A *zero-day threat* is an attack method that was unknown prior to it being launched. Zero-day threats are very difficult to defend against, but also very costly to research and develop.

State-sponsored actors are most likely to steal information related to intellectual property or conduct electronic espionage. Not only are the types of information they are looking for are different, but their behavior during and after an intrusion is different as well.

First, criminals don't care if their activities and tactics are discovered after they've accomplished their objectives. State-sponsored actors are often as covert as possible. If they use a novel exploit and they cover their tracks well, they can re-use that exploit against another target. They also take great pains to cover their tracks and make attribution difficult. Sometimes the intrusion is detected, but it is often difficult to trace it back to who sponsored the attack. Very sophisticated attacks are often attributed to the state-sponsored category, but identification of the actual sponsor is rare.

Second, if the attack is successful and the actions are not discovered, state-sponsored actors are not motivated to disclose their activities after the breach. It is rare that state-sponsored groups will brag about a successful operation or that the information they stole will be made available on the dark web.

Third, state-sponsored actors are patient. In some cases, if they do not have an intended offensive objective, they will simply compromise an environment and lay dormant and undetected in case they choose to launch an attack later. In other cases, the objective is surveillance. They simply want to see what their ally or adversary is doing or saying.

State-sponsored operations are either designed to do damage or to steal information. It would be rare for a state-sponsored actor to engage in an extortion campaign. The next group we will discuss, hacktivists and terrorists, deploys tactics used by other groups, but their motivations are different.

Hacktivists and terrorists

Hacktivists are threat actor groups that attack organizations they disagree with to make a political statement. The most well-known hacktivist group is *Anonymous*. Hacktivists and terrorists are very similar. An argument could be made that hacktivists are a subset of terrorists, but terrorists generally have a broader set of tactics and aims. We will start by talking about hacktivists.

Hacktivists tend to be technically savvy and have access to broad networks of actors with significant capabilities. They normally launch attacks against groups with whom they disagree to make a statement. Because they are trying to gather attention, they often claim responsibility for their attacks. Also, because they make public statements, you can anticipate which hacktivists groups may target your organization. Many organizations are unlikely to be targeted by hacktivist groups.

Hacktivist groups generally target information meant to expose people or tactics or focus on system damage. Taking down or defacing public websites is a favorite tactic because of the visibility it has. Also, using stolen information to expose an organization is common.

Terrorists aren't often seen as a cyber threat, but the ability to cause real damage through offensive cyber operations is increasing every day. When the **Islamic State of Iraq and Syria** (**ISIS**) was at its peak, they used social media for recruiting and propaganda to great effect. In an example case later in this chapter, we will explore an attack on the Ukrainian power grid that caused a widespread outage across the capital city of Kiev. An attack by a terrorist group on a hydroelectric dam could flood a community. As the world becomes more connected, the opportunity for terrorists to wreak havoc using cyber operations increases.

We discussed insider threats in detail in *Chapter 2*, *The Human Side of Cybersecurity*. However, they are also a threat actor group that should be discussed in the context of threat actor groups.

Insider threats

Insider threats are an important threat actor group because they have a significant advantage over other threat actor groups. Insider threats do not need to gain access to the network or the information because they already have it. There are many insider threat examples. Among the most compelling is the Becton Dickinson case.

Example Case: Becton Dickinson Theft

Becton, Dickinson, and Company is a large medical device manufacturer in Franklin Lakes, New Jersey. BD, as it is commonly known, is among the oldest medical device manufacturers in the United States. In 2013 and 2014, BD was working on a next-generation epi-pen injector that was expected to be a major revenue-producing product globally. As part of this development effort, they hired a number of full-time and contract resources to aid in the development project. Among the engineers working for the company was Ketankumar Maniar.

During his employment, Mr. Maniar decided to steal secret information from Becton Dickinson and move back to India. Fortunately for Becton Dickinson, they had deployed controls that allowed them to identify Mr. Maniar's suspicious activity and take action quickly. Following a rapid response from BD resources, the Federal Bureau of Investigations served a search warrant for Mr. Maniar's hotel room and rental car and arrested him before he could leave the country.

As the legal process played out, Mr. Maniar eventually pleaded guilty to stealing trade secret information from Becton Dickinson for his own economic benefit. During the investigation, it was discovered that Mr. Maniar also worked for a competitor of Becton Dickinson, *C.R. Bard Inc.*, and stole trade secret information from them. The difference between Bard and Becton Dickinson is that Becton Dickinson had a proper insider threat program and response capability in place that allowed them to detect the unauthorized behavior and respond. Bard was unaware of the theft until the investigation demonstrated Mr. Maniar had stolen from them as well. If Becton Dickinson had not discovered this insider attack, Bard likely would have never known how their intellectual property was misappropriated.

Ketankumar Maniar is the rare example of an insider threat that likely had malicious intent from the time he was hired. Since he had previously stolen similar information from a competitor, it appears that he joined *Becton, Dickinson, and Company* intending to steal their trade secrets for his own economic benefit. Mr. Maniar is also a poster child for insider threats. He lived and worked in the New Jersey community with his friends and co-workers. Few people would have predicted that their co-worker would be stealing information from their mutual employer, potentially putting their jobs at risk. The challenge with insider threats is that you cannot predict who they are, so you must monitor everyone who could potentially cause harm to the organization (United States Department of Justice, 2014).

Insider threats present unique challenges. They also have a much shorter attack chain than external actors because they often start with access to the systems and information they are targeting. Every other group must go through a process to accomplish their objective. Next, we will address how to build a risk treatment plan for cybersecurity.

Risk treatment planning

As one of my leaders, Steven Drew, is fond of saying, *You shouldn't spend a dollar to protect a nickel.* Effective cybersecurity is a risk management exercise. When building a risk treatment plan, there are four choices a company can make for each risk on the risk register:

- **Risk Acceptance**: This is the default mode. If an organization does nothing about an identified risk, they are accepting the risk. If an organization fails to identify a risk, they are accepting the risk. Risk acceptance is an appropriate strategy, but only if the risk is identified and the person accepting the risk on behalf of the organization has the authority to do so. It is rarely a security practitioner's responsibility to make risk acceptance decisions. Risk acceptance authority is generally granted at different levels of business leadership. There will likely be a threshold for risk acceptance for the VP level, another threshold for the C Suite, and some levels of risk that should be reviewed and accepted by the board.
- **Risk Avoidance**: The second option for an organization is to avoid risk. An extreme example of risk avoidance is if a company does not want to comply with **Payment Card Industry** (**PCI**) rules, the organization can choose to no longer accept credit card payments. Clearly, this choice would have business implications and would not necessarily be the right fit for a business. Similar to risk acceptance, it would often be a member of the business leadership team making risk avoidance decisions, not the security team. Risk avoidance always has a cost, but that cost is associated with lost productivity or a reduction in revenue, not a cash outlay.
- **Risk Transference**: The third option is for an organization to transfer the risk to someone else, in exchange for money. Insurance policies are a risk transference strategy. In most cases, cyber insurance does not cover all the costs associated with a breach. Most estimates indicate that 50%-75% of the costs of a data breach are indirect costs. These include reduced sales or loss of brand reputation. These costs are difficult to quantify and, therefore, difficult to insure.

- **Risk Mitigation**: The final option is to mitigate the risk. Risk mitigation means to lessen the impact of the risk should it manifest, or to lessen the likelihood it will manifest. Cybersecurity is risk mitigation for risks to sensitive information or systems. Risk mitigation always has a cost. Defining the benefit of mitigating a risk is key to making effective information security budgeting and purchasing decisions.

If you choose to mitigate a particular risk, it is important to understand different attackers, the tactics they use, and their intended goals to assess the likelihood and potential impact of a certain type of attack. Doing so will help prioritize cybersecurity investments. Too often, cybersecurity technologies are purchased based on what is perceived to be the hot new technology or the types of attacks a company fears most, rather than a thoughtful analysis of the risk landscape. If you believe your data will be targeted by criminals, understanding the stages of the attack will help you deploy the proper countermeasures to decrease the likelihood those criminals will successfully steal your information. If the risk you intend to mitigate is a disruption to a critical system, there is a different set of countermeasures that would be appropriate to protect those systems.

Next, we will discuss the process of how an external attacker would exploit an organization.

Stages of an attack

There are a few popular models to describe how attackers compromise an organization and achieve their objectives. One is the *Cyber Kill Chain* (Lockheed Martin), which was developed by Lockheed Martin and is mostly focused on **Advanced Persistent Threats** (**APTs**), who are often state-sponsored or very sophisticated organized criminals. Another very detailed model is the MITRE ATT&CK Framework.

Both frameworks are good. The MITRE framework is very detailed, and the Cyber Kill Chain is very specific to one type of threat actor. For the purposes of this discussion, there is a separate process for each of the three primary objectives – extortion, stealing information, and damaging systems. We will start with extortion schemes. The most common cyber extortion scheme is a ransomware attack.

Extortion

Extortion means to gain something of value using force or threats. Ransomware is an extortion tactic that threatens a person or company's access to their information. Ransomware is a specific type of malicious software that is delivered as a virus or a worm. The most successful ransomware attacks do not infect a single machine and make demands. Instead, the most successful lie dormant for a period so they can spread throughout a network. Next, they quietly begin encrypting as many files as the software can access. Only once a significant number of files have been encrypted do they notify the user, normally through a pop-up message, and demand payment.

> **Ransomware 2.0**
>
> Extortion through ransomware today is an attack against access to files. While it may be disruptive or distressing to lose access to important information, ransomware could be much worse in the future. The world is more connected than ever. The average person has dozens of devices in their house or that they wear that are connected to the internet. All of those devices are potentially vulnerable. Many electric car companies are connecting their cars to the internet to allow for software updates and telemetry. While this is much more convenient than going to a mechanic, it also increases the average person's attack surface. What if ransomware were able to infect your vehicle and make demands of you in exchange for control of the car you were driving? The *Internet of Things* offers exciting capabilities for humanity. It also offers a very scary opportunity for organized crime.
>
> It should be noted that none of this is intended to scare you. I drive an electric car with over-the-air updates enabled. Some very smart people work tirelessly to protect us. There are two key lessons with respect to connected devices and ransomware, however. First, you should evaluate the security posture of any company you purchase a connected device from. If you don't understand and believe in their cybersecurity posture, you should question whether you want or need their device. Second, the stakes for ransomware are increasing. You must remain vigilant at home. The next generation of ransomware could allow criminals to threaten people's lives, rather than simply gaining access to information.

How do ransomware attacks happen? The first step is to gain access to the target system or network.

Gaining access to target systems

The first step of a ransomware attack is to gain access to the target systems. Ransomware is often delivered through a phishing attack and is mostly deployed by criminals who are not specifically targeting a single organization. As a result, there is little reconnaissance done upfront. Instead, the attacker will send a phishing lure to many people. The phishing lure will either have an attachment that contains malware or will be designed to trick a user into providing credentials in a fake portal. Often, credential phishing campaigns targeting organizations will mirror password reset emails as closely as possible.

Once access is gained, the attacker may try to escalate privileges or move laterally throughout the environment to gain access to the systems that are most likely to make their attack successful. Attackers are looking for systems with access to as much information as possible. Organizations that give users too many permissions make it easier for attackers to find systems with the access they need.

Next, we will explore what attackers will do with the access they have gained. In the case of an extortion event, the objective is to install malicious software.

Installing malicious software

With proper privileges, installing malicious software is easy. Without privileged credentials, attackers will need to trick someone with privileged credentials into installing the malicious software. Both cases are common in ransomware attacks. The common delivery methods are viruses and worms. Viruses require an end user to install and help propagate the malicious software. They are less sophisticated and easier to develop than worms. Sophisticated ransomware actors may use worms as a delivery method. These worms, once installed on a single computer, can propagate themselves through the network without additional human activation.

Some basic defenses against the remote installation of malicious software can be put in place with little expense or effort. First, enabling **User Account Control** (**UAC**) will warn the user when software requiring administrative permissions is being installed. If a user is opening a document and they get a UAC message, they should pause to wonder why a document would need to install software. Second, most users do not need local Administrator privileges on their machines. Limiting Administrator privileges directly limits the attack surface, or the number of accounts that an attacker could compromise to install malicious software. Third, for users who are going to be a local Administrator, it is the best practice to give those privileges to an account that is different from their main user account. Doing so ensures their primary account cannot be used for administrative functions.

In the case of ransomware, the most effective pieces of malicious software do not act as soon as they are installed. Instead, they spread the infection while lying dormant for some time.

Spreading the infection

Once the ransomware is in the environment, it is often designed to harvest as many credentials as it can, to allow it to spread as widely through the environment as possible. Often, ransomware is designed to attempt to spread to a Domain Controller or a Domain Administrator account, which are generally controlled by the information technology team in an organization. Once the ransomware has compromised a Domain Controller or Domain Administrator account, it can propagate across an environment and locate and encrypt backup files. This is a key portion of the attack. If the ransomware does not successfully infect the backup files, the organization can restore their information from backup without paying the ransom.

Network segmentation is an effective defense against the rapid spread of ransomware. A properly segmented network makes it difficult for ransomware to spread and successfully move laterally and attack backups. Second, ensuring user accounts only have access to the minimum resources necessary to perform their function will also help contain an infection if one were to occur.

Once the ransomware has attacked key objectives, it must notify the victim that they have been attacked and make demands for payment.

Notifying the victim and making demands

Once the infection has spread throughout the environment, the attacker needs to notify the victim of what has transpired and make a payment demand. While ransomware attacks vary, there are common elements across all of them. The elements are as follows:

- A pop-up message designed to create fear
- A description of what has happened
- A time limit and a countdown to create urgency
- Instructions for payment and recovery

We will briefly describe each of the elements of the ransomware notification.

Pop-up message

The first element of the notification is the pop-up message itself. Most of the time, there is a scary-looking logo at the top. Common choices are the skull and crossbones logo, or a logo of a lock. The colors are often selected to be ominous as well. Common choices are black backgrounds or red backgrounds. As time goes on, more ransomware criminals are building a brand and putting that brand on their pop-up messages. It is critical for the ransomware business model for the victim to believe that if they pay the ransom, they will get their files back. If the victim believes their files are gone regardless, there is no motivation for them to pay the ransom.

Once the attacker has gained the victim's attention, they need to quickly help the victim understand what has happened.

Ransomware description

The next portion of the notification tells the victim what has happened. The message will tell the user that their files have been encrypted and they won't be able to access them. They also notify the victim that they can recover their files, but only if they pay for the decryption key. There is often a warning to the victim that instructs them not to try to recover files themselves or rename them. Often, the threat is explicit that unless the victim follows the instructions explicitly and quickly, they will lose their files forever.

The next portion of the ransomware notification is designed to create urgency on the part of the victim. Creating urgency is an important tactic in the attacker's toolbox. The theory is that when people are rushed and afraid, they do not think rationally about their actions, and are more likely to behave in a way that benefits the attacker.

Time limit and countdown

Urgency in ransomware is created by a countdown. Often, the victim is given a time limit to pay. There is usually a countdown clock on the pop-up notification. In some cases, the threat is that the decryption key will be deleted forever at the end of the countdown clock. However, if an attacker destroys the files, the cyber crime version of shooting the hostage, they will not profit from the attack. As a result, it is becoming more common for the price for the decryption key to escalate based on the time frame. For example, a ransomware attack may demand payment within 3 days, with the price doubling each day after the clock expires. In any case, the countdown creates urgency for the victim.

The next portion of the notification is designed to help the victim understand how they can pay the attacker and restore access to their files.

Instructions for payment

The last portion of the notification is designed to help the victim transfer funds to the attacker if they decide to pay the ransom. Attackers often demand payment in cryptocurrency because it is easy for them to track if the victim has paid them, and it is outside the purview of national governments who monitor transactions for illicit activity. However, victims may not be familiar with cryptocurrency or how to use it. As a result, attackers will provide instructions to the victim on how they can convert their money into the proper amount of cryptocurrency and how to transfer it to the attacker. Successful ransomware attackers provide clear instructions and support for victims who decide to pay the ransom.

Once the victim has paid the ransom, the attacker will then verify the payment and restore the systems. As ransomware actors continue to act more like a business, it is important to them to gain a reputation for restoring victims' systems after they have paid the ransom.

Verifying payment and restoring systems

Once payment has been received and verified, attackers help systems restore their systems. In many cases, attackers have built a technical support division to help victims restore their systems if they encounter issues. Ransomware actors are like organized crime syndicates that were running protection rackets. If you did not pay the criminals for protection, they may attack you themselves. However, if you paid them, you became their customer and they would not only not attack you, but they would also ensure others didn't attack you as well. A shop owner may not be happy about paying for protection, but it was important for the illicit business to ensure that nothing bad happened to shop owners that paid. Ransomware criminals are similar. They want to ensure that people who pay the ransom have a good experience to motivate other victims to pay the ransom.

Example Case: Colonial Pipeline Attack

Colonial Pipeline operates the largest fuel pipeline in the United States. The pipeline transports 100 million gallons of gasoline every day and supplies 45% of the fuel consumed on the East Coast of the United States. In May 2021, Colonial Pipeline was hit by a ransomware attack that led to fuel shortages across the eastern and southern portions of the United States. It was discovered that the attack was caused by a single compromised password purchased from the dark web. Since there is no known password compromise from Colonial Pipeline directly, the root cause of the infection can likely be traced to an employee re-using credentials from a compromised site as their corporate password.

While the employee clearly made a mistake, if a single employee's mistake can cause a large-scale incident, it is the fault of the process and the technology as well as the user. This is true in the Colonial Pipeline case as well. The **Virtual Private Network (VPN)** allowed remote access to Colonial Pipeline systems with only a username and password. No multifactor authentication was deployed. For many years, threat researchers have continuously reminded the community that most breaches could be stopped by eliminating publicly facing systems and services that allow access with a single factor of authentication. Multifactor authentication is an important measure to help limit the damage caused by stolen passwords.

In response to the attack, Colonial Pipeline proactively froze their IT systems and networks to limit the spread of the infection. For 6 days, from May 6 to May 13, Colonial Pipeline attempted to contain and eradicate the infection. On May 13, they gave into the attacker's demands and made a Bitcoin payment equivalent to roughly $5 million.

The attack was launched by a known group known as DarkSide, and the targeted systems were on the business side, not the operational side. As a result, the attack was designed to generate revenue from the payment of a ransom, not to damage systems. However, because of the decision to proactively shut down the systems while they were evaluating the attack, the attack resulted in the failure of critical infrastructure and a disruption to daily life for millions of consumers.

DarkSide claims that they are apolitical and were not trying to target critical infrastructure. Instead, they are in the ransomware business to make money. DarkSide is a well-known ransomware actor. Their decryption keys have been leaked in the past, but it appears they use a new key for each attack because the previously leaked keys were provided to Colonial Pipeline and did not decrypt the affected files.

Example Case: Colonial Pipeline Attack

Because of the disruption to daily life caused by the attack, the response from the United States government and Colonial Pipeline themselves was aggressive. President Joe Biden even made statements referring to the United States offensive cyber capability and refusing to rule out a strike against DarkSide. In response to the pressure, DarkSide announced they were shutting down on June 8th. It is unlikely that the people associated with DarkSide will cease criminal operations. Instead, DarkSide as a brand will cease operations while the people will either reconstitute under a different name or join other criminal organizations.

The response to the Colonial Pipeline attack represents a change in the response to large-scale attacks. In the past, law enforcement advised victims not to pay the ransom to prevent motivation for more attacks. Outside of limited assistance in recovery, there was little coordinated response from the government. In response to Colonial Pipeline, the aggressive targeting of people associated with DarkSide and DarkSide as an organization indicates that critical infrastructure is a line criminals should be wary of crossing. However, since the response was successful at shutting down the group and recovering some of the ransom payment, why wouldn't a similar response be appropriate for any large-scale ransomware attack? (Schwirtz, 2021), (Osborne, 2021), (Turton, 2021)

While ransomware gets many of the headlines, it is not the most common way that criminals make money. It is also not the preferred attack method for the most sophisticated actors. While ransomware is an attack on the availability of information, attacking the confidentiality of information is more lucrative. For this reason, the largest attacks and the most sophisticated actors are focused on stealing information.

Stealing information

Information theft falls into two categories. The first is regulated information such as **Protected Health Information** (**PHI**) and **Personally Identifiable Information** (**PII**), while financial information such as credit card numbers is often targeted by criminals to make a profit. The second is intellectual property, which is often targeted by more sophisticated actors. While some elements of the attack are the same between malicious software attacks and information theft attacks, elements are necessarily different.

When performing an extortion attack, the target is indiscriminate. It doesn't matter what the information is if it is important to the victim. When stealing information, the information must be targeted, either as information that is valuable in a dark web marketplace, or information that is valuable to the attacker. As a result, the first step is for the attacker to identify what information they may want to target and who has the information they want.

Identifying what to steal

Each threat actor has a different objective and, as a result, will have a different set of targets. When stealing information, indiscriminate attacks are often not effective. Since certain types of information are targeted, the first step for the attacker is to find out who has the information they want. In the case of intellectual property theft, they are looking to steal a very specific piece of information that is only held by a single organization. In the case of regulated information, the volume of information that is held by the target determines the profitability of the attack. While attacking small victims may be easier, the attack is less lucrative. This is why large organizations that store large volumes of information are constantly under attack. Other organizations that conduct research or contain very valuable intellectual property are often targeted by nation-states or industrial espionage actors and insider threats.

Once the attacker has identified the target, the next step is to determine how they will gain access to the targeted information.

Gaining access to information

There are many methods in which an attacker can gain access to information they would like to steal. In some cases, attackers may look for vulnerabilities in an environment. It is not difficult for a company to identify known vulnerabilities in their systems using scanning tools. It is also not difficult for attackers to identify known vulnerabilities with known exploits using similar tools. As a result, it is often a race between the defender and the attacker. The defender must identify and patch the vulnerability before the attacker identifies and exploits the vulnerability.

In other cases, attackers will gain access to information by compromising accounts using previously discussed techniques. Once an attacker has access to an environment, they can use the credentials to discover what types of information can be accessed. If accounts are overly permissive, attackers may have all the access they need. If accounts are provisioned properly and networks are segmented, the attacker may have to move laterally or escalate privileges to achieve the objective.

Another method is to utilize a malicious insider. Malicious insiders may be disenfranchised employees or people motivated by their own self-interest. In some cases, they may be bribed. In others, they may be cultivated by the attacker. Cultivating a source involves befriending a target and trying to slowly turn them against their employer. This is a common practice in law enforcement and statecraft.

Once an attacker has access to the information they want, it is often not all in one place. Therefore, the next step is for the attacker to aggregate the information to make it easier to exfiltrate.

Aggregating information

Aggregating information is a necessary step before the exfiltration event. In some cases, such as an attack directly against a database housing sensitive information, all the information is already in one place. In other cases, the information must be gathered from multiple sources. When information is aggregated from a variety of sources, attackers may choose to launch a *low and slow* attack. A low and slow attack is designed to avoid detection by moving small volumes of information over a long period of time, rather than moving large volumes of information quickly. The objective is to aggregate as much information as possible before packaging it for exfiltration.

In other cases, attackers will rely on their ability to move faster than defenders and will move as much information as possible as quickly as they can. The key metric in preventing low and slow attacks is to reduce the dwell time of an attacker. Dwell time refers to the amount of time an attacker can remain in an environment undetected. Stopping attacks where the attacker is moving as much information as they can as quickly as possible relies upon the metrics of **Mean time to Detect** (**MttD**) and **Mean time to Respond** (**MttR**). These metrics measure how quickly an organization can detect and respond to attacks. The faster the response, the less an attacker can steal.

The type of attack used is often linked to the sophistication of the attacker. Sophisticated actors often use low and slow attacks because it is important to them that their attack is not detected until it is over, or ideally, if the attack is never detected at all. Less sophisticated actors who are less confident in their ability to remain undetected indefinitely will often use methods designed to steal as much as possible as quickly as they can.

Once the information that has been targeted is aggregated in a single location, the next step is for the attacker to move the data outside the target environment and into an environment they control. This process is known as exfiltration.

Exfiltrating information

Information exfiltration often involves encryption and movement. The information is often encrypted to make it less likely to be detected and blocked at the perimeter. Many organizations have solutions in place to block certain types of information as it leaves the environment. Encrypting the information can help defeat these types of rules. As a result, many organizations block encrypted file transfers using encryption methods not deployed by the organization or block large file transfers out of the environment. However, in most organizations, there is a method in which an attacker can transfer a large volume of encrypted information outside the organization. Sometimes, the attacker will use protocols designed to transfer large volumes of information, such as **File Transfer Protocol** (**FTP**). In other cases, the attacker can transfer information to a cloud service and share it externally. There are countless methods of exfiltration attackers can use.

The key idea for defenders is to understand what methods of transmission are necessary to conduct business. Any transmission mechanism that is not necessary for business should be blocked. Blocking protocols and transmission methods that are unnecessary is one way in which an organization can shrink its attack surface. Attack surface is a measure of how an organization can be attacked, and therefore a measure of how difficult it is for the organization to defend itself. If a transmission method is necessary, it should be monitored. The organization should be able to analyze the source, destination, and content of any transaction. If the transaction cannot be analyzed, it should be blocked, or at least quarantined and reviewed. This monitoring and enforcement is commonly referred to as the *Information Protection discipline* and is among the most important and difficult challenges faced by modern organizations.

Once an attacker has full control of the data and has moved it outside the target environment, they must generate economic benefit.

Generating economic benefit

In the case of intellectual property theft, the economic benefit is often achieved as soon as the information is exfiltrated. In the case of regulated data, it is often offered for sale in dark web marketplaces. Many companies that are targeted for information theft discover the breach when the information is put up for sale, and it is often discovered by a law enforcement agency, rather than the target organization itself.

Information is available for sale on the dark web every day. There are large databases of information that can help criminals commit identity theft, financial fraud, or target their phishing attacks better. There are many ways in which a creative criminal can use stolen information. There is no shortage of buyers for stolen information, which is one of the reasons why the proceeds from cybercrime continue to rise with each passing year. The efficiency of the dark web marketplace allows attackers to understand the value of different information types similar to how commodities markets allow traders to understand the real-time value of commodities such as oil and corn. This value per record drives the illicit economy and helps attackers decide which types of data to target. While organizations do not need to closely monitor the dark web, it is worthwhile knowing what types of information the organization may possess that could be valuable to an attacker to build proper defenses around that information.

Not all attacks are focused on information. Extortion schemes focus on the availability of information and information theft attacks focus on attacking the confidentiality of information. The next attack type is focused on the integrity of systems.

System disruption or destruction

Attacks against the integrity of systems are rarely focused on economic benefit for the attacker. Instead, the attacks are focused on harming the victim. As a result, these types of attacks are often the domain of hacktivists, terrorists, and nation states. These attacks are designed to deface or destroy systems.

The first type of attack is an attack on critical infrastructure.

Attacks on critical infrastructure

Many people believe attacks on truly critical infrastructure are the worst-case scenario. It could be argued that the Colonial Pipeline attack was the closest to a critical infrastructure attack we have seen in the United States. However, there have been large-scale critical infrastructure attacks in other parts of the world. The Colonial Pipeline attack was a ransomware attack. Attacks on critical infrastructure that are designed to cause damage rather than to compel a company to pay a ransom can be far more destructive. A very good, and very scary, example happened in Ukraine.

Example Case: Industroyer Attack on the Ukrainian Power Grid

Attacks designed to destroy systems are rare, but they pose an immediate and catastrophic threat for people around the world. The December 2016 attack on the Ukrainian power grid that is widely attributed to Russia's offensive cyber capability is one such attack. On December 23, 2016, the power grid operator in Ukraine, Ukrenego, experienced a cyber attack that caused all of the circuit breakers in a distribution center in Kiev to open simultaneously. The attack caused an orchestrated blackout across a significant portion of the Ukrainian capital. About an hour later, the power was switched back on. Overall, the disruption was significant, but not catastrophic.

After further investigation, it has become clear that the malware, Industroyer, did not function as it was designed. The intention was never to cause a short-term disruption. The malware was designed to disable some of the protective systems that prevent physical damage to electric transmission equipment. The apparent intention of the attack was for the Ukrainians to re-energize the systems in an effort to restore power, not knowing the protective systems had been disabled, therefore causing catastrophic damage to the power grid. Ultimately, the most destructive portion of the attack did not work properly for reasons that are not fully understood (Greenberg, 2019).

The key learning point from Industroyer is not studying what happened, but instead studying what the attackers intended to happen and the type of damage that could be caused by a successful cyber attack. While it is still rare to see destructive malicious software attacks in the wild today, it is possible that they will become more common, especially as sophisticated actors launch escalating attacks against each other.

There are international agreements that govern the rules of warfare, such as the Geneva Conventions, that are designed to limit collateral damage to civilians, among other things. No such rules exist for cyber warfare and many countries, including those that may be considered rogue nations, are beginning to develop the types of capabilities that would allow them to launch attacks that could cause major harm to people as well as economies. The question is, how would a targeted country respond? Would the retaliation remain digital, or would it become kinetic? At what point is a cyber attack truly an act of war?

Increasingly, cyber attacks can be used to attack countries. This opens the door for cyberwar and cyber terrorism. These types of attacks that can inflict harm in the physical world because of a cyber attack raise the stakes for cybersecurity.

The next attacks we will explore are attacks motivated by revenge rather than attacks against a real or perceived adversary.

Revenge attacks

Most attacks are motivated by financial gain or espionage. Sometimes, the motivation for the attack is based on righting a perceived wrong. As the *Lennon Ray Brown and Citibank case* from *Chapter 1, Protecting People, Information, and Systems – a Growing Problem,* demonstrates, any employee can become an insider threat based on a perceived slight. In Mr. Brown's case, it was a poor performance review that triggered the malicious turn. In other cases, someone could feel slighted by not getting a raise or being passed over for a promotion.

Revenge attacks are also not limited to insiders. Hacktivist attacks could be classified as revenge attacks. **Distributed Denial of Service** (**DDoS**) attacks, which leverage large numbers of computers to simultaneously flood a server so that legitimate traffic cannot be processed, are designed to damage or embarrass a company, not to steal information or extort the victim. The motivation for these attacks is often a real or perceived slight. The behavior of the attackers is different as well. In many types of attacks, the attacker does not want the attack attributed to them. In revenge attacks by third parties such as hacktivist or terrorist groups, the attacker will often claim responsibility for the attack.

In some cases, the attacks are covert or overt acts of war, intended to destroy systems that are of critical importance to the target country.

Cyber weapons of war

Most countries are developing or have developed an offensive cyber capability. Countries around the world are frequently probing the defenses of allies and adversaries daily. In some cases, it may be preferable to use cyber means to attack a country rather than using conventional military power. The Stuxnet attack is one of the most high-profile examples of using an offensive cyber capability instead of a conventional military attack.

Example Case: Stuxnet

In 2010, a very sophisticated computer worm was discovered that appeared to be intended to destroy systems. This was the first time an offensive cyber weapon with the sophistication to be considered a military weapon had been discovered. This worm, which would later become known as Stuxnet, was perfectly designed as an offensive weapon.

Stuxnet is a worm, which means it can spread and infect computers without being explicitly installed by an end user like a virus. Stuxnet is not only a worm, though, but also a worm that is specifically designed to accomplish a military objective. Stuxnet operates in three stages. First, it infects a Microsoft Windows machine and replicates itself to other Windows machines. It does not affect those machines, and it would be difficult to know whether a machine was infected with Stuxnet. In the second stage, the worm specifically targets Siemens STEP7 software, which also runs on Windows devices. Siemens STEP7 is software that controls industrial systems, which control devices such as centrifuges, much like the centrifuges that were central to Iran's nuclear enrichment capabilities. The third step was to compromise the logic controllers for the centrifuges. Once they were compromised, Stuxnet allowed operators to monitor the centrifuges remotely, and could even modify the controllers to cause the centrifuges to destroy themselves.

It is believed that the United States and Israel collaborated to create Stuxnet to monitor and disrupt Iran's nuclear enrichment activities. It is believed that Stuxnet infected 14 Iranian sites, including at least one of the three known nuclear enrichment sites. Iran denies Stuxnet degraded any of its capabilities, but reports indicate that numerous centrifuges were destroyed in Iran's Natanz facility. If this is true, Stuxnet would be the first known successful cyber warfare operation. It will not be the last. The story of Stuxnet is a mix between traditional statecraft and new cyber warfare. Reports indicate that spies and double agents were used to introduce the malicious code into the facility. These agents were necessary because the original introduction of Stuxnet required physical access to a computer since the worm was delivered on a USB device. The world is much more connected today, and it would likely be possible to introduce a worm into an environment using phishing or other social engineering techniques.

The story of Stuxnet does not end with the successful attack on Iran's nuclear program. Stuxnet was more effective at spreading than its creators anticipated, and it escaped into the wild. United States companies and government agencies began to see Stuxnet attacks in 2012. Since Stuxnet, there have been several exploits developed for military or statecraft purposes that have been leaked and used in the private sector. As a result, even companies that are unlikely to be targeted by very sophisticated actors such as nation states must be prepared to defend themselves against very sophisticated pieces of malicious software (Kushner, 2013) (Anderson, 2012).

The United States and Israel could have attacked Iran directly to degrade their capability to create nuclear weapons. However, had they done so, they would have started a large-scale war that would have cost countless lives on both sides. By using a computer worm instead, it could be argued the lives saved justified launching the attack.

The other side of the argument, however, is that the attack opens a new type of warfare that can escalate out of control. In fact, there is evidence that the United States and Israel lost control of Stuxnet, and it could theoretically be used by others to attack victims who don't know they're infected. Malicious software created as a weapon of war can be very dangerous, and there is little international agreement regulating how these weapons can be used and how they should be controlled.

In 2017, hacking tools created by the United States National Security Agency, including the powerful hacking tool Eternal Blue, were stolen from the agency. In the years since, the stolen tools have been used in many attacks, causing billions of dollars of damage (Perlroth, 2019). There is a legitimate question about whether the United States government should be liable for the damages that stem from attacks using the tools they developed and lost control of. When weapons of war of any kind fall into the wrong hands, they can create a very dangerous situation for organizations that do not have the resources necessary to defend themselves from these sophisticated weapons.

The next topic to discuss is directly related to the increased sophistication of the average cyber attack. Some attackers are becoming more sophisticated based on education and experience. Other attackers are launching sophisticated attacks without being sophisticated themselves. How are they doing so? They are hiring the skills that they need through an illicit marketplace.

Attackers for hire

On the dark web, you can hire attackers with specialized skill sets. In fact, you could launch attacks in the modern world with little technical expertise. All the skills necessary to launch a sophisticated attack are available to lease or purchase.

Dark web forums

The dark web is a common theme throughout much of the cyber criminal's value chain. The need to hire accomplices is no different. Offensive cyber criminal experts offer their services on dark web forums. A person with little capability outside of nefarious intent could purchase everything they need to launch a cyber attack on dark web forums. An individual could purchase a list of potential victims with contact information, purchase a well-crafted phishing lure, a sophisticated piece of malicious software, and services to deliver the malicious software, collect the payment, and help victims restore their files in the case of a ransomware attack.

This cooperation and specialization among attackers make the digital world a more dangerous place for organizations and individuals.

The most meaningful service offered on the dark web is malicious software as a service.

Malware as a Service

Some criminal organizations do not attack organizations directly. Instead, they have specialized in creating and distributing malicious software. Many of them control botnets or distribution networks and provide capabilities for their customers to orchestrate and control the attacks they launch, using the provider's malicious software infrastructure. Many times, the package includes support in case the purchasing criminal experiences technical issues with the package they purchased.

These companies operate similarly to legitimate **Software as a Service** (**SaaS**) companies. In fact, many parts of the illicit marketplace, especially when it comes to organized criminals, operate similarly to the legitimate business world. There are risk versus reward decisions, a cost versus benefit analysis, a marketplace for labor, a marketplace for technology, and a marketplace to monetize the information that is stolen or to collect payments from victims.

Summary

After reading this chapter, you should be more familiar with the types of threat actors that exist, and the ways that common attacks happen. You should also be aware of the dark web and how any attacker can gain sophistication through the dark web marketplace. Through our example cases, we explored how the different types of attacks can cause catastrophic damage both intentionally and through collateral damage.

In the next chapter, we will begin to discuss how an organization can protect itself. First, we will discuss some very well-known best practices that are rarely deployed. Most do not require advanced technologies, but they do require effort and thought. These often-ignored best practices can greatly decrease the likelihood of a successful attack and mitigate the damage caused, should such attacks occur.

Check your understanding

1. Describe the major threat actor groups and how they differ from each other.
2. What are the stages of a ransomware attack?
3. How does an information theft attack differ from a ransomware attack?
4. Which threat actor groups are likely to launch attacks with the intention of disrupting or destroying systems?
5. How would an attacker use the dark web to launch a sophisticated attack?

Further reading

- Anderson, N. (June 1, 2012). Confirmed: US and Israel created Stuxnet, lost control of it. Retrieved from ARS Technica: `https://arstechnica.com/tech-policy/2012/06/confirmed-us-israel-created-stuxnet-lost-control-of-it/`
- Greenberg, A. (September 12, 2019). New Clues Show how Russia's Grid Hackers Aimed for Physical Destruction. Retrieved from Wired: `https://www.wired.com/story/russia-ukraine-cyberattack-power-grid-blackout-destruction/`
- Kushner, D. (February 26, 2013). The Real Story of Stuxnet. Retrieved from IEEE Spectrum: `https://spectrum.ieee.org/the-real-story-of-stuxnet`
- Lockheed Martin. (n.d.). The Cyber Kill Chain. Retrieved from Lockheed Martin: `https://www.lockheedmartin.com/en-us/capabilities/cyber/cyber-kill-chain.html`
- MITRE. (n.d.). ATT&CK. Retrieved from MITRE: `https://attack.MITRE.org/`
- Osborne, C. (May 13, 2021). Colonial Pipeline paid close to $5 million in ransomware blackmail payment. Retrieved from Zero Day: `https://www.zdnet.com/article/colonial-pipeline-paid-close-to-5-million-in-ransomware-blackmail-payment/`

- Perlroth, N. A. (May 25, 2019). In Baltimore and Beyond, a Stolen N.S.A. Tool Wreaks Havoc. Retrieved from The New York Times: `https://www.nytimes.com/2019/05/25/us/nsa-hacking-tool-baltimore.html`
- Schwirtz, M. A. (June 8, 2021). DarkSide, Blamed for Gas Pipeline Attack, Says It Is Shutting Down. Retrieved from The New York Times: `https://www.nytimes.com/2021/05/14/business/darkside-pipeline-hack.html`
- Turton, W. A. (June 4, 2021). Hackers Breached Colonial Pipeline Using Compromised Password. Retrieved from Bloomberg Cybersecurity: `https://www.bloomberg.com/news/articles/2021-06-04/hackers-breached-colonial-pipeline-using-compromised-password`
- United States Department of Justice. (October 16, 2014). Former Engineer at Two Global Medical Technology Corporations Sentenced to 18 Months in Prison for the Theft of Trade Secrets. Retrieved from United States Department of Justice: `https://www.justice.gov/usao-nj/pr/former-engineer-two-global-medical-technology-corporations-sentenced-18-months-prison`

Section 2 – Building an Effective Program

This section is dedicated to building on the foundational knowledge in *Section 1* to build or improve an information security program. There are some timeless information security best practices that are as relevant today as they were decades ago. Interestingly, these timeless best practices are the ones that are routinely ignored in security programs. Next, it is important to address the weakest link in the program by building an effective security awareness program. Most companies perform security awareness training. Few succeed in educating their workforce. We will explore what they're doing wrong and how to do it better. Finally, there are additional capabilities that should be deployed to secure the modern enterprise that may not have been necessary previously.

This part of the book comprises the following chapters:

- *Chapter 4, Protecting People, Information, and Systems with Timeless Best Practices*
- *Chapter 5, Protecting against Common Attacks by Partnering with End Users*
- *Chapter 6, Information Security for a Changing World*

4
Protecting People, Information, and Systems with Timeless Best Practices

In the preceding chapters, we have defined the problem of information security, discussed the human side of cybersecurity, discussed what makes cybersecurity challenging, and analyzed the anatomy of an attack. All those chapters defined problems. This chapter is all about solutions. Fortunately, some timeless information security best practices are as relevant today as they were decades ago. Interestingly, these timeless best practices are the ones that are routinely ignored in security programs. If these ideas are not novel or difficult to understand, why are they so often ignored? The ideas are simple, well-known, and effective, but they are not easy to implement. These best practices are difficult, and the complexity of implementing them grows exponentially with the size of an organization. As a result, the companies that are most likely to be attacked are least likely to have implemented these best practices.

They are difficult because no technology will automate the process. These best practices rely primarily upon strong processes and well-trained people. In security, it is generally easier to deploy technology than it is to design intelligent processes and build a team of skilled professionals.

The consequences for ignoring these best practices are severe. To limit the economic damage due to breaches and to secure our future, we must build our security programs on solid foundations that have stood the test of time. Before diving into the best practices themselves, we need to discuss the most business-critical technology application in most organizations and the most important threat vector from a security perspective, email.

In this chapter, we will cover the following topics:

- The most important threat vector
- Time-honored best practices that could stop most breaches
- Capabilities necessary in the remote world
- The role of human behavior
- The everything, everywhere world

The most important threat vector

Email is the most important business communication method. The mainstream adoption of fax machines and then email changed the business world and greatly accelerated economic activity. Email is largely responsible for shrinking the globe. Before email and fax machines, if a US company wanted to communicate with a company in India, the team would either need to make very expensive trips or phone calls or send messages through traditional mail and wait 30 days for a response. The fax machine enabled near-instant communication, but it was an imperfect technology. Email allowed messages to be sent around the globe in 30 seconds, which greatly accelerated the global business cycle. It could be said that globalization as we know it today would not be possible without email.

Since email is so widely used and critical to business operations, it is also the most attacked part of a corporate infrastructure. Because email is a business-critical application, organizations usually prioritize uptime and availability of email infrastructure over security. This does not mean that attackers are instead targeting your email infrastructure, but rather using the email infrastructure as it is designed to efficiently deliver threats, just as your employees and business partners use it to deliver legitimate messages. How prevalent are email-based attacks? Let's look at the numbers.

Email attacks by the numbers

Unlike other types of communication protocols, most businesses have a need to allow emails from unverified third parties to be delivered to their users. Because email is rarely blocked, and it is such a critical application, many attacks start with email. Most statistics state that more than 90% of attacks start with email, and up to 96% of social engineering campaigns are delivered through email (Verizon, 2021).

Protecting users on the email channel is the single most impactful security step an organization can take. These protections come in many forms. In some cases, technology can be implemented to limit the damage that can be done if a user is tricked into clicking on a link. In other cases, harm from a user opening an attachment that contains malicious software can be limited by technology. Other types of technology can use machine learning to warn a user that a message may be suspicious or contains elements that are common among **Business Email Compromise** (**BEC**) schemes. In any case, the technology should be developed to support the end user and to make it easier for them to perform their business functions without putting the organization at risk.

Partnering with end users to protect information and systems is important. Users must be part of the solution. However, relying solely upon the end user to never make a mistake is not an effective information security strategy, regardless of how effective the end user's training may be. Next, we will look at the common types of email attacks that exist in the hope that this information can help you build defenses against these common tactics.

Types of email-based attacks

Most common attacks can be launched by email and the methods for the attacks are limited only by the imagination of the attacker. However, there are a limited number of ways that attackers can use email to harm a victim or create an economic benefit for themselves. In our discussion of email attack types, we will focus on those moments of truth, or the action the victim must take for the attacker to be successful.

It is of note that most attacks that are launched are still human-activated. What that means is that the purpose of the attack is to trick the victim into doing something that allows an attacker to be successful. In the context of email attacks, this means the recipient must do something and if they do nothing, the attack will fail. In *Chapter 5, Protecting against Common Attacks by Partnering with End Users*, we will discuss how organizations can decrease the likelihood that an end user will activate the attack, but for the purposes of this chapter, we will focus on the types of attacks and what the organization can do to protect themselves in case the user does activate the attack.

First, we will look at malicious links.

Malicious links

Malicious links are the most common form of email-based attacks. The attacker is trying to convince the user to click on a link. In many cases, the link text is changed to make the user think they are going to a legitimate website when they are instead being directed to a website controlled by the attacker. There are two common purposes in having an end user click on a link from the attacker's perspective.

First, attackers may want a user to click on a malicious link to install malicious software such as ransomware. These are often referred to as drive-by downloads. When the user clicks on the link, the software is downloaded, and the attacker attempts to convince the end user to install it. This software payload may be a virus or a worm and could be designed to carry out a variety of functions.

Second, the malicious link may be designed to harvest information from a victim. This is common in credential phishing techniques. A common example is trying to spoof a popular banking website. For the sake of example, we will use Chase. If an attacker can spoof an email address to make the message look like it is coming from Chase Bank and draft a message that appears to be legitimate, the attacker has an opportunity to trick Chase customers into clicking on the link. Often, the message itself will be designed to create urgency in the hope that the user will act quickly and not think critically about what they are doing. For example, the message may tell a user they need to log in and update their information to receive a payment or avoid a fee. If the user clicks on the link, they will be taken to a website that looks like the Chase Bank login screen in the hope that they will enter their credentials to Chase.

From the attacker's perspective, they will send this email to as many people as possible. Those who do not bank at Chase will ignore the message because it will be obvious to them it is not legitimate. Anyone who clicks on the link is likely a Chase customer. If they enter their credentials, the attacker now has the login to their banking website. With access to the financial institution, the attacker can perform several harmful actions.

It should be noted that Chase and other financial institutions have made great efforts to ensure these types of attacks are not successful. For example, they have implemented multifactor authentication for consumer accounts when the login is coming from an unrecognized computer. The example I used is unlikely to compromise a Chase customer. However, there are consumer applications with access to financial or sensitive personal information where the provider has not taken extraordinary measures to protect their customers. Attackers can find out which financial institutions have and have not implemented multifactor authentication for remote access to accounts, as an example. This is a good example of why consumers should use the provider's cybersecurity posture as one of their evaluation criteria.

Next, we will look at malicious attachments.

Malicious attachments

Malicious attachments are often designed to entice the user into clicking on them, and when they do, they run malicious code. A classic example is the payroll spreadsheet. An attacker will create a macro-enabled Excel file and name it something like *Next Year's Payroll*. They will then spoof an internal finance user's email address and pretend they mistakenly sent it to everyone in the company. If someone receives it, they may be enticed to open the attachment out of curiosity regarding what other employees in the company are being paid or out of curiosity for their own compensation. If they open the attachment, malicious code will run, and malicious software will be installed on their machine. Countless similar schemes using different file types have been identified. The attacker only needs a user to click on the attachment to deliver their malicious payload.

There are many technologies that can identify and block malicious attachments, but they are not universally deployed, especially in personal email services. The best advice is to not click on an attachment you are not expecting. For corporate environments, BEC has become more popular because it is more difficult to prevent using commonly deployed security technology.

Business Email Compromise

Business Email Compromise (**BEC**) is difficult to detect because the messages do not contain links or malicious software. BEC is essentially a scam. Most often, the attacker will send a message that appears to be from a legitimate source, asking the recipient to do something that appears to be a legitimate business action. For example, an attacker may impersonate a vendor and ask to update a mailing address or wiring instructions. In other cases, an attacker may impersonate the CEO and ask someone to purchase gift cards for an employee visit and send them to their hotel. These attacks are difficult to detect because they are human interactions, not technical compromises.

Because BEC defeats most of the countermeasures deployed by most organizations, it is among the most popular attack types in the modern threat landscape. It also accounts for almost half of the financial losses due to cybercrime.

There are two defenses against BEC.

First, training end users responsible for making payments or processing transactions to verify these types of requests will be a good first defense. Second, emerging technologies are being developed to help flag potential scams to raise an end user's awareness level. Some technologies have the ability to identify potential threats and warn the user before they interact with the message.

BEC is a very specific type of fraud attack. However, there are more general types of email fraud that exist and can cost organizations dearly.

Fraud

Executive fraud can be used in BEC but can be used more broadly as well. When attackers research executives, they can often spoof their email address and even speak in a common tone for that person so they can trick employees into following their instructions, believing the instructions came from an executive. If an attacker can convince a user the message originates from an executive and create urgency in their messaging, they are more likely to convince the user to take any action that benefits the attacker.

Example Case: Magellan Health

In April 2020, Magellan Health fell victim to a fraudulent request from an attacker posing as a client that resulted in the attacker being granted remote access to Magellan Health systems. Over the next 5 days, attackers exfiltrated sensitive data belonging to employees and installed ransomware on Magellan Health systems.

On April 11, 2020, Magellan Health was made aware of the ransomware attack when the attackers demanded payment, and they hired the incident response team from Mandiant to help them respond to the breach. By the end of the investigation, it was determined that over 1.7 million people had had sensitive information stolen in the breach. Those people were both internal and external to Magellan Health.

Between the initial investigation in April 2020, the Health and Human Services disclosure of 365,000 patients in July, to the final tally of over 1.7 million victims disclosed in August, the number of people impacted continued to grow. Every time a new number was reported, there was a public relations impact on Magellan Health. While the Magellan Health response once they were made aware of the breach appears to be robust, the failure to understand the scope of the problem initially led to self-inflicted brand damage.

This multi-stage attack shows how damaging a single successful social engineering attack can be. Once the attackers had access to Magellan Health systems, they chose to install ransomware and steal as much data as they could. As a result, the damage to Magellan Health was massive. Based on publicly available reports, the ransomware attack was not as damaging as the data breach. The result for Magellan Health was a loss of brand reputation as well as a class action lawsuit launched against them by victims of the attack. The Magellan Health case highlights the dangers of fraud in email-based attacks (Toms, 2020) (HIPAA Journal, 2020).

As evidenced by the Magellan Health example case, attackers can impersonate clients as well. This type of attack is interesting because the victim would need to be sure the request is illegitimate if they were to ignore the message. This approach places a lot of pressure on the victim organization to respond and represents a sophisticated social engineering attack.

Now that we've established some common attack types launched via email, we will discuss some best practices that have stood the test of time.

Time-honored best practices that could stop most breaches

The following best practices are well known in the security community and time-honored. We know these best practices are effective in making the work of attackers far more difficult. In most cases, only the most sophisticated actors could defeat these countermeasures on a large scale. However, they are rarely implemented.

First, let's examine the Concept of Least Privilege.

Concept of Least Privilege

The **Concept of Least Privilege**, sometimes referred to as the Principle of Least Privilege, states that a user should not be granted any permissions beyond the minimum they need to perform their job function. While this sounds simple and rational, implementing least privilege is very difficult. Most organizations don't maintain a list of specific permissions each user needs to perform their job function. Second, when trying to implement least privilege, the default mode is blocking. As a result, if a mistake is made, the permissions granted will be insufficient for a user to perform their business function. As a result, the user will be frustrated, and harm could be caused to the organization. To prevent this negative business impact and the feedback that comes along with it from business units, IT teams often give users every permission they *might* need, which is the opposite of least privilege. In some cases, they give every user administrator rights to ensure they never encounter a situation they don't have the privileges to overcome.

These over-permissive accounts become perfect targets for attackers. Now all an attacker must do is compromise *any* user account and they have the proverbial keys to the kingdom. Over-permissive accounts make the attack surface the organization must defend very large. Instead of having very few administrative accounts that have the permissions necessary to make changes to systems, all accounts can now install software and access sensitive data, regardless of whether the account owner needs to perform those functions or even knows that their account has those capabilities. It is easy to see how organizations make these choices. It is also easy to see how it results in massive data breaches or ransomware incidents.

Implementing the Concept of Least Privilege requires discipline and effort to define the permissions each user needs to perform their function. It also requires strong information security leadership to explain to the business why it is so important that some minor business disruptions should be tolerable if a business unit fails to properly define the permissions necessary for one of their team members.

Some helpful tips make least privilege easier to implement at scale. First, rather than treating every account as an individual, it helps to set up roles for people who need like permissions and to assign permissions based on their role rather than the individual. There are technologies available, broadly defined as Identity Governance solutions, that are designed to make this process easier. Then, when a change must be made, it can be made to the role and replicated to all users assigned to that role. This approach also helps to address permissions accumulation. Permissions accumulation happens when long-tenured employees move around the organization. I am a good example. I have been with my organization for over a decade. I have worked in every part of the business except for finance.

When I moved from operations to sales engineering, I needed new permissions for my new role. Every organization understands that part. I also no longer needed the permissions I had as part of the operations group, and in fact, it would be inappropriate for me to have them. Most organizations never remove the old permissions in that scenario, and people who move around slowly accumulate permissions that make them a lucrative target. Assigning permissions to roles rather than people means that when a user moves roles, their permissions change to match their new role. This is different than having the additional necessary permissions added to an existing permissions list.

Second, it helps to build a baseline set of permissions that every user should have and a set of permissions that no user account should have. Once you have a minimum set of permissions and a maximum set of permissions, you can better define the roles in between those baseline profiles. The permissions that are denied in the maximum permissions set should be applied to domain administrator accounts and the people with access to those permissions should use them with an account that is different from their primary user account. This reduces the likelihood that these permissive accounts will be compromised in an attack.

The Concept of Least Privilege is difficult and time-consuming to implement, especially in a large complex organization. However, it also makes it far more difficult for an attacker to do their work, which makes it among the most effective best practices an organization could implement. Since the Concept of Least Privilege is both well-known and difficult to implement, whether an organization has implemented least privilege is an indicator of how committed that organization is to information security.

Example Case: Sage Data Breach

In 2016, the UK accounting software company, Sage, suffered a data breach that compromised the personal information of employees at 280 businesses, who were Sage's customers. A 32-year-old employee was arrested at the airport in London and charged with conspiracy to defraud the company. It is not clear how the employee intended to profit from the theft.

While Sage did not release many details of the data breach, they did mention the data was accessed by an internal account. That, coupled with the arrest of a Sage employee and the subsequent charges that were filed, indicates that it is likely the breach was the result of a malicious insider.

The other lesson learned from Sage is the need for the Concept of Least Privilege and Need to Know. While the employee in question likely needed access to some systems to do their job, it is unlikely that they needed access to all the data and systems to which they were granted access. Implementing these best practices, which are simple to understand but can be difficult to implement, limits the harm that can be done with a single compromised account or the amount of information that can be stolen by a single rogue employee (Wright, 2016) (Tech Sapiens, 2016).

Need to Know

Need to Know is a best practice that is often associated with the Concept of Least Privilege. Least Privilege is related to permissions to systems. Need to Know governs access to information. Need to Know states that a person should only have access to the minimum information they need to inform their decision-making process or to perform their critical job functions. Most organizations have some information that is sensitive and could be attacked. However, few people in the organization need to interact with that information. In too many data breaches, accounts are compromised and have access to far more information than is necessary for that user to perform their job functions. As a result, many data breaches are much larger than they should be.

Since the cost of data breaches is often measured in cost per record, implementing least privilege and Need to Know effectively could reduce an organization's residual information security risk by a significant percentage.

Role-Based Access Control

Role-Based Access Control (**RBAC**) is focused on the types of access a user is granted to a system. Where least privilege covers whether a user needs access to a system, RBAC determines what specific actions a user should be permitted to take inside the systems they are granted access to. Most technologies can build RBAC into the permissions that are granted to a user, but they differ in terms of how granular that access can be. Defining the precise functions that a user must perform inside a system is required to implement RBAC effectively.

Many organizations that fail to implement the Concept of Least Privilege struggle to implement RBAC effectively because too many users have access to the system. Consequently, it is difficult to define the precise permissions each user needs since so many users have access. The result is often all users being granted access to the same profile, which is often a profile that is granted all permissions to the system.

Poorly implemented RBAC controls are closely related to a failure to implement the Concept of Least Privilege. These poor access control policies build on each other and compound to make some organizations a soft target for attackers.

Effective RBAC is dependent on understanding the roles and responsibilities of users inside the organization. Next, we will talk about Identity Management.

Identity Management

The preceding best practices are focused on proper access control, which is a foundational element of an effective security program. However, Identity Management is focused on managing the process of identifying, authenticating, and authorizing the user. If access control is ensuring users have access to the resources they need and nothing more, identity management is about ensuring users are who they say they are when they attempt to use the permissions they have been granted.

Effective identity management is designed to be seamless and must balance the need to guard against compromised accounts with the need to make the user experience as smooth as possible. Multifactor authentication is often necessary, but it can be onerous if a person must perform multifactor authentication for every service they need to use. As a result, many companies have embraced **Single Sign On** (**SSO**) technologies that allow a user to authenticate once and have access to a suite of applications provided by their organization.

Identity management requires a balance between security and usability and there is a constant tension between the two. Solutions that can simultaneously improve the security posture of the organization and the experience for the end user offer a compelling value proposition.

Next, we will discuss another best practice, vulnerability management and patching.

Vulnerability management and patching

A zero-day exploit is a new attack against a system or vulnerability that has never been seen before. True zero-day exploits are expensive to research and develop and require sophistication to deploy. Also, once they have been used in the wild, they are no longer zero-day exploits. As a result, true zero-day exploits are used by only the most sophisticated actors against the highest value and best defended targets. Most readers will never face a true zero-day threat. However, understanding how they are created can yield valuable insight that can be useful in a security program.

How vulnerabilities are created

One important concept to understand is that software is written by people. Vulnerabilities are introduced into code in two ways. First, many organizations develop software with little emphasis on developing secure code or programmers inadvertently introduce vulnerabilities into code by accident. Not all organizations emphasize the need to develop secure software. Certain organizations provide emphasis on feature enrichment, stability over security. Also, code libraries are often re-used, so a single vulnerability can be present across many software products and across operating systems, security vulnerabilities can creep into software when security is at the forefront of a development team's priorities, so, when security is an afterthought, the risk of this goes up exponentially.

Secondly, there are several use cases where vulnerabilities in software are introduced by accident. Developers will inadvertently introduce vulnerabilities into their software, opening doors for attackers to exploit these vulnerabilities to exploit target systems. In fact, the MITRE organization tracks disclosed vulnerabilities within various applications that have been found and reported.

Researching a zero-day attack

Sophisticated actors have research teams that are constantly researching software looking for undisclosed vulnerabilities in applications and operating systems. Often, the same scanners and tools that organizations use to scan code for security vulnerabilities can be used by attackers to find vulnerabilities in software that is exploitable. These vulnerabilities can be lucrative, but are not zero-day vulnerabilities. By definition, if a vulnerability is loaded into a scanner, it is a known vulnerability. True zero-day researchers are reviewing the code in detail trying to find holes in the software that can be exploited. The process usually begins by using software debuggers. When a programmer loads software into a debugger, they can see how a program interacts with the computer, and what instructions the code uses to perform its functions, which allow the attacker to identify potential vulnerabilities that can be exploited. Meticulously going through lines of code can take days, weeks, or maybe even months, which is why true zero-day attacks are rarely encountered.

Exploiting a zero-day vulnerability

Once an attacker identifies a zero-day vulnerability, they must devise a method to exploit it. This exploit could be written into a malicious software package or it may be a technique that an attacker can use to exploit the vulnerability if they can acquire proper access to the target system. Attackers know different vulnerabilities give them different methods for extracting information from a system, taking control of a system, damaging a system, or spying on activities that are taking place on the system or the network. The methods attackers can use to exploit a vulnerability depend on the type of vulnerability identified.

Most organizations will never face a true zero-day exploit due to the cost and effort involved in researching one. However, many organizations will face threats that were zero-day threats at one time. The following model is one I have built to showcase the threat life cycle:

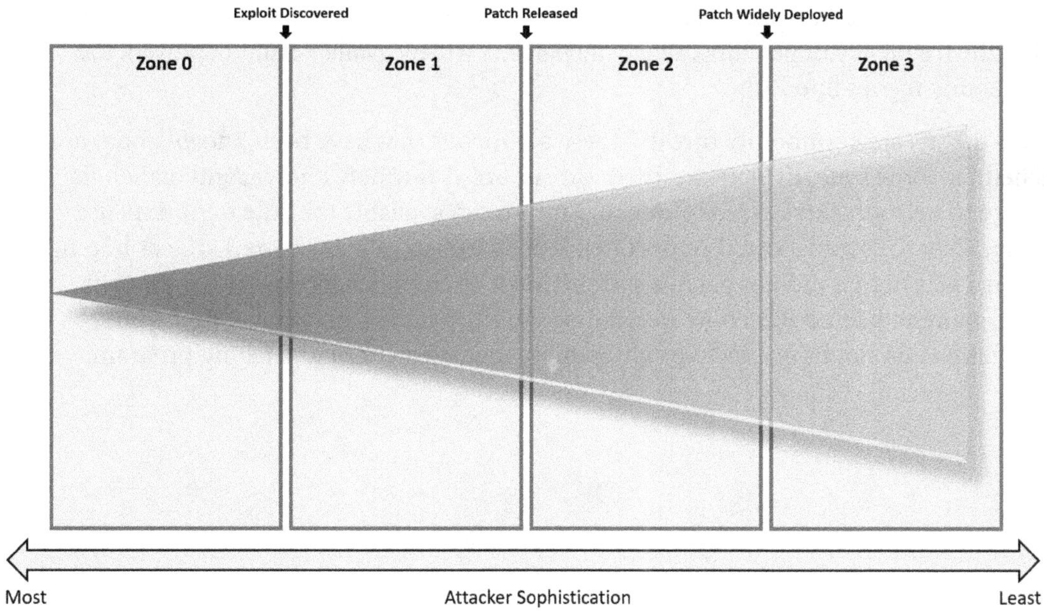

Figure 4.1 – Zone model for classification of threat sophistication

From left to right is the length of time the vulnerability has been known. As you move to the right, vulnerabilities have been known longer. The longer a vulnerability is known, the easier it is to defend against, and the easier it is to attack. I classify threats into four zones.

Zone 0 is a true zero-day threat. Very few attackers can exploit it, and there is no countermeasure yet available. True zero-day threats are *only* known by the attacker. As a result, there is no way to defend against the vulnerability. As soon as someone else discovers the vulnerability, it crosses into Zone 1.

Zone 1 constitutes threats that have been discovered but have not yet been patched. There could be effective countermeasures for Zone 1 threats. In many cases, a pattern for how the vulnerability could be exploited could be programmed into a monitoring system in Zone 1. This will not prevent the vulnerability from being exploited but will provide an early warning when this type of exploit is happening. Threats are usually in this zone for fewer than 3 days, but this is a period where organizations can be vulnerable. Skilled actors who are not sophisticated enough to find their own zero-day threats may be able to launch Zone 1 attacks if they act quickly. Once a patch is released, the threat crosses into Zone 2.

Zone 2 covers the period between when a patch has been released and when most organizations have deployed it. Many threat actor groups will launch Zone 2 attacks in the hope that they can outmaneuver their victims. Many times, patches are applied monthly. In those cases, a threat could stay in Zone 2 for up to 31 days, assuming the patch is widely deployed. In some cases, patches are deployed even more slowly. The length of Zone 2 is tied to the frequency of patching. Once the patch is widely available and deployed, the vulnerability moves into Zone 3.

Zone 3 threats are commodity threats. These are threats that have been known about and patched for some time. Exploits for these threats are also widely known, and malicious software to help attackers exploit these threats is often available for little to no expense to an attacker. Unsophisticated actors often launch indiscriminate Zone 3 attacks hoping to catch a victim that did not patch a system. Most often, this happens with unknown systems or systems that somehow were missed in the patching rotation. Other times, organizations do not have effective vulnerability management or a patching program.

Example Case: Equifax

Equifax is one of the three major credit reporting bureaus in the United States. Equifax, TransUnion, and Experian are in a unique position because they gather potentially sensitive information about millions of people without their explicit consent. Because they are entrusted with large volumes of information, and the data subjects are given little control of what information is collected about them and how it is stored, there is a high degree of public trust necessary for these companies to operate. In March 2017, that trust was shattered when Equifax suffered a data breach that affected hundreds of millions of people.

The fact that information belonging to so many people was breached and the information that was breached made those people easy targets for identity thieves was bad. The response was far worse. Equifax leadership tried to blame a single well-intentioned employee for a failure to patch a critical system against a widely known vulnerability. While the employee could have made a mistake, it was Equifax that was grossly negligent in not having an effective vulnerability management process that would have highlighted the fact that a key system was vulnerable.

Second, it was clear that attackers were able to gather such large volumes of information because the network was not segmented, and they could move laterally once they had gained access to the environment.

The outrage caused by the breach was significant, but the situation was made worse when details of the behavior of Equifax executives were made public. It is alleged that Equifax did not disclose the breach for a month, and during that time, key executives sold Equifax stock.

Everything about the Equifax breach was egregious. The way the intrusion happened showed a lack of due care for their security posture. The way the attackers were able to move laterally and steal data undetected for 76 days shows a lack of basic security capabilities and operations. The behavior of executives who allegedly saved themselves from significant financial losses by trading on non-public information shows a lack of concern for shareholders. The lack of SEC action against those executives or meaningful policy change related to the credit reporting agencies shows a lack of meaningful reform based on the lessons learned.

However, for all the negative impacts of the Equifax breach and subsequent response, the event brings one thing into sharp relief. Organizations must identify vulnerabilities, patch their systems, and verify they were patched appropriately. A failure to do so is the responsibility of the organization and cannot be blamed on an individual (Fruhlinger, 2020).

It is important to understand how Zone 3 attacks happen. As previously mentioned, large-scale indiscriminate attacks against commodity vulnerabilities are often launched by unsophisticated actors. Other times, actors will use tools that allow them to scan the public-facing infrastructure a company has looking for known vulnerabilities. Attackers have the advantage in this scenario. A defender must patch all their systems to defend effectively. An attacker often only needs to find a single unpatched system to accomplish their objective.

The best tools a defender can use to defend themselves from Zone 2 and Zone 3 attacks are known as **vulnerability management** tools. Vulnerability management allows an organization to scan all their systems against a database of known vulnerabilities to see whether there are any vulnerable systems in their environment. This allows an organization to patch these vulnerabilities before an attacker discovers them. It is important to run an effective vulnerability management program to identify vulnerabilities, patch them, and ensure the patching was successful by re-scanning the environment. An effective vulnerability management program will harden an organization's systems considerably.

Capabilities necessary in the remote world

As the world continues to shift from an environment where people accessed systems locally in an office or a data center to a world where people primarily access systems and resources from remote locations such as their home office or a coffee shop, it is becoming increasingly apparent that information security systems must evolve. While many of the best practices we have discussed previously are relevant in all configurations, a number of additional best practices should be implemented to secure remote systems and remote users. The first best practice deals with how users are authenticated.

Factors of authentication

In *Chapter 3*, *Anatomy of an Attack*, we highlighted several attack types that are made easier for attackers to execute by single-factor authentication systems. Multifactor authentication techniques are often an effective countermeasure, especially when part of the attack chain involves account compromise. Many organizations deploy multifactor authentication to help solve this problem. However, there are some misunderstandings about multifactor authentication that should be addressed.

First, there are three factors of authentication – **Something you know**, **Something you have**, and **Something you are**. Each of these factors of authentication represents a category of authentication methods, and there are several techniques under each. It is important to understand that multifactor authentication requires authentication techniques from more than one *category*, not simply more than one method from a single category. An example is if you were to enter your username and password into a website. The website then says, to confirm your identity, please tell us the make and model of your first car. While this is more secure than just the username and password, this *is not* multifactor authentication, since both methods fall into the category of something you know.

Since something you know is the most common factor of authentication, we will address it first.

Something you know

Something you know can be thought of as a secret. The password is the most common authentication method in this category. If you have password reset questions that ask things such as *What is your favorite sea animal?* or *What is your mother's maiden name?*, those are also something you know. Other common examples are passphrases that ask a user to type a sentence rather than a password. If you are prompted to type something in exchange for access, there is a good chance the authentication method you are using is something you know. This is the most common method. Most organizations that are deploying multifactor authentication are seeking to deploy a second factor.

The most familiar second factor is something you have.

Something you have

Something you have is an authentication method that proves to a system that you possess something. In some military systems, there are identification cards with computer chips that must be inserted into a system while a password is typed. This is something you have. Many people are familiar with RSA tokens, which are hardware devices that generate a random number key string at a frequency. Typing those numbers into a system to look for a match is also something you have. Many modern systems use push notifications to enrolled smartphones. When you tap your smartphone, you are confirming you have it.

Something you know and something you have is the most common true multifactor authentication combination. Next, we will explore the third factor of authentication – something you are.

Something you are

Something you are, also known as **biometrics**, is the act of identifying a user based on a characteristic about them that cannot be changed. Common examples are fingerprints or iris scans. Something you are is often considered the most secure factor of authentication and the most difficult and expensive to implement. Many mobile devices are now equipped with fingerprint readers or facial recognition for authenticating their users. As a result, it is more common to see biometrics used as a factor of authentication than it used to.

Why your password is meaningless

There are billions of usernames and passwords available for sale on the dark web. Many people reuse their favorite passwords between their personal accounts and their corporate accounts, so credential stuffing attacks, which is when attackers try multiple username and password combinations across popular services, are often successful. An analysis of these stolen passwords shows that most passwords are not complex anyway, so even when attackers do not have stolen passwords, they can use common passwords to gain unauthorized access to systems.

I recommend that all people use a password manager and that they let their password manager create a long, complex, and unique password for each of these services. However, many people will not. As a result, a password as a factor of authentication is meaningless. This does not mean that a password can't be effective; it simply means an organization cannot rely on a password to identify a user in the modern world.

There is no meaningful debate about whether using a password as a single factor of authentication to sensitive systems is a good practice. It is not. There is a meaningful debate over whether passwords should be used at all though. Alternative solutions are to build multifactor systems based on something you have and something you are, eliminating the password entirely. Other emerging approaches that are interesting involve monitoring a behavior profile on a device and mapping it to normal behavior for that user. If the pattern matches completely, the system allows access with no authentication. If it matches mostly, the system requires one additional factor of authentication. If it matches with a little less confidence, it may require two. If it doesn't match at all, the system may suspend access until the user calls a helpdesk.

Other organizations still use something you know, but do not use passwords. Instead, perhaps, they may use a series of questions or passphrases. These alternative methods are still prone to being stolen as something you know as a factor of authentication is the weakest. In general, multifactor authentication is a best practice. Many companies have been working to make the multifactor experience more user friendly. In the modern world, multifactor authentication is not difficult to implement and does not degrade the user experience.

Multifactor authentication

Most data breaches begin with compromised credentials accessing a system with a single factor of authentication. Single-factor authentication is so bad that the United States Cybersecurity and Infrastructure Agency named it among the most exceptionally risky practices for access to remote systems (Hope, 2021).

As previously mentioned, multifactor authentication requires authentication methods from two or more of the preceding factors of authentication. In some cases, very secure systems may use all three.

Deploying multifactor authentication makes the attacker's job much more difficult as they need to perform several successful attacks against the same target to compromise an account. While such attacks are not impossible, most threat actors will simply seek a softer target.

Many organizations still use single-factor authentication for access to sensitive information and systems. As a result, many attackers will not go through the trouble of defeating multifactor authentication and simply find an easier target. The next best practice, network segmentation, is designed to make an attacker's job more difficult once they have gained access to an environment.

Network segmentation

Network segmentation is designed to make it difficult for unauthorized users to move between portions of the network. In a flat network, there are firewalls separating the internal network from the external network, but once an attacker is in, they can access any resource they choose. Network segmentation separates those parts of the network from each other to limit the number of resources that can be accessed from a single network segment.

Setting up network segmentation with proper access controls between those segments is how we can mitigate risk and stop the spread of malware attacks. Network segmentation makes it much harder for an attacker to launch a successful ransomware attack because ransomware must spread throughout an environment to be successful. Network segmentation paired with appropriate access controls between segments makes it much more difficult for that spread to occur. Similarly, in an information theft attack, an attacker is often looking to gather as much information as possible before exfiltrating that information. Network segmentation makes it more difficult for the attacker to gain access to large volumes of data.

Most types of attacks that don't involve a malicious insider are more difficult when network segmentation is implemented. Network segmentation increases the amount of work for the attacker. Another effective best practice is allowing applications.

Allowed applications

Allowed applications is a technique that can be very effective, but difficult to implement. Allowed activity, in general, is a better approach than trying to anticipate all the bad activity and stop it. It is better to say these are the activities that are allowed, and I want to prevent anything else. Allowed applications, then, define the applications that are allowed to run on a system and blocks all other applications from running. It is simple and effective, so why is it not used more?

Allowed applications is easiest to implement in small organizations. As organizations become larger and more complex, it becomes exponentially more difficult to define what applications each job function or user needs to run. As that list grows, it takes more time to administer the list, and worse, the likelihood that end users will be impacted in a negative way grows. However, an effective allowed applications program has the potential to stop all ransomware attacks, as well as malicious software attacks, more broadly. Because of the enormous potential benefit, allowed applications should be considered. Because of the enormous potential costs associated with both work effort and potential disruption, these projects should be approached with caution.

Example Case: Cognizant

Cognizant is the largest managed services company in the world, employing hundreds of thousands of people and generating $15 billion in annual revenue. They are Fortune 185, which makes them the 185th largest company in the United States by revenue according to the 2021 Fortune rankings. On April 17, 2020, Cognizant notified their customers that they were under attack from Maze ransomware and customers should disconnect themselves from Cognizant's networks to prevent the infection from spreading to their networks.

Cognizant was detailed in the notice they sent to their customers, providing helpful details such as the indicators of compromise associated with the attack and IP addresses associated with the suspected attackers. This information was designed to help Cognizant customers quickly identify and respond to an infection that crossed over from Cognizant's network to any of its customer environments.

The ransomware that infected Cognizant was designed to threaten to publicly release sensitive information if a ransom is not paid, rather than encrypting information and demanding a ransom in exchange for the encryption key. As a result, it is more difficult for the victim to know for sure how pervasive the attack was.

All indications are that Cognizant responded well to the attack that compromised their systems. The information they provided to their customers was helpful and timely. However, it is the attack itself that offers some insight into a lesson learned. Had Cognizant deployed allowed applications on their systems, it would have been more difficult for the ransomware to take root and spread (Abrams, 2020).

The Cognizant data breach shows that even the largest and most sophisticated IT operations can suffer a data breach. It is the response when these events occur that shows the maturity of the security program in place at the organization. Comparing the story of Equifax and the story of Cognizant should clearly show the difference between an immature security posture in Equifax contrasted with the mature security posture and response from Cognizant.

Next, we will explore the role of human behavior in these best practices.

The role of human behavior

By this point, it should be clear that human behavior analysis is an important part of an information security program. Most people think of human behavior analysis in terms of the detection of anomalies, but there are other ways in which behavior analysis can be used to build an effective information security program.

The first has been mentioned previously, and it is using human behavior as part of the *something you are* factor of authentication.

Behavior analysis for authentication

The way people interact with devices has changed significantly in the last 20 years. Before smartphone technology, people used computers to perform a function, much like a tool. After the invention of smartphones, technology has become more like a personal assistant than a tool. In fact, many people spend more quality time with their devices than they do with their own family members. I am not arguing in favor of these technology addictions or trying to downplay the potential impact on society; I am simply stating a fact.

As a result, technology companies build machine learning algorithms designed to get to know their users to make meaningful suggestions to them or to enrich their experiences in the hope that the users will become even closer to their devices. In many cases, no person knows a user better than their technology devices do.

Some innovative thinkers have begun to wonder, if your device knows you so well, could that behavior profile for a set period be shared with an authentication system to verify not only that this is the device belonging to the end user that is trying to authenticate, but that the user is behaving in a way that is consistent with their normal behavior.

This approach must mature before it is widely adopted, but the possibilities are interesting. The next use of behavior analytics is in use currently and has proven to be among the most effective ways of identifying malicious insiders and compromised accounts.

Behavior analysis for anomaly detection

It is very difficult to predict how a user will behave when they become malicious, or exactly how an attacker will behave when an account has been compromised. However, it is almost certain that the behavior pattern will change when compared to the previous behavior pattern. Even if an attacker wanted to emulate a user's behavior to avoid detection, it would be difficult for that attacker to know the user's behavior pattern, and in order to steal something or infect a system, they will have to do something different than the user would do since those activities would not fit the user's behavior pattern.

In fact, in any attack, something must change when the environment goes from a normal state to an abnormal state. Detecting and responding to that change is the role of the information security program. Using behavior analysis to detect those changes is among the most effective techniques currently available.

Detecting the behavior change is the first step in the equation. However, taking automatic action based on that change is a logical next step.

Adaptive security in human behavior

Adaptive security should be the long-term goal for all behavior analysis capabilities in information security. The ability to accurately identify changes in behavior and respond instantly with changes to the security profile is among the most effective ways to protect against insider threats. There are technology companies that have tried to begin this journey, but the technology is still in its infancy.

The goal should be that all security controls are adaptive. When everything is normal, there should be little interference with the user's job function. As anomalies occur, the security systems should tighten in response to the potential threat. This type of adaptive approach will result in the right protections being applied to the right technology and information assets at the right time with minimum disruption. Static defenses are less effective than they've ever been.

The everything, everywhere world

The modern world is very different from the world that existed even a few years ago. The COVID-19 pandemic has changed the way we live and work in a profound way. While it is difficult to predict exactly which changes will be permanent and which will fade away post-pandemic, it is clear to most people that a wholesale return to pre-pandemic normalcy is unlikely.

Even before the pandemic, workers were demanding more flexible work arrangements. For many years, employers had the power in employment negotiations and could dictate terms to employees. In the modern world, there are more jobs than qualified applicants to fill them in many fields. As a result, the balance of power is shifting. Employees are in a better negotiating position to demand flexible working arrangements. Even if they don't, employees who travel need access to sensitive corporate systems or information remotely. All these factors have contributed to the death of the traditional castle and moat approach of protecting a physical data center where all the crown jewels were housed.

In the modern world, employees need access to everything, and they need it from everywhere. This puts a strain on traditional security models and technologies. Interestingly, some of the oldest security techniques, the timeless best practices highlighted in this chapter, are more relevant in this modern world than they have ever been.

Security infrastructure and technology should be built in a way that allows an organization to protect information and systems regardless of the location of the source or the destination. There are reference architectures and concepts that seek to help organizations achieve this goal, but it is the goal that is critical, not the implementation methodology.

Summary

In this chapter, we have discussed some of the basic best practices that can form the foundation of an effective security program. You have learned why email is the most important threat vector and the types of attacks that often originate in email. You have also learned some best practices that have stood the test of time and are as important now as they have ever been. You have learned about capabilities that are more important as the business world has become a remote access paradigm, and you have learned how human behavior analysis can help identify anomalies, secure systems, and create an adaptive security posture.

In the next chapter, we will highlight techniques that help end users become part of the solution rather than being seen as part of the problem.

Check your understanding

1. Describe Business Email Compromise in your own words.
2. What is the Concept of Least Privilege? What is Need to Know? How are they the same and how do they differ?
3. What are the three factors of authentication?
4. Describe how human behavior analysis can be used to enhance your security program.
5. In your own words, describe the challenges associated with granting users access to systems and information remotely.

Further reading

- Abrams, L. (June 17, 2020). IT giant Cognizant confirms data breach after ransomware attack. Retrieved from Bleeping Computer: `https://www.bleepingcomputer.com/news/security/it-giant-cognizant-confirms-data-breach-after-ransomware-attack/`
- Fruhlinger, J. (February 12, 2020). Equifax data breach FAQ: What happened, who was affected, and what was the impact? Retrieved from CSO: `https://www.csoonline.com/article/3444488/equifax-data-breach-faq-what-happened-who-was-affected-what-was-the-impact.html`

- HIPAA Journal. (July 1, 2020). Extent of Magellan Health Ransomware Becomes Clear: More than 364,000 Individuals Affected. Retrieved from HIPAA Journal: `https://www.hipaajournal.com/extent-of-magellan-health-ransomware-becomes-clear-more-than-364000-individuals-affected/`
- Hope, A. (September 13, 2021). CISA Adds Single-Factor Authentication to the List of Bad Cybersecurity Practices. Retrieved from CPO Magazine: `https://www.cpomagazine.com/cyber-security/cisa-adds-single-factor-authentication-to-the-list-of-bad-cybersecurity-practices/`
- Tech Sapiens. (August 16, 2016). Sage Data Breach 2016: what you need to know. Retrieved from Tech Sapiens: `https://techsapiens.com/blog/sage-data-breach-what-you-need-to-know/`
- Toms, L. (October 15, 2020). Cyber Autopsy Series: Phishing Attack on Magellan Health. Retrieved from GlobalSign: `https://www.globalsign.com/en/blog/cyber-autopsy-series-phishing-attack-magellan-health`
- Verizon. (2021). 2021 Data Breach Investigations Report. Retrieved from Verizon: `https://enterprise.verizon.com/resources/reports/2021-data-breach-investigations-report.pdfx`
- Wright, A. (August 19, 2016). Employee Charged with Fraud after Data Breach at Sage. Retrieved from SHRM: `https://www.shrm.org/resourcesandtools/hr-topics/technology/pages/employee-charged-with-fraud-after-data-breach-at-sage.aspx`

5 Protecting against Common Attacks by Partnering with End Users

If people are the weakest link in an organization, and cybersecurity attacks consist of people exploiting people, it stands to reason that enabling your people to be assets to your security posture is a good thing. Traditional models of annual security awareness training are useless and obsolete. To actually train people, the training must be frequent and realistic. Also, types of training such as simulations and tabletop exercises help to ensure people know what is expected of them and what they should do to fulfill their obligations.

In this chapter, you will learn how an organization can partner with end users to help improve their security posture. You will learn how to structure employee training programs, how to make your end users active participants in the program, and how to train executive and incident response teams to work together seamlessly to execute a coherent response to a potential incident.

In this chapter, we will cover the following topics:

- A framework for effective training
- Making your people your partners
- Training people to protect against common hacking techniques
- Tabletop exercises

A framework for effective training

Effective information security training does not happen by accident. It requires an intentional effort to improve the cybersecurity awareness of the average employee. There are numerous topics that should be covered in an information security awareness program, but not all of them are relevant to every employee. For example, if a small percentage of employees handle personal information, those employees need to be trained on the proper handling of that information, but the same training that may be critical for those employees may be irrelevant to others. Defining what training modules are relevant based on roles will help tailor the program to roles properly. Tailoring the program is an important point. Generic training where much of the content is irrelevant to most attendees results in poor engagement and little progress. The more tailored the content is, the more likely it is that attendees will gain something valuable from the experience.

Once the roles have been evaluated to identify the proper training topics, it is important to ensure the training is effective. Effective training takes three key characteristics into account: frequency, content, and scope. First, we will explore the frequency of effective training.

Frequency

Neuroscience research from 2014 suggests that people forget 50 percent of information presented to them within 1 hour, 70 percent within 1 day, and 90 percent within 1 week (Kohn, 2014). This data alone makes the case that training must be frequently reinforced. Other neuroscience data suggests that you must recall a memory 30 times to commit it to long-term memory (Oaklander, 2015). Recalling a memory means that someone has reminded you of it, or more powerfully, you need to access it to accomplish a task. The data is clear that annual security awareness training is mostly useless. Asking employees to read security policies also has little value.

It is more effective to choose a few training topics that are most relevant to the employee's role and reinforce those concepts frequently and in various ways.

An example may be that an employee logs in and they are assigned an interactive training module that lasts 5 minutes. The training module is a mix of video and interactive content. When the training is complete, they get up to go to the restroom. They see a poster on the wall that reinforces the same message. When they log onto their machine, they are presented with a tooltip that reminds them what they should do if they identify an illegitimate email message. A week later, they are sent a simulated phishing attack. If they click on the link, they are routed back to the training module along with some feedback on how they could have avoided falling victim to a similar phishing scheme. If they take the proper action, they are presented with positive reinforcement.

Consistent and real-time feedback is more meaningful than a one-time training event. Spot training can be helpful to reinforce the message. Developing training that meets the need for frequency requires messaging discipline. Too often cybersecurity awareness training is generic and overly ambitious in terms of scope, which makes it more difficult to reinforce the messages with the proper frequency to allow employees to retain meaningful information. To accomplish this objective, it is important to curate the proper content for the proper people at the proper time.

Content

Content discipline is important when developing an effective employee training program of any type. One of the most meaningful ways to maintain content discipline is to break all the possible training content into smaller modules. For example, rather than giving a generic presentation about the danger of social engineering, modules could be built for each of the common techniques, such as one module focusing on phishing email messages. Breaking up content in this way will likely yield several categories of modules, which sets the foundation for the organization to assign modules to employees that are most relevant to individual job functions.

Ensuring the content is relevant to the person's job role is important to developing employee engagement. If security training is something that must be done but the employee is not engaged, it is unlikely to be effective. Developing interesting content that is relevant is critical to success. The last part of the framework is the scope of training events.

Scope

Effective training should be frequent and relevant, but it also must be consumable. Running traditional annual training events more frequently will only make the problem worse. Training programs that have modules lasting for an hour or more are unlikely to make a meaningful difference. Training events that focus on a single idea that can be covered in 10 minutes or less are more effective. Training that incorporates video has a higher retention rate than text, and training that requires the user to take an action is more effective than video. Some of the most effective training repeats a simple message multiple times and requires a person to take action and put what they have learned into practice.

Shorter, more frequent events allow for training to be repeated if the performance metrics do not indicate that employee behavior is improving. If the simulation metrics are acceptable, the organization can choose to move on to another topic. The frequency and scope of a modular training program will allow an organization to be more flexible and data-driven in its approach.

Programs like the ones previously described are not common. Too often information security awareness training consists of two elements. First, during onboarding, the employee is given a virtual stack of information security policies and procedures that they must attest to reading. This information is delivered in text format, and most people do not read the policies at all. Some skim the policies that are most impactful to them in their job function, and a select few may actually read the policies. Neuroscientists suggest the most studious group will retain up to 10% of the information presented. Then, in most organizations, there is an annual event, lasting an hour or two, where someone from the security team lectures employees and presents them with slides. Within an hour, much of the information is forgotten.

Effective training programs look different. They employ small, consumable pieces of information that are curated for specific roles to deliver content that is relevant to the role and requires the employee to take action. The lessons are integrated with technology to provide reinforcement, and simulations are conducted at random to evaluate whether employees can execute their responsibilities effectively. In short, effective training asks employees to become security partners.

Making your people your partners

Training people about the dangers of cybercrime or the best practices associated with security could be meaningful but including a call to action and engaging users as part of the solution helps make people true partners in cybersecurity. The first step in making employees partners is to encourage them to get off the sidelines and get actively involved in the defense of the organization.

Making people active participants

People like to play games and engage in friendly competition. Cybersecurity simulations offer a great opportunity to reinforce training while gamifying the process to make what has historically been mundane training into something people enjoy and look forward to. Creating a friendly competition between groups that has prizes a department can win can also be a fun way to drive engagement.

Training that calls people to take action when they see something happening offers the opportunity to simulate those types of events and measure how effectively an individual or group is retaining the information they have been presented with.

Simulations are better than presentations

Presentations can be a necessary way to communicate information, but people will retain a fraction of what they are presented with. Simulations that allow users to put what they've learned into practice in a realistic but safe environment enrich the learning experiences for employees.

Simulated activities should not be announced and should be conducted during the course of the normal workday. The simulations should be designed to be as realistic as possible while reinforcing a key concept from a recent training session. Employees who successfully complete the simulations should move on to the next module the next time training is scheduled. Those who do not perform as they have been trained should be re-trained and the simulation can be run again.

If large groups of employees do not pass the simulations, the training should be reviewed and critiqued to make it more effective for subsequent teams.

Educating about data

Often, information security awareness training focuses on tactics and attacks and neglects to teach people about the value of information and how it is used by an attacker. Understanding what types of information a person will encounter are sensitive and why they are sensitive helps users understand why the training they are about to receive matters.

Simon Sinek gave a powerful TED Talk focused on messaging for brands and used Apple as an example. There is a large volume of meaningful information in the talk, but the key concept is people respond better when they understand the purpose of what they're doing, or the *why* behind the *what*.

Many information security training programs would be more successful if they started by teaching users why information has value and teaching them about the cybercrime economy. When I share statistics about the global proceeds of cybercrime or show people real dark web marketplaces where identities are bought and sold, they pay more attention to the content being presented. Sharing examples like the example cases in this book can help people focus on the importance of what they're learning and draw parallels between what they're learning and what they may have seen in the news.

One thing I have long said is *familiarity breeds commoditization*. This phrase does not roll off the tongue, but years later I have not found a better way to make this point. If you rarely work with medical information or financial information, when you come across it, you intuitively know it is sensitive and you should ensure you handle it carefully. If your job is to process medical claims and you deal with nothing but medical information and financial information, the information is normal to you, and you may exercise less care with the information over time.

However, if you are reminded of individual stories of people who were hurt by identity theft or fraud, you are more likely to be reminded how improper handling of the information you are interacting with can cause harm to others. If I were building a cybersecurity awareness campaign for a group of these employees, I may include a monthly story about an identity theft victim with a specific call to action that would have prevented this person from being exploited. This type of reminder helps people remain vigilant.

Example Case: City of Calgary

In 2016, a class-action lawsuit was filed against the City of Calgary in Canada alleging a privacy breach. An employee of the city sent an email to another Alberta municipality that contained the personal information of 3,716 municipal employees. The information was related to Workers' Compensation Board claims and contained significant amounts of sensitive information. The staffer was accused of negligence.

It is clear that in the moment, the staffer was not thinking about the sensitivity of the information they were sending and the potential harm that could result from the action. There is no evidence that the staffer had malicious intent. This case highlights the need for ongoing training about the sensitivity of information a person may encounter, and the proper handling and due care associated with that type of information. It cannot be assumed that all employees understand the sensitivity of the information they encounter. It can also not be assumed that one-time training will be sufficient education for the entire course of a person's employment (Grant, 2017).

Negligent is a harsh word, but it is difficult to find a word to better describe employees who do not handle sensitive information with due care. There are technologies, such as Data Loss Prevention technologies, that can identify and prevent accidental exposures like the one detailed in the example case about the City of Calgary. This is aligned with the theme that should be clear by now: people are our greatest asset and can be our weakest link. We should invest in our people, but we should also use technology and processes to support those people.

Previously, we have explored various ways attackers trick their victims into activating their attacks. As we discussed previously, *all but the most sophisticated attacks are human activated, which means the majority of attack techniques rely upon an end user to do something they shouldn't for the attack to be successful.* The next section of this chapter will focus on methods to help reduce the likelihood that your team members will activate the attacks launched against them.

Training people to protect against common hacking techniques

In a broad sense, social engineering techniques have changed little over the years. The techniques have evolved and become more effective over time as attackers continue to hone their craft. However, the core techniques change little because they are effective.

The first thing to understand about social engineering is the techniques are not designed to exploit technology, *they are designed to exploit people*. Social engineering techniques depend on the study and exploitation of strong human emotions such as fear or hope. Effective social engineers study human psychology and try to implement techniques that will produce a predictable human response. They know how the human brain works and understand their victims are more prone to making mistakes if they are thinking quickly and relying on emotions or survival instincts to guide their actions rather than using the rational parts of their brain that can only be accessed if they slow down to think before they react. As a result, they seek to create urgency in their victims. They understand their targets have a strong loss aversion, so they create messages to threaten victims with a painful loss if they don't take an action. Since social engineering techniques are designed to use an understanding of human nature to exploit our tendencies, the first method to defend against them is to teach people about the social engineering tactics they may face. Once a person understands the techniques that are likely to be deployed against them, the attacks themselves become almost comical because the person receiving the message understands what the attacker is trying to accomplish. Also, training users on attack methods helps them identify malicious messages quickly because they understand what the message is trying to do. Often, there is no motivation for a legitimate sender to create urgency or play on fear to engage with their customers. Marketing communications can be an exception.

The first part of training people is to help them understand the social engineering techniques that underpin many attack methods.

Social engineering awareness

In *Chapter 2*, *The Human Side of Cybersecurity*, in the *People exploiting people* section, we detailed several common social engineering attack types. We will not cover them again in this section. Instead, we will discuss the most effective ways to teach users about these attack types.

Mechanical descriptions of social engineering types can be interesting, but they are not useful or memorable. It is more effective to follow a three-step model for educating users about social engineering.

First, a description of what the technique is and what it is designed to achieve is important. For example, phishing is designed to trick a user into taking an action they would not normally take to give the attacker access to a system they would not normally have. There are much deeper explanations of phishing, but keeping the descriptions brief and to the point helps people who don't focus on security every day understand the technique. There is a common saying often attributed to Albert Einstein, *If you can't explain something simply, you don't understand it well enough*. Information security professionals sometimes overcomplicate concepts in a way that alienates end users.

Second, it is important to describe the human tendency that the attack is designed to exploit. This is often not included in information security awareness training, but the training is far more effective and memorable when it is. For example, many phishing training programs will talk about how phishing messages are designed to create urgency. It is more effective to tell users how the messages are designed to make them feel and the reaction the attacker hopes it will produce, using examples that create empathy between the victim and the people attending the class. Too often, training makes attacks seem obvious and the victims seem unintelligent. This approach leaves attendees with the mistaken impression that if they simply act with common sense, they will be safe. That perception is dangerous. Instead, it is better to communicate that these types of attacks can happen to anyone, and everyone must remain vigilant to protect themselves and their organizations. Using concepts from Daniel Kahneman's book *Thinking Fast and Slow* can also help people understand how they can counteract what the attacker is trying to do. Teaching people how their brain works and how they can intentionally slow down to maximize their ability to think rationally and make good decisions will help people better defend themselves against social engineering. It will likely have additional benefits in their personal and professional lives as well.

Third, it is important to empower end users with actions they can take to protect themselves. For example, for phishing attacks, you could tell users to not click links or attachments from unknown senders, to read a message twice before they respond, and to report suspicious messages appropriately using their security tools or contacts inside the IT security team. Keeping these recommendations simple and easy to remember is important. Finding ways to remind people in their daily lives will help reinforce the message. These tips should not be designed to be comprehensive but should focus on being memorable. It is not appropriate to expect every person in an organization to become an expert on social engineering countermeasures. It is appropriate to expect every user to exercise basic due care when they are handling the resources they are given access to.

Example Case: Snapchat

Snapchat is a popular social media platform that specializes in short-form video and photo messages. Snapchat currently employs almost 4,000 people. In 2016, Snapchat was the victim of a **Business Email Compromise (BEC)** attack that tricked a Snapchat employee into sharing sensitive personal information belonging to employees. Specifically, the information requested was W-2 forms, which are tax forms in the United States that allow employees to file their income tax returns. If an attacker had an employee's W-2, they would have all the information to file a fraudulent tax return and much of the information necessary to steal a person's identity.

The message was sent by an attacker pretending to be Snapchat CEO, Evan Spiegel. The message was reportedly simple and may have seemed legitimate to the end user. Essentially, the message asked the employee to send over a PDF copy of the employee's W-32 so he could review them. This is information that the CEO could legitimately access. However, this is an odd request. In this case, the urgency required to make the recipient not question the request was implied, given the request appeared to originate from the CEO. Also, the direct nature of the request gave the recipient less to scrutinize. The result was a successful attack.

BECs can be difficult to defend against because there is a power imbalance that the attacker is aware of and is preying on. This request is unusual, and it should give the recipient pause, but the attacker is hoping the recipient does not want to question the CEO. The recipient should have reached out to the CEO directly to verify the request. They could do so in a non-confrontational way. For example, the recipient could call the CEO and say something like *I received your request for W-2 information on our employees. Due to the sensitivity of the information requested, could we set up a secure share rather than sending over email?* If the request were legitimate, the phone call would confirm that, and it is unlikely the employee would receive negative feedback from the CEO. If the request was not legitimate, the CEO's response would make it clear that the message was a scam.

It is important that employees that have access to very sensitive employee information or have access to capital resources for the organization receive additional training related to BEC. According to the United States Federal Bureau of Investigation, BEC causes losses that are 64 times worse than ransomware. While many BEC stories are less dramatic and sensational than ransomware incidents, BEC caused $1.8 billion of the $4 billion in losses related to internet crime reported by the FBI in their 2020 cybercrime report. BEC is by far the costliest type of cybercrime for organizations. (CSO Magazine, 2016) (Cluley, 2021) (Federal Bureau of Investigation, 2020)

Phishing training and prevention

Phishing is a type of social engineering, so all the guidance in the preceding section is applicable. However, because phishing is so prevalent and has devastating consequences for organizations that do not adequately train their people on how to avoid falling victim to phishing schemes, it is worthwhile to explore the elements of an email message that should give a person pause when they exist. It is important to note that no one of these techniques is sufficient to identify all phishing messages by itself, but the combination of these factors helps to identify suspicious messages. First, we will talk about examining the sender's address.

The sender's address

The first red flag that's easiest to identify in a phishing message is the sender's address. This is the first thing I cover with my family members when trying to educate them on common scams. When there is an email in your inbox claiming to be from Amazon, your first step should be to look at the sender's address and see if it comes from an Amazon.com address. A significant percentage of consumer-targeted phishing campaigns will not have the sophistication to spoof a real email address or compromise a legitimate account. They will simply change the display name to say *Amazon* in this example, but the actual email address is a nonsensical domain or a personal account such as Yahoo or Gmail.

Legitimate messages sent to customers from most businesses will use the standard business domain name. If Apple is doing customer outreach, the sender address will come from `apple.com`, as an example. If the sender address does not match the sender display name, it is best to delete the message immediately. If it was sent to a corporate account, it is recommended that you also report the message to your IT security team.

Next, we will talk about the message itself.

Style and tone

It is important to consider the style and tone of a message and ask yourself if it is normal for the sender. If the sender is someone you know and their communication style is different than normal, it is possible the account has been compromised. If the communication is claiming to be a business, ask yourself if the way the message is written is consistent with the brand voice.

Greetings can be a red flag as well. If a greeting seems unusual, it is advisable to read the message closely and check for other red flags. Also, spelling and grammar can be important. There are many variations of English spoken throughout the world. If a message is using words in a strange context or words are spelled differently than normal for communications you receive, that message may not be from a legitimate sender.

Next, we will talk about the concept of creating urgency.

Urgency

Creating urgency is an important element for attackers. While some legitimate communications, such as marketing messages, may be designed to create urgency, messages from people you know or companies you already do business with rarely are structured that way. If you read a message that requires you to act immediately to avoid something bad happening, do not click on the link. If you think the message may be legitimate, call the person or the business to ask about the issue. Do not use a contact number listed in the message, but one you already have or one that is available from a public source such as a corporate website.

Legitimate messages are not designed to scare you. If the message feels aggressive, it should give you pause. Next, we will talk about links.

Links

The first rule of links in an email is do not click on them. The second rule of links in an email is do not click on them. Some links are legitimate, but links should be treated as illegitimate until you can verify otherwise, rather than the inverse. Instead of clicking on links, if the link is a simple website, it is better to type the link into your address bar yourself, rather than linking from the message.

If you are inclined to click a link, which I do not recommend, there are a few things that should be done prior to clicking. First, make sure that the link in the text and the redirect link match. In most email applications, if you hover over a link, you can see where it will actually redirect to. It is possible to make a link look like it is going to `www.chase.com` in the text, but it actually takes you to an entirely different website if you click on it.

There are exceptions. Sometimes people you know well will send you links to documents or resources. In these cases, you should be expecting the link. If you are not expecting it, you can reach out to the sender by some method other than replying to the email to verify the link is legitimate. In general, be very suspicious of links.

Next, we will discuss attachments.

Attachments

Attachments, like links, can be dangerous. Many people are accustomed to receiving attachments and open many attachments they receive. Attackers understand this behavior and use attachments to deliver malicious software. Attachment schemes are generally designed to prey upon a person's curiosity instead of fear. There are attachments that can be sent to corporate users that have very high click rates. For example, attachments that look as if they contain salary information are very popular. In general, the campaigns that appear to be accidentally sent to you containing information you may be interested in are often successful.

Next, we will cover a very general red flag, unusual requests.

Unusual requests

Unusual requests are covered last because defending against them requires a person to rely on their intuition. However, it is a meaningful element. If something seems off about the message or the request, slow down and think about what you are being asked to do. This is generic but can be useful guidance.

Example Case: Saudi Aramco

In 2012, Saudi Aramco, a major petroleum company in Saudi Arabia experienced what was called the worst cyberattack in history. A group that identified itself as the Cutting Sword of Justice claimed responsibility for the attack that caused severe disruption to the oil giant's operations. The attack was launched during the holy month of Ramadan when most of the employees were not at work. Malicious software known as Shamoon was deployed, which eventually stole passwords and destroyed data from more than 35,000 computers. Employees scrambled to contain the damage and took most of the systems offline. Oil operations continued, but most of the other business operations of the company were forced to be conducted on paper or cease altogether.

It is suspected that the attack was sponsored by Saudi Arabia's regional rival, Iran, and if true, is another example of a state-sponsored attack designed to cause damage rather than steal information or generate profit. This attack was targeted at the largest oil company in Saudi Arabia working in the sector that provided the vast majority of revenue to the kingdom at the time. Saudi Aramco is actually the largest oil producer in the world.

It is believed that the Shamoon malware was introduced to the environment when a well-meaning employee fell for a phishing email that contained a malicious link. Once the employee clicked on the link, the infection spread. It is also believed that an **Enterprise Resource Planning** (**ERP**) technology project linked the information technology network to the operational technology network, which were previously segregated, which made the attack far worse and the damage more widespread.

The Saudi Aramco case is among the best cases in the history of cybersecurity because it highlights many important lessons. First, a phishing attack only needs to fool one employee if the appropriate technologies are not in place to support end users. You can and should train employees on phishing and how they can be vigilant and good stewards of the systems and data they are entrusted with. However, the best training will not guarantee no employee will fall for a scam. Technologies can help support those users and limit the risk exposure for the company. Second, network segmentation is important. Properly segmented networks act like compartments on a ship. In the event of a compromise, network segments contain the damage and make it more likely that the organization can continue to function in the event of an incident. (Pagliery, 2015) (Council on Foreign Relations, 2012)

The Saudi Aramco attack shows the damage that can result when a well-meaning user is fooled by social engineering. Next, we will look at an example of a phishing message sent to one of my personal email accounts as an example. Coincidentally, I received this message as I was writing this chapter.

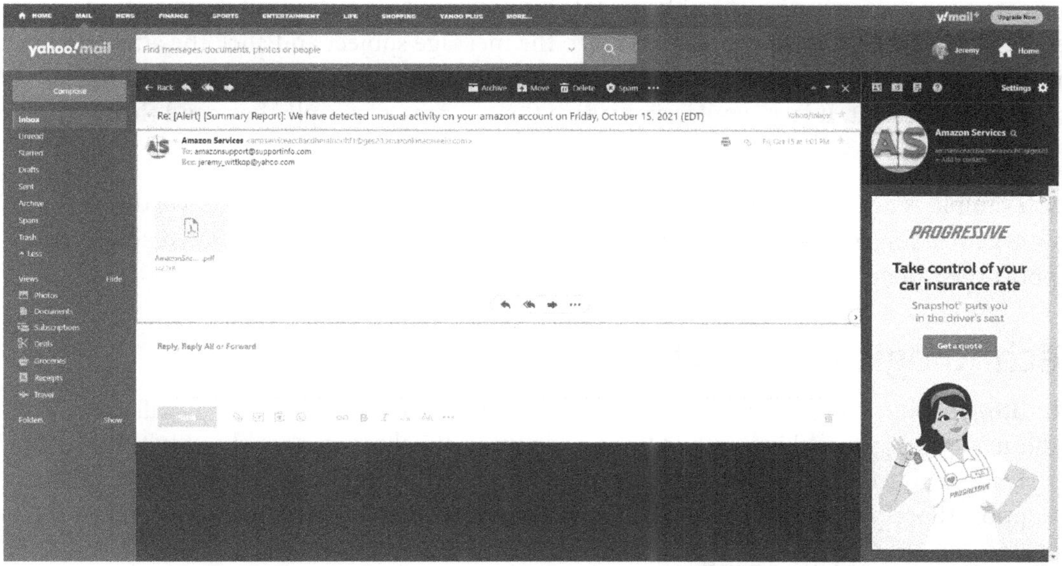

Figure 5.1 – Example attachment phishing message

First, the message display name says it comes from Amazon Services, but the email address is clearly not an Amazon email address. The attacker created a domain that has the word Amazon in it to make it look more legitimate, but it is clear from the mangled domain name, strange username, and misspelled words in the domain name that the sender is not associated with Amazon.

Second, the subject line is designed to create urgency. In this case, the attacker tried to scare me into thinking there is unusual activity on my Amazon account and attached a PDF document that allegedly will detail the information. I did not open the attachment, but it is reasonable to assume it does not contain security details associated with my Amazon account.

Interestingly, the attacker tried to make the message seem more legitimate by copying an email address they want me to believe is an Amazon support email address. It is not an Amazon.com domain though.

Other telltale signs are the fact that there is no message. If there were really unusual activity on my Amazon account that Amazon wanted me to know about, isn't it reasonable to assume they would write a message to explain more?

This message does not stand up to scrutiny. That is why there is a need for an attacker to create a sense of urgency. They likely sent this message to hundreds of thousands of people in the hopes that a few would react to the message subject and click the attachment without slowing down and thinking critically. The attacker may or may not know I have an Amazon account. It is a popular service, so the majority of people they send this message to will.

This example is not a sophisticated attack, but it is a common one. Next, we will discuss how organizations whose people are likely to be attacked by more sophisticated actors can support their people using technology.

Technologies supporting people

Educating people is important, but even the most effective training programs will not result in zero people clicking on bad links or opening attachments they shouldn't. When people inevitably do make mistakes, it is important to have the proper technology in place to support those people and prevent their mistakes from causing widespread harm.

First, we will look at URL rewriting.

URL rewriting

A **Uniform Resource Locator** (**URL**) is the text string that users put into their browser window to access resources on the internet. In most cases, the URL for legitimate businesses is recognizable. For example, most people know Amazon websites use a URL that is some variation on `amazon.com`. When an attacker is trying to fool a user, they will often disguise a link to appear as if it is going somewhere different than where it is actually going.

To combat this technique, some technologies will re-write all link URLs to show where the link is actually taking the user rather than only showing the link text that is placed into the message. URL rewriting technology makes it easier for users to identify where the links they are sent will take them. Please note, even if you have URL rewriting technology, I still recommend that you do not click links in emails.

Next, we will explore attachment sandboxing.

Attachment sandboxing

Attachment sandboxing is designed to ensure users that click on malicious attachments are protected. Essentially, the technology opens attachments in a safe, disposable environment rather than executing the action on the user's local machine. If the attachment is malicious, it will not cause harm to the user, and the sandbox environment will be destroyed, and with it, the malicious code.

Next, we will talk about a similar technology that focuses on protecting users from malicious links, rather than attachments.

Browser isolation

Browser isolation is similar to attachment sandboxing in that it creates a safe environment for users in case they make a mistake. With browser isolation, when a user clicks on a link, instead of being taken to that link in their browser, and thereby being exposed to whatever code is running on that site, they are directed to a secure browsing instance that allows them to interact with the desired web page without allowing direct access to their machine. In this case, if a user were to click on a malicious link, they would be protected.

Next, we will explore a technology that helps prevent malicious emails from being delivered in the first place, reputation blocking.

Reputation blocking

Reputation blocking focuses on the sender's reputation. Based on the volume and types of emails sent by the sender's domain, and a variety of other factors, the email security system will block some senders it believes to be illegitimate. These senders could be suspected criminals or spammers. This blocking helps to reduce the volume of illegitimate emails a user must sift through.

Finally, we will explore some emerging approaches that leverage machine learning.

Emerging machine learning approaches

Much is made of security technologies and their use of **Artificial Intelligence** (**AI**) and **Machine Learning** (**ML**). Much of the time, these claims are overblown and many of these capabilities are solutions searching for a problem. AI is the development of computer systems or code to perform functions that usually require human involvement. ML is a subset of AI focused on machines learning from inputs to make decisions that no longer require human intervention.

In cybersecurity, the most widespread form of AI is ML. When discussing social engineering techniques, astute observers may have noticed that identifying the difference between legitimate and malicious messages relies upon pattern recognition. ML is well suited for pattern recognition. Emerging technologies have begun using ML to identify patterns associated with risky communications to help stop more sophisticated attacks.

A good example is BEC. BEC is difficult for traditional countermeasures to protect against because there is no payload. However, there are patterns in BEC messages that users who have significant authority are trained to recognize. Some technologies are now training machines to recognize BEC patterns to better support end users. These techniques will likely grow in scope as the cybersecurity talent shortage continues to worsen and the pressure to respond quickly to security incidents continues to increase.

Next, we will explore a training technique designed to educate leadership rather than end users, known as tabletop exercises.

Tabletop exercises

I have had the opportunity to conduct numerous tabletop exercises with executive teams of different types of organizations of all shapes and sizes. The teams all came from different places in terms of awareness and maturity, but all of them provided value for the participants. It is one thing to have a plan for how to respond to a breach. It is quite another to ensure everyone has clarity on their role and the confidence to execute in a high-stress situation.

Tabletop exercises should not be conducted as an evaluation, they should instead be conducted as a learning opportunity. The first mistake I see people make is to run them as a test of whether people know what to do. This causes unnecessary stress and limits learning. I find it to be more effective to step through the response to a real-world scenario while asking participants to challenge the plan and find better ways to respond. We have found meaningful insights from team members going through the process and asking questions about why we are doing things a certain way.

A tabletop exercise can be very expensive, but it doesn't need to be. A team could research a recent incident and anonymize what happened and turn it into a tabletop scenario with minimal effort. The next step is to ensure there is an incident response plan that advises the people involved on what should happen during an incident and what their responsibilities are. This incident response plan should be distributed prior to the exercise. The details of the scenario should not be.

The tabletop exercise itself should be conducted with all the members of the response team in the same room, if possible, with minimal distractions. The scenario should be structured in a way that simulates reality and should be delivered in phases. In phase one, there may be limited information available, which is realistic. With each subsequent phase, more information should be revealed, and team members should be allowed to act differently considering new information. The response should be cross-functional. For example, the exercise should not only cover what the IT and security teams will do, but who will handle crisis communications and how communication will flow throughout the executive team.

After each phase, the exercise should be paused, and the team should be asked to think critically about the response and what could be done better. In military circles, this is known as an **After Action Review** (**AAR**), but it is a good practice for all types of organizations seeking to learn lessons and improve after each experience. The purpose of the exercise is to allow people to make mistakes in a safe and controlled environment, allow team members to become familiar with their role in the program, and improve the incident response plan. The intention should not be to evaluate the individual's ability to respond. Successful tabletop exercises are learning events, not evaluations.

Example Case: Uber Breach and Cover Up

Uber is a technology company that is well known for its popular ride-sharing service. Uber, under the guidance of founder Travis Kalanick, was also known for many events that revealed questionable ethics. The events related to the cyberattack against them in 2016 are a good example.

It was not until 2017, when Dara Khosrowshahi was the CEO of Uber, that the true events of 2016 became publicly known. In 2016, data about Uber's 57 million customers, including mobile phone numbers, names, and driver's license numbers was stolen by an attacker. Rather than report the breach, Uber chose to pay the attackers in exchange for a promise that they would destroy the information. There is no way Uber could have verified the information was actually destroyed and there were no remaining copies of the information. The idea to pay off the attackers was silly on its face. What they were able to secure in exchange for their payment, however, was the attacker's silence.

There is a saying that the cover-up is always worse than the crime. In the case of Uber, that is certainly true. Had Uber admitted they were a victim of a cyber-attack, it may have been embarrassing to the company, but they would have been a victim. When they chose to pay the attackers and cover the breach up, they became an accomplice and a perpetrator.

While the story of these events is in character for the leadership team at Uber in 2016, no reasonable person would respond to this attack in this way. Anyone who had been properly trained would know that bribing the attacker is not a reasonable response to an information theft attack. An effective tabletop exercise would have ensured that the people responding to a breach understood what to do and the potential result of each potential action they could take. If someone were to suggest paying the attacker in exchange for destroying the stolen information in this setting, it is likely that the group would have seen the error in that approach. (Muncaster, 2017)

As evidenced by the Uber breach and attempted cover-up, if people are not clear on how to respond to an incident, they may make improper decisions. The purpose of a tabletop exercise is to train executives on the proper response to an incident. An effective response can reduce the overall cost of a cybersecurity incident while allowing the organization to return to normal operations as quickly as possible when the incident is over. Many companies do frequent and effective employee training but have never done a tabletop exercise to ensure senior leadership is properly trained on how they should respond to an incident.

Summary

In this chapter, we have reviewed the framework for effective training, discussed strategies to partner with your people against cyber threats, and how to build training programs effectively. Now you have the necessary skills to build a more effective training program in your organization and to select technologies that can help support people, so their mistakes do not cause harm to the organization.

In the next chapter, we will revisit how the world is changing and how that puts pressure on traditional security controls. This time, we will examine specific solutions that help organizations set up flexible security programs to meet modern and emerging threats.

Check your understanding

1. What are the three elements of a framework for effective training?
2. Which are more effective, simulated exercises or informative presentations? Why?
3. Describe some of the elements of a message that could be a red flag that the message is a phishing attempt.
4. Describe some of the technologies designed to support end users in the event of a mistake.
5. What is a tabletop exercise and why would one be valuable to an organization?

Further reading

- Cluley, G. (2021, March 18). 64 times worse than ransomware? FBI statistics underline the horrific cost of business email compromise. Retrieved from The State of Security: `https://www.tripwire.com/state-of-security/featured/fbi-statistics-underline-orrific-cost-of-business-email-compromise/`
- Council on Foreign Relations. (2012, August). Compromise of Saudi Aramco and RasGas. Retrieved from Council on Foreign Relations: `https://www.cfr.org/cyber-operations/compromise-saudi-aramco-and-rasgas`
- CSO Magazine. (2016, March 4). This is what the CEO spoofing attack on Snapchat looked like. Retrieved from CSO: `https://www2.cso.com.au/article/595279/what-ceo-spoofing-attack-snapchat-looked-like/`

- Federal Bureau of Investigation. (2020). Internet Crime Report. Washington, D.C.: Federal Bureau of Investigation.
- Grant, M. (2017, October 3). $93M class-action lawsuit filed against City of Calgary for privacy breach. Retrieved from CBC: `https://www.cbc.ca/news/canada/calgary/city-calgary-class-action-93-million-privacy-breach-1.4321257`
- Kohn, A. (2014, March 13). Brain Science: The Forgetting Curve–the Dirty Secret of Corporate Training. Retrieved from Learning Solutions: `https://learningsolutionsmag.com/articles/1379/brain-science-the-forgetting-curvethe-dirty-secret-of-corporate-training`
- Muncaster, P. (2017, November 22). Uber Shock: Firm Hid Breach of 57 Million Users. Retrieved from InfoSecurity Magazine: `https://www.infosecurity-magazine.com/news/uber-shock-firm-hid-breach-57/`
- Oaklander, M. (2015, September 29). The 5 Best Ways To Improve Your Memory. Retrieved from Time: `https://time.com/4042569/how-to-improve-memory/`
- Pagliery, J. (2015, August 5). The inside story of the biggest hack in history. Retrieved from CNN Business: `https://money.cnn.com/2015/08/05/technology/aramco-hack/index.html`

6 Information Security for a Changing World

The world is changing quickly and some of the changes are inherently more secure, while others are less secure. Most changes are benign from a security perspective but require a different approach and render previous technologies and techniques obsolete. While we cannot abandon timeless information security best practices, failure to meet the challenges of a changing world can also result in catastrophe.

At a time where the security talent gap is reaching crisis levels, the changing technology landscape demands more from people who are already stretched thin. Understanding the modern threat landscape is a key element in building an effective security program and reducing the strain on overburdened teams. Trying to apply antiquated technologies and approaches to the modern world creates unnecessary work and stress for cybersecurity practitioners.

Meeting the challenges of today and tomorrow in a thoughtful way will help build resilient systems and processes that can adapt to the changing environment. This chapter will discuss the unique challenges of the modern world using techniques that are timeless and independent of the underlying technology. We will begin by talking about the security triumvirates that provide different perspectives for how a person can evaluate the efficacy of an **information security program**. Then, we will discuss each of the three disciplines that make up the modern information security landscape. Those three disciplines are securing the workloads that store, process, and transmit sensitive information, securing the endpoints that people use to access them, and managing the identities, access, and behavior of entities that have been granted access to those systems. The disciplines are defined by ambiguous terms in this section intentionally. In the future, just as terminals were replaced by desktops and eventually laptops, computers may increasingly give way to tablets and smartphones or other devices that have yet to be invented. Regardless, there will be an endpoint, or a point of interaction where the intentions of a human being are digitized for the first time. Similarly, just as mainframes gave way to data centers and are currently moving to cloud services, those cloud-hosted workloads may move to a distributed edge and ultimately to an architecture yet to be invented. Regardless, there will always be workloads that store, process, and transmit information.

The key to understanding information security holistically is to look at the objectives and challenges from a high level, rather than focusing on tactics, techniques, and technologies. Tactics, techniques, and technologies change, but the fundamentals rarely do. In fact, it could be argued that the fundamentals are actually thousands of years old. How is that possible? Much of information security is analogous to the military, which has a rich history. To help understand information security at a high level, let's explore frames of reference that may be helpful.

In this chapter, we will cover the following topics:

- Frames of reference
- Challenges with the traditional information security model
- Protecting information
- Securing networks and workloads
- Securing identities and granting access
- Securing endpoints

Frames of reference

Information security is a large problem. It is difficult to understand it holistically without using a **frame of reference**. Those who try to tackle information security without a frame of reference often retreat to silos and individual disciplines. As a result, many people understand endpoint security, network security, vulnerability management, cloud security, or information protection, but far fewer people understand information security holistically.

The good news is that information security is not that complex when you focus less on technology and focus more on actors and objectives. When you do, you will see parallels between information security and military operations.

Military connection

The connection between information security and military operations makes sense when you think about it and can be useful. In some cases, attacks are, in fact, **military operations**. In those cases, you could envision the attackers and defenders as cyber armies with similar roles as in a traditional conflict. One is trying to capture an objective and one is trying to defend it, with both sides deploying weapons and tactics to prevent their adversary from accomplishing their objective.

Even in cases where the adversary is a criminal, the operations themselves are not dissimilar from counterinsurgency or counter-terrorism operations. Like counter-insurgency operations, stopping criminals is difficult because they will steal credentials and blend in with the legitimate user population. Countermeasures must be designed so they can prevent the insurgents from accomplishing their objectives while impacting the legitimate user population as little as possible.

I served the United States Army and was deployed to Iraq in 2004 and 2005. Since beginning my information security career, I have been struck by similarities between defending information in an organization and defending the local Iraqi population from insurgents and eventually sectarian violence. The challenges are similar, and the solutions are akin to each other. This is important because while information security is relatively new, and novel techniques and technologies are being created every day, the principles of military operations are well established. This means we can learn lessons from military history and military thinkers that we can apply to modern information security challenges. Additionally, books such as *Robert Greene's The 33 Strategies of War* and *Sun Tzu's The Art of War* are useful for both understanding the strategies employed by attackers and developing defensive strategies for your program. There are countless other military strategy books that are as useful as, or more useful than, any information security book when designing an information security program, if you can apply your imagination and see the parallels.

The next way to look at information security from a holistic perspective is the common security triumvirates that I will introduce in the next section. There are more, but in the spirit of the triumvirates, I chose three.

Security triumvirates

The rule of three is a timeless rule used in writing and spoken word that says characters or ideas are more satisfying or memorable when they are presented in groups of three. A **triumvirate** is a concept that comes from ancient Rome where three people would share power equally. It was rarely equal, but when you think of a triumvirate conceptually, you can imagine three equally powerful concepts that work together.

Many information security concepts are presented in groups of three. I am not certain if these concepts are intentionally presented in sets of three due to the rule of three, or if the rule of three makes concepts presented in groups of three more memorable. Regardless, there are triumvirates that help provide a lens through which to view information security. The first we will examine is perhaps the most widely used: people, process, and technology.

People, process, and technology

People, process, and technology is a fascinating example of a triumvirate because it has all the challenges that real triumvirates had in ancient Rome. In a conceptual triumvirate, each of the three would have equal power. This is rarely the case in the real world, and people, process, and technology is no different. While the three should be equally important and command equal attention from **information security architects**, that is not what happens. By far, more time, effort, and resources are spent on technology than people and process. An overreliance on technology causes many of the problems we see in information security. Few technologies can protect against modern threats without the people and processes necessary to maximize the value of the technology.

The people aspect of cybersecurity gets the second most attention and resources in most information security programs. Most security leaders know that they need people to make their programs successful. However, due to the global cybersecurity talent shortage and the pace of technology change, it is more difficult than ever for organizations to hire, train, and retain the people they need to optimize their programs. Service providers, including **Managed Security Service Providers** (**MSSPs**), help fill the void, and many organizations are outsourcing security expertise out of necessity rather than desire.

The portion of the triumvirate that is often overlooked is the process section. Process is critically important, but it is often an afterthought. Most people would prefer a multiple-choice test over an essay test if given the choice. Technology selection is a multiple-choice test. A person can look at the market and choose the technology they think is best suited to solve their problem. People selection is similar. In good times, you post a job opening and you get a list of applicants. Once the initial screening process is complete, you essentially have a list of qualified candidates to choose from. Process creation is an essay exam. You must build processes to solve complex and multifaceted problems with few guidelines. It requires creativity and critical thinking. Many organizations do not focus on process because doing so is difficult.

Looking at security through the lens of people, process, and technology is useful when evaluating a program to compare how well the programs are built in each area. The next triumvirate looks at security through a different lens. Instead of defining the elements necessary to be successful in information security, **confidentiality**, **integrity**, and **availability** is a triumvirate designed to define information security through the lens of what the program is designed to accomplish.

Confidentiality, integrity, and availability

Confidentiality, integrity, and availability focuses on the three primary objectives of a security program and all three revolve around information. Otherwise known as the **CIA triad**, it speaks about the confidentiality, integrity, and availability of information. Every information security technology or program is designed to protect against threats to one or more of the three.

Confidentiality deals with ensuring that only authorized people can view sensitive information. **Information protection solutions** are designed to protect against attacks on the confidentiality of information. The most common way confidentiality is breached is when information is stolen or when unauthorized parties gain access to systems.

Integrity ensures that information is not modified by unauthorized parties. The **Solarwinds attack** is an example of what can happen when integrity is compromised. Solarwinds customers thought they were updating legitimate software, but the integrity of the software had been compromised by a threat actor.

Example Case: Solarwinds

Solarwinds is an IT software company that provides monitoring tools for many organizations around the world. Solarwinds customers saw what appeared to be a routine update from Solarwinds for one of their popular products. However, the update was not routine, and it was not created by Solarwinds. It is believed the **Russian intelligence agency** compromised Solarwinds' network and planted malicious software in the update that allowed them to compromise any Solarwinds customer who updated their software. As customers applied the update, which they believed came from Solarwinds, the attackers gained access to systems.

This attack was very sophisticated and highly intelligent. Rather than trying to compromise very well defended networks by using vulnerabilities, they chose to compromise a softer target that had access to their target networks as well as many other networks around the world. This is similar to the idea that caused the target breach through the compromise of an **Heating, Ventilation, and Air Conditioning** (**HVAC**) vendor, but at an exponentially larger scale, since Solarwinds was a vendor to thousands of organizations, including national governments.

This attack is devastating for information security professionals. It is difficult for a company to have a deep understanding of the security practices of all their software providers. Also, if people don't trust updates, they will update more slowly as they verify that no malicious software is contained in the update. That means they will be vulnerable for longer, and the time between discovering a vulnerability and patching that vulnerability will lengthen. This gives attackers of all kinds a larger window of opportunity. The Solarwinds attack shows that attacks against integrity are uncommon but can have devastating consequences that reach around the globe and change the way we think about best practices, such as patching systems (Temple-Raston, 2021).

Other integrity attacks include modifying information in a system for some kind of gain. An easy-to-understand, although highly unlikely, example is if I were to break into systems belonging to a financial institution and modify the balances in my accounts or credit cards. Ensuring the information that is in the systems is accurate and has not been tampered with is the goal of the integrity portion of the triad.

Availability deals with ensuring information or systems can perform their intended function. The classic attack on availability is the **Denial of Service** (**DoS**) attack. A DoS attack is when an attacker floods a legitimate service with so many requests that it cannot process legitimate requests. This type of attack is often used to take down websites and often uses bot networks in what is known as a **Distributed Denial of Service** (**DDoS**) attack. **Ransomware attacks** are also attacks on availability. The attacker denies legitimate access to files until a ransom is paid.

You could evaluate an information security program holistically by classifying technologies and countermeasures based on whether they were designed to protect the confidentiality, integrity, or availability of information or systems. The next triumvirate we will explore is **people**, **data**, and **threats**.

People, data, and threats

People, data, and threats is a new triumvirate that is gaining traction as a lens through which we can view information security. This triumvirate deals with the indicators that can help an organization identify anomalous activity.

The people element of cybersecurity deals with human behavior analysis. This portion is important because it helps identify insider threats, which have been a blind spot for organizations for many years. In the modern world, people work from anywhere and the information they access is not often located in a corporate-owned data center. As a result, the need to identify imposters and insider threats is magnified. Human behavior analysis helps you to understand the patterns of the people that access information and systems. Behavior analysis is not focused only on insider threats, though. Behavior analysis is an effective way to spot imposters using compromised accounts and may be used to highlight users who need additional training before they accidentally expose data or systems.

Data deals with the need to distinguish between the movements of sensitive information and commodity information and to apply selective controls based on the sensitivity of the information. Not all information is of equal value or equal risk to an organization. Some types of information are necessary to perform the intended business function but represent residual risk. Examples could be health-related information for a hospital. The hospital could not provide the necessary services without the health-related information, but the information itself is not likely to be monetized by the hospital. Other types of information allow an organization to profit from its exclusivity. For example, an innovative business practice or trade secret offers an opportunity for increased revenue and profitability. If others had access to this information, it could result in diminished financial performance. In both cases, protecting that information is critical.

Threats deals with internal and external actor groups and understanding the ways they are likely to attack and the information they will likely target. Threat data alone is rarely meaningful. However, understanding specific threats that are likely to target a specific organization or type of data can help you design effective countermeasures and build effective monitoring systems.

Now that we have established some lenses that can be used to evaluate information security programs, we will explore some of the challenges associated with traditional security models in the modern world.

Challenges with the traditional information security model

Traditional security models often are techno-centric and do not use the security triumvirates discussed previously. Instead, they focus on the technology used and therefore are vulnerable to change. With the current pace of change in the technology landscape, the shelf life of a techno-centric model is shorter than at any previous time in history. It is said that technological change is a flywheel, and we are likely to see a perpetually accelerating pace of change. As a result, techno-centric models don't work.

For decades, there has been a pendulum of trends in information technology swinging between **centralized** and **decentralized** infrastructures. Mainframes with terminals were a centralized architecture. All the computing power was in the mainframe, and the terminal was used only to access the mainframe. With the advent of personal computers and laptops, processing power was increasingly decentralized. The cloud computing revolution was a shift back toward a centralized infrastructure. Current conversations about edge computing are conversations about shifting back to a decentralized infrastructure. This pendulum continues to swing faster. Any frame of reference that is specific to an information technology strategy will continue to have a limited shelf life.

However, any of the security triumvirates can be applied in either a centralized or decentralized IT architecture. Effective security programs must be flexible and resilient by building their foundation on timeless principles rather than tactics and technologies. To underscore the fallibility of a security program built on current technology, we will next talk about the pace of technological change.

The Pace of Change

Famous futurist Ray Kurzweil predicted in 2001 that change is exponential and as a result, we will not experience 100 years of change in the next century, but rather 20,000 years of progress at the 2001 rate. It is difficult to comprehend how much change that would be, but most people who study technological change would agree it has never been linear in human history. Technological advancement has been accelerating throughout history. Here are some examples highlighting the pace of change in the new millennium.

The first smartphone with a touch screen and mass-market appeal (*iPhone*) was released in *2007*. Now, the smartphone is the center of most people's worlds. It is difficult to imagine life without them. In some cases, governments have identified smartphone access as a human right, ensuring even the poorest of their citizens have access to them.

In the *1990s*, the most popular storage devices were 1.44 MB floppy disks. The average base-level smartphone now has over 177,000 times the storage capacity. People rarely use physical devices to store information, though. Cloud services offer virtually unlimited storage for most people. In the case of social networks, people can use that storage for free, although they must trade access to their personal information to use the service.

In *2005*, **Google Maps** was launched. Before Google Maps, people had to either know where they were going, or print out turn-by-turn directions. Now, most people use their phones to navigate to most destinations.

In the year *2000*, the average household with high-speed internet was running at 56k speed. In most metropolitan areas, gigabit internet is widely available. The modern household download speeds are over 17,000 times faster than they were in the year *2000*.

The **Apple iPod** was invented in *2001*. While it was not the first portable MP3 player, it was the one that became popular enough to change the way most people purchased and stored music. Before *2001*, people would carry large books of CDs in their cars, and people working out who wanted to listen to music had to carry a portable CD player that was prone to skipping. If someone wanted to change the album they were listening to, they would have to remove one CD and insert another. People paid for music on a per-album basis and subscription services for both music and movies did not exist. Now, most people have access to millions of entertainment choices through a monthly fee using services such as **Netflix** and **Apple Music**.

The pace of change around us makes it easy to lose perspective. All indications are that the pace of change is increasing and will continue to increase exponentially. Therefore, being flexible and adaptable to change is a key trait if a person wishes to be successful in any endeavor (Hammond, 2020).

Next, we will discuss a discipline that is critical to an information security program, but difficult to execute effectively: protecting information.

Protecting information

I have dedicated most of my adult life to protecting information. I believe that the exclusivity of information is the bedrock of the Western way of life. Without the ability to protect and profit from ideas, you cannot have individual freedom and entrepreneurship. Without the ability to protect a person's identity and creditworthiness, you cannot have an efficient consumer economy. Many organizations run information security programs that focus on everything except protecting information. Many security teams are so focused on systems, vulnerabilities, and threats that they forget the general premise of what they are trying to accomplish. All the people, processes, and technologies that make up an information security program should be focused on protecting the confidentiality, integrity, and availability of information.

A core part of building an effective information security program is to value the information you are protecting. There is an expression I first heard from my long-time CEO *Steven Drew* that says, *You shouldn't spend a dollar to protect a nickel*. That sounds obvious, but many organizations deploy expensive security controls without ever assigning value to the information they are trying to protect. If that is the case, how do they know if they are making good investments? I am not naïve, I know it is difficult to create a return-on-investment calculation for security investments, *but it is possible*. I will give one example of an approach, but there are many possible ways to value information.

I like to use a valuation technique for cost-benefit analysis similar to how an insurance company would gauge risk and risk mitigation for natural disasters or fires. Essentially, the exercise is designed to predict potentially damaging events related to a threat of a data breach in this example. It is important to identify the cost of a single event. In many cases, this would be the cost of a specific record being lost. In this example, there is third-party research, such as the **Ponemon Cost of a Data Breach study**, that can help value a record. In other cases, such as intellectual property cases, it is more difficult to determine an absolute value, but it is possible to estimate. Then, the exercise would ask participants to estimate how many records would be lost if nothing were to be done. It is generally expressed in the number of records lost per year. Sometimes, the number could be less than one if the event were to occur less than once per year. Then, the cost per record can be multiplied by the frequency to calculate an annual risk exposure in financial terms. The equation could be expressed like the following:

Annual Risk = Financial Risk of a Single Event x The Number of Times it Would Occur (Annually)

Then, the organization can run the same calculation, assuming the proposed countermeasure is being put in place. The difference between the two calculations is the benefit side of the cost-benefit analysis. Is this an exact science? No, but it is better than making no effort to scrutinize security investments.

What would happen if this level of scrutiny was applied to information security investments? I think there would be more of a focus on information protection programs and less of a focus on programs and technologies that are more exciting, but less financially consequential. Protecting information would have the highest return on investment for most organizations.

Now that we've discussed why it is important to protect information, let's talk about why protecting information is difficult.

Challenges of information protection

Information protection is difficult. There is no technology you can buy and deploy that will automatically protect your information. **Data Loss Prevention** is a great example. One of my early mentors in the space told me that this is not a technology tool, it is a business tool that is facilitated by technology. That statement has proved itself accurate through my years of experience. Technology deployment is easy. It is more difficult to align with business unit leaders to define how information should be used in an acceptable manner and tune the technology to find any deviations from those acceptable business processes.

Modern information protection tools are more powerful than early Data Loss Prevention technologies, and the need to coordinate with business units to define normal and acceptable behavior is more necessary than ever before. With increasing visibility into the behaviors that lead up to an information exfiltration event comes the need to have a deeper understanding of normal behavior for a business unit or role. Understanding these behavior patterns and making a qualitative analysis in near real time is an interesting opportunity for automation in information protection as well. However, effective automation in this space requires capturing and analyzing behavior patterns. Even if that technology existed, it would still be critical to define acceptable behavior by working with business units to understand what should be happening.

It is difficult to protect information. It is much easier to deploy technology such as an antivirus or **Intrusion Detection Systems** (**IDS**) because there is little process design and discovery necessary. However, even though it is difficult to protect information, it is a critical capability for organizations to build.

Protecting information is a critical capability

We live in the information age. Information drives the economic engine of most organizations. There are countless articles naming data as the world's most valuable commodity, calling it the new oil. Yet, most organizations outside of Silicon Valley have little insight into the value of the data they hold.

In most organizations, the only way data or information is assigned a value is based on the cost of a data breach. While it is important to understand risk exposure, it is more important to understand the value of information holistically. What types of information are necessary to generate revenue or operate your business? Of those information types, which are only valuable if they are kept private? Of those information types, how much revenue do they contribute to? These are key questions to answer to properly value information.

It is no surprise that organizations that have not valued their information struggle to protect it. If you don't know what to protect, why you should protect it, or what the consequences are if you don't, it is difficult to set objectives for an information security program. Many organizations that do not have the ability to value their information rely upon regulations to tell them what to protect. It is good to comply with regulations designed to protect information. In my view, those regulations serve a necessary purpose in society and the economy. However, those regulations are designed to protect information the loss of which could harm the public or the economy through financial fraud or identity theft. Those regulations are not designed to help an organization protect information that they use to generate revenue or maintain a competitive advantage. Like many other aspects of business, developing and maintaining a competitive advantage using information is the sole responsibility of the organization.

For more than a decade, I have been helping organizations define the information that's important to them and build a strategy to protect it. More than 90% of the organizations I have worked with have intellectual property of some type that can be tied directly to revenue-producing operations. **Intellectual property** is not just patents, trademarks, and copyrights. **Business processes**, **customer lists**, and **trade secrets** are also intellectual property. While **patents**, **copyrights**, and **trademarks** have legal protections that preclude others from using them against their owner, other types of intellectual property do not, and those types of intellectual property need to be protected more.

To protect data appropriately, you must understand how it flows through the environment during the normal course of business. The best way to do that is to map data flows in the context of an information life cycle.

Mapping data flows

One of the most important ways to protect information is to understand how it should flow through your environment. There are different ways to visualize the information life cycle. The following diagram is an easy way to think about it:

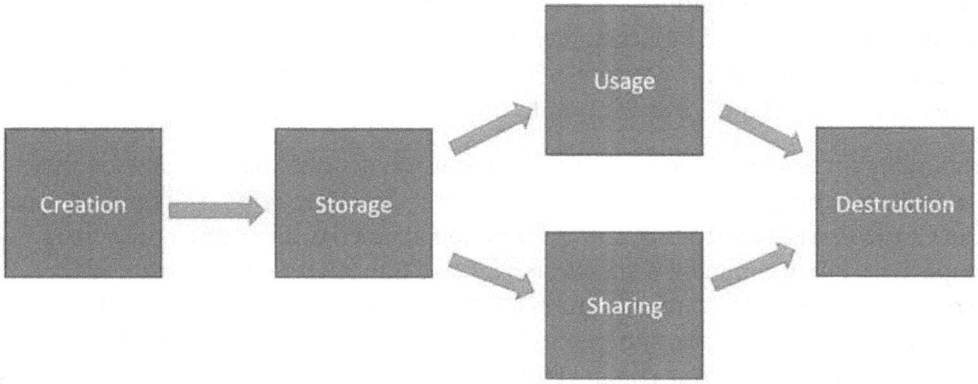

Figure 6.1 – Simple information life cycle

The idea behind mapping data flows is to map how data should move throughout an environment. This distinction is important because an organization that only maps **data flows** and does not monitor them is naïve. I have never seen an organization that can map its data flows so well that when monitoring is put in place there are no deviations from defined authorized behavior. **Monitoring** and **enforcement** are key; however, data flow mapping allows an organization to define its information protection rules and communicate with employees handling sensitive information effectively. Communicating processes and procedures with end users is a foundational element of an effective security program.

Next, we will spend some time defining each stage in the cycle, beginning with creation.

Information creation

Creation refers to the origination of the information in an electronic system owned or operated by the organization. All information an organization controls entered its environment at some point. That point can change based on the information type. For example, intellectual property may be created in a literal sense. It did not exist yesterday, but a member of our organization created it today. Other types of information, such as health data, may be provided by a customer using a form. Financial data, such as credit card data, may be captured at a point-of-sale system. In any case, information and its associated duty of care have a starting point.

Understanding these starting points is critical because as soon as that information enters the environment, there is an implied duty to protect it. However, you cannot protect what you don't know exists. Controlling how information enters the environment becomes very important. Every company that collects sensitive information from customers or partners should have a well-defined process for information collection, and controls to ensure information cannot leak into the environment through other channels. Common examples are customers sending personal information through email or ticketing systems designed to solve problems containing sensitive information. In the case of intellectual property, organizations must define who might create intellectual property and what the process will be if they do. For example, I may not be able to define the next product an automotive engineer creates, but I can probably surmise who will create it, what the file type will be, and where it will be stored. If I cannot define that process, it will be difficult to understand what intellectual property exists and therefore protect it. Protecting intellectual property is difficult, but it is not impossible. The reason most organizations struggle is they cannot define the property or the process of how it is created. This is another example of why security cannot operate in a silo.

Next, we will discuss the next logical step, which is **information storage**.

Information storage

Once information is created, it must be stored somewhere. This is obvious. However, the method and location of information storage are critical. **Physical information** was easy to control. Copy machines notwithstanding, data could be moved, but did not often propagate. **Digital information** is very different. It is often copied as it is moved, and it is not uncommon for hundreds of copies of a single piece of information to exist.

Many organizations can define a location where sensitive information is stored. Most cannot define all locations where sensitive information is stored. This makes powerful technologies such as **File Activity Mentoring** (**FAM**) less effective. In the past, monitoring the storage of information was very difficult. Essentially, an organization would have to scan all its storage repositories to generate a report of where sensitive information was located. Those scans could take weeks or months. By the time the scan was completed, the results were outdated, and even the best organizations were constantly chasing the problem. It was very difficult to get ahead. These challenges put tremendous pressure on the data destruction discipline we will discuss later and directly led to over-retention, which indirectly led to regulations such as the GDPR.

Modern technologies such as **Cloud Access Security Brokers** (**CASBs**) using **Advanced Programming Interface** (**API**) capabilities and some **Cloud Security Posture Management** (**CSPM**) solutions allow an organization to monitor the storage and movement of sensitive information in cloud repositories in near real time. There was a time where people were reticent to move information to cloud services because many of the security controls they relied upon were not available. At this point, there are many powerful security tools in the cloud that are not available on-premises. It is important to understand, however, that information in cloud services carries different responsibilities and risks, which we will cover in the *Securing cloud workloads* section of this chapter.

The determination of how and where information should be stored, whether it should be encrypted at rest, and who should be able to access it should be an intentional decision made by the organization.

A great example is a company I was working with that color coded data repositories based on the most sensitive information they could contain, and then built its access models based on that information. A *red* data repository contained information that had access restrictions based on government regulations, meaning some employees were legally not allowed to access that information. An *orange* data repository contained sensitive information but could be accessed by any employee with a need to know in accordance with least privilege. *Green* data repositories did not contain sensitive information. The company then would scan all orange repositories to ensure there was no red information, and scan green repositories to ensure there was no orange or red information. This approach is ideal in my opinion because it covers several best practices and includes recurring enforcement.

After information storage, there is a natural dovetail. The information will be used internally or shared with a third party. However, for the information to be valuable, someone needs to use it in some way. Therefore, we will start with defining the authorized use of information.

Information use

Understanding the **use of information** is critical. Many organizations focus solely on who should be able to access information, and once a person is granted access, there are few restrictions placed on what that person can do with that information. The problem is that malicious insiders and compromised accounts can then steal that information with impunity. It is important to monitor how sensitive information is used. However, doing so well requires the discipline to define which data is important and how it should be used.

There are roles and regions where monitoring all employee behavior is acceptable. In most jurisdictions, it is either required by law or expected by custom that such intrusive monitoring is only applied with just cause. It is preferable to define what is authorized with respect to how information should be used in the course of normal business and to alert on deviations from that behavior. Doing so requires the security team to map the use of information with the business unit. If you don't know what normal behavior is, how can you identify abnormal behavior? There are few cases of information theft where the behavior did not cross the threshold of obviously abnormal, but the question is whether the organization had the necessary controls in place to identify that abnormal behavior.

Next, we will talk about **information sharing**.

Information sharing

Information sharing is often necessary to maximize the value of information. However, when information is shared, the organization often loses visibility of the information and control over how it is subsequently used and shared. For types of information where that visibility and control are necessary, there are tools that allow an organization to retain those rights. However, deploying them can be time-consuming, costly, and onerous. Therefore, it is important to apply those controls only when necessary.

For some types of information, contractual agreements that govern how the information can be used are deemed sufficient. It is important to understand the information, the risks, and the legal protections in place to define the authorized methods of sharing the information. It is then critical to ensure the monitoring and enforcement capabilities are in place to restrict other methods of sharing. In the modern world, sharing has become very easy. There are many methods a user can employ to share information.

Like water and electricity, most users will take the path of least resistance. An effective information security program focuses on making it easy for users to share information properly, and to make it difficult for users to share it improperly. It is often infeasible to make it impossible to improperly share information. For example, in all but the most restrictive environments, there is little to prevent an employee from taking a picture of a computer screen with a phone and texting the picture to someone else. However, it is easier to put the file on a cloud service and invite a collaborator, unless you make it difficult to do so. The best way to guide behavior is to apply resistance to things you don't want to happen and eliminate barriers to productivity using authorized methods. Users will learn where the resistance is and naturally avoid it in most cases. Shaping behavior in this way can reduce risk considerably.

Finally, we will talk about **information destruction**.

Information destruction

Information destruction deals with the inevitable point in time when information has outlived its usefulness. For many years, there were no regulations that mandated that information should be destroyed. At the same time, storage became cheaper with every passing year. There were regulations that mandated that information should be stored for a minimum amount of time. The response was that most organizations didn't delete anything. The result is that for most organizations, retaining information with no business value is the largest pool of residual risk in their environment. The following example case demonstrates this problem well.

Example Case: Sony Pictures Entertainment

In *2014*, *Sony Pictures Entertainment's* systems were breached by a group calling itself the **Guardians of Peace**. The group, widely believed to be backed by the government of *North Korea*, stole large volumes of information from Sony servers. Most of the information was used to try to embarrass Sony Pictures Entertainment. Emails were released that detailed conversations between executives making disparaging remarks about each other, and important people who worked with Sony Pictures Entertainment, such as high-profile actors and directors. The motivation for embarrassing Sony Pictures Entertainment indicates it is unlikely a criminal organization was behind the attack. Most of this information had no business value. The question is, why would they have it? The Sony Pictures Entertainment case highlighted the residual risk carried by most organizations because they over-retain information that has no value. This case highlights the need for an effective data destruction policy.

While the information released was embarrassing, the business disruption was catastrophic. Sony Pictures Entertainment lost all faith in their electronic systems and took most of them offline. Teams resorted to communicating with each other using written notes and whiteboards. For weeks, the organization was crippled and forced to operate its business in the modern world without access to modern technology. The attack was devastating and highlighted the importance of an effective business continuity plan (VanDerWerff, 2015).

Most of the damaging information from the Sony Pictures Entertainment data breach had no business value, but still presented a risk to the organization. The GDPR mandates that personal information that has no business value and no legal retention requirement must be destroyed. This is important because it means that organizations must have a data destruction and certification process in place. Also, it requires that organizations understand information storage and information flows so they can be sure all the copies of the information are destroyed. This sounds easy. In practice, it is very difficult and requires a change in the way organizations think about information and risk.

Once every stage of the life cycle has been defined, you will understand how data should be used in an authorized manner. Now, you can build an information protection program that looks for anything outside those allowed practices. In some cases, the practice may be necessary but was not defined up front. This is fine as programs tend to mature. However, starting with a defined authorized behavior is the most effective way to build an information protection program. I should emphasize that defining authorized behavior and detecting everything else is the most effective way to build any security control. The number of bad things that could happen is infinite. The only thing that is possible is to define what should happen and then to put in controls that detect deviations from those authorized processes.

Successfully establishing a program that understands authorized interactions with information requires input from departments outside information security and ongoing cross-functional collaboration.

Cross-functional collaboration

Cross-functional collaboration, where people from multiple business functions work together to achieve a common goal, is a feature of the most successful information security programs, but it is rare. Few organizations are sufficiently committed to information security to dedicate resources from business units to advance the security program. Few information security programs have the discipline and maturity to make good use of cross-functional collaborators, even if the will exists. However, since cross-functional collaboration improves the security program significantly, it is a worthwhile pursuit to build it into the program, at least up front while objectives are being defined.

Information protection specifically is largely dependent on this collaboration. I was told by one of my early mentors that information protection is not a technology solution, it is a business solution facilitated by technology. Rules governing the creation, use, storage, sharing, and destruction of information are business rules. We simply use technology to enforce them. When framing the problem that way, it is natural to ask for business unit involvement.

If you are responsible for an information protection program, one of your first steps should be to get buy-in from leadership and start building your cross-functional collaboration workflows. These cross-functional collaboration teams will be critical in identifying information, the proper sharing of information, and other items related to keeping information safe in your organization. Now that we understand how and why we should protect information, we will turn our attention to securing networks and workloads.

Securing networks and workloads - past, present, and future

Securing networks and workloads is a heading that is intentionally vague. The methods we use to transport information and who owns them have changed significantly since the early *2000s*. Then, people's access to high-speed internet was mostly provided by their employer, who owned the infrastructure, the path to the internet, and the internet circuit itself. Most people either physically came into an office or used a **Virtual Private Network** (**VPN**) to access the network remotely. In either case, the organization owned the path to the internet and could put controls in place to monitor its use for a variety of reasons. In the modern world, most people have multiple methods of high-speed access to the internet. Home internet download speeds are often higher than the speeds at work. Most people in developed countries have high-speed internet access on their mobile phones. Many workers never come into their office, and VPN connections are used only for access to specific resources. Organizations have lost control over the path their teams take to the internet.

Workloads have changed as well. In the early *2000s*, the term "workload" did not exist because there was no need for it. Workloads were run primarily on physical servers. The first virtual server technology was brought to market in *1999*, but virtual servers behaved like physical servers from a security standpoint. Servers were deployed in environments owned by the organization. Many owned and operated large data centers full of servers. Others used colocation facilities, but most organizations had complete control over how systems were built and how information was stored, processed, and transmitted. According to a recent report, 85% of organizations had most of their workloads in the cloud in 2020 (*AllCloud, 2020*). This means most workloads are no longer owned by the organization; they are renting computing power on demand from others. While this makes sense from a business perspective, it introduces new challenges to security teams.

Next, we will explore how to **secure networks**.

Securing networks

Securing networks is increasingly challenging when the organization no longer has ownership of the route to the internet and, often, the device being used to connect or the workload the user is connecting to. Further, modern protocols such as **Transport Layer Security** (**TLS**) 1.3 make it more difficult to intercept and inspect traffic in transit. TLS is a protocol that ensures traffic is encrypted. If you were to browse to an internet site that starts with the prefix `https`, you would be using TLS to access that site. Most modern sites use TLS. The change to TLS 1.3 made it difficult for traditional approaches to network security to operate. Traditionally, organizations would use a proxy server. Any user who wanted to access the internet would go through the proxy server, which would read the traffic and the destination and decide whether to allow the transaction to happen. The problem is that this is identical to a **Man-in-the-Middle** (**MitM**) attack. TLS 1.3 makes MitM attacks more difficult, which in turn, makes it more difficult to execute an effective proxy strategy for network security.

In response, many organizations are turning toward cloud-based **Secure Web Gateway** (**SWG**) solutions. However, when users are accessing the internet through their own networks and on their own devices, it is very difficult to force them to use an SWG. Therefore, modern SWG controls are a partial solution. It is part of a company's duty of care to ensure that if they are providing access to the internet, the access is secure. However, gone are the days where a company could rely upon SWGs as a comprehensive control governing internet access and data movement.

Securing cloud workloads

In *Chapter 1, Protecting People, Information and Systems – a Growing Problem*, we introduced the **shared security model** for cloud computing environments. We are going to revisit that model as we focus on solutions to secure cloud environments. Cloud computing is a centralized IT model. History tells us we will move back to a decentralized model in the future. The most discussed decentralized IT model for the future is edge computing. When you hear edge computing, think of a transition back to a decentralized model. However, the dominant IT model currently is the centralized model broadly referred to as cloud computing. Cloud computing is different than previous centralized models in that the actual server infrastructure and data centers are owned by third parties. This idea of outsourcing workloads is new in the history of computing. However, when discussing edge computing, while decentralized, it is likely that it will be offered as a service, meaning the idea of outsourcing workloads does not appear to be a passing phenomenon. Why is this important? Because it means that shared security models are also here to stay. A shared security model means there are two or more entities responsible for the security of a workload. Misunderstandings of who is responsible for what, especially on the customer side, are the root cause of most data breaches involving cloud environments.

Therefore, understanding the following model is critical for securing cloud workloads. Having and understanding a similar model any time you are consuming anything as a service is similarly important:

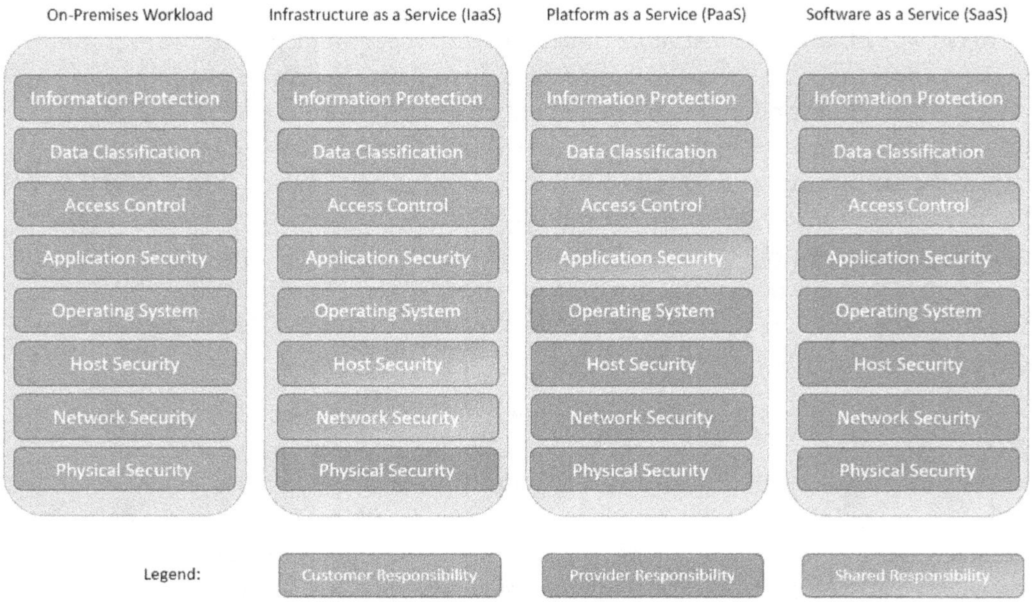

Figure 6.2 – Shared security model for various cloud computing environments

As you can see, depending on which type of cloud computing you are consuming, there are different responsibilities for you and your service provider. **Software as a Service (SaaS)** is the most widely used and understood model. In this model, the cloud provider provides the underlying infrastructure, compute power, and application to you as the consumer, and you simply use it. If you have ever used **Salesforce**, **Box**, **OneDrive**, **Exchange Online**, or **Gmail**, you are using SaaS. Since the provider is in control of most of the stack, they have most of the responsibilities. However, even when consuming SaaS, you are responsible for protecting your information, classifying it if necessary, and controlling who has access to the environment and what permissions they have. In fact, in any model, you cannot outsource responsibility for these disciplines. The reason is that each of them requires some knowledge of your business and what is allowed. There is no way for the provider to know who should have access to a specific document, for example. **Cloud Access Security Brokers (CASB)** were built specifically to solve the SaaS challenge of providing capabilities to control these three things across many SaaS applications that exist.

Infrastructure as a Service (**IaaS**) is almost completely the opposite of SaaS. IaaS simply provides computing power on demand. You as the consumer decide what operating system to deploy, what applications to install, and what the intended purpose of the workload is. If you have ever worked with **Amazon Web Services** (**AWS**), **Google Cloud Platform** (**GCP**), or **Microsoft Azure**, you are probably consuming IaaS. I say "probably" because all three offer services that are not IaaS, which we will discuss in the next paragraph. In IaaS environments, the provider is responsible for the physical security of their data centers, and they share responsibility with the consumer for securing the networks and the hosts themselves. Everything else is the consumer's responsibility. Broadly, **Cloud Workload Protection** (**CWP**) solutions are designed to help customers meet the security needs of an IaaS environment.

Platform as a Service (**PaaS**) offerings are in between SaaS and IaaS, which leads to confusion. Also, many popular PaaS platforms are offered by companies better known for their SaaS or IaaS offering, adding to the confusion. For example, Salesforce is a popular SaaS application. The underlying `Force.com` platform, which all Salesforce customers have access to, is a PaaS offering. AWS is IaaS. However, services on the platform, such as **Beanstalk**, are PaaS offerings. It gets very muddy. Solutions such as **Cloud Security Posture Management** (**CSPM**) are designed to help customers meet their PaaS responsibilities. However, it is difficult for customers because most are using PaaS, but most think their PaaS platforms are actually IaaS or SaaS.

The best way to secure cloud workloads is to create an inventory of every cloud service consumed in the environment, classify it as SaaS, PaaS, or IaaS, and define strategies and tools to secure each environment. Most organizations do not have this kind of cloud computing register, but they should. Most breaches involving cloud computing are the customer's fault, and most of those breaches stem from a misunderstanding of the shared security model. The tools are also purpose-built. For example, a CASB solution can help you discover what cloud services are in use, and even have connections to services such as AWS, which is IaaS, but the controls are built for the responsibilities you have in an SaaS environment. Therefore, using a CASB to secure AWS leaves major gaps in your responsibilities in the shared security model.

Next, we will discuss how we can secure identities and grant them access.

Securing identities and granting access

Securing identities and granting access are critical functions for a security program. It is always your responsibility to grant access to systems and information to identities and to build controls to ensure the people requesting access through a login are who they say they are. We discussed **Multifactor Authentication** (**MFA**) in *Chapter 4, Protecting People, Information, and Systems with Timeless Best Practices*, so we will not discuss it in depth during this chapter. However, we will briefly discuss the importance of **verifying identities**.

Verifying identities

It is important for every organization to have the ability to identify who is requesting access and to verify they are who they say they are. In a world where most people access resources remotely, and many resources are accessible from anywhere because they are cloud based, it is more important than ever to verify identities. Also, with the prevalence of password theft, MFA is a critical capability. Before a user is granted access to a system, we must have the capability to identify that user and be sure the user is not an imposter.

Next, we need to grant access to the information or workloads they must access.

Granting access

Once we can identify the people who are requesting access, we need to grant that access. In *Chapter 4, Protecting People, Information, and Systems with Timeless Best Practices*, we discussed the concepts of *least privilege* and *need to know*. Granting access is where those disciplines come into practice. There are two underlying causes of over-permissive accounts in most environments, **fear of business disruption** and **credential accumulation**.

Fear of business disruption is the idea that it is better to give a person more access than they need rather than less. The theory is if I am denied access to a resource, the security team has harmed business productivity and I need to request access before I can accomplish my job function. While understandable, this practice leads to an unacceptable level of risk in my opinion. We should grant access to the resources we know a user will need to perform their intended function. Too often, we grant permissions to all the resources a person *might* need. Then, if that account is compromised, the attacker has access to more resources than they should, and the damage of the breach is magnified. While it may be a minor annoyance to the end user to have to request access to a resource when they are using it for the first time, the risk posed by over-permissive accounts is much greater.

Example Case: Tesla

Tesla is one of the most innovative companies in the world, led by an outspoken innovator named *Elon Musk*. Elon has been vocal about instances where he believed employees were stealing from Tesla, which has provided a window into insider intellectual property theft that was rare prior to Tesla's disclosures. Intellectual property theft by insiders is not rare. However, most companies don't have the controls to identify it, and when they do, they rarely disclose the events publicly. The disclosures by Tesla provide security professionals a better ability to understand insider threats.

One such disclosure was made at the end of *2020*. In *December 2020*, Tesla hired an engineer named *Alex Khatilov*. During the two weeks he spent as an employee of Tesla, Khatilov is accused of stealing more than 6,000 files that help Tesla automate its operations. It was said that these files had nothing to do with his job, but he had access to them and copied them to a SaaS service that he could access from his personal computer, and therefore exfiltrate. During the investigation, thousands of files were found, and it is difficult to determine if or how Mr. Khatilov used them.

There is a key lesson learned from this incident. If the files truly had nothing to do with Khatilov's job, why did he have access to them? If the proper controls were in place, Tesla could have stopped the files from being uploaded to Dropbox. It is clear that some of the controls were in place because the activity was detected. In general, Tesla does a great job of protecting its intellectual property and identifying when it is being stolen. It is important to remember that those who disclose many incidents compared to their peers, such as Tesla, are not inherently lax in their security controls. In most cases, the opposite is true. The most insecure organizations think they don't have a problem and don't have the capabilities to prove otherwise.

Tesla is a great example of monetizing intellectual property. Tesla accounts for about 2% of the United States automobile market, but has a total market capitalization, roughly translated to value, that's bigger than all other United States car manufacturers combined. Some of that can be attributed to Elon Musk's leadership, but much of it can be attributed to innovation and intellectual property (Houcheime, 2021).

Next, we will discuss **permissions accumulation**.

Permissions accumulation

During my time at *InteliSecure*, a cyber-security services company that I was with for over 10 years, I served in a variety of roles, and I was the poster child for potential credential accumulation. As I moved from operations to sales, to marketing, and eventually to the C suite, I needed access to different resources. I no longer needed access to other resources. In most organizations, I would be granted access to the new resources I needed, but my access to resources I no longer needed would not be removed. As a result, over time, I accumulated permissions that made my account over-permissive and made me a major risk to the organization. It is important to focus on what a user no longer needs when they change functions as well as the new permissions they need in their role.

It is more difficult than ever to verify identities and grant access properly. Next, we will discuss how human behavior analysis can help with both.

Human behavior

In most cases, I think the applications and effectiveness of **machine learning** and **artificial intelligence** capabilities are overstated. **Behavior analytics** is a notable exception. Behavior analytics is a capability that uses machine learning to analyze human behavior patterns. This application is perfect for machine learning. Machines are very good at recognizing patterns from large datasets, and that is exactly what behavior analytics is designed to do. There are many effective applications for behavior analytics, and it is one of the most promising new technologies in my opinion. It has a special role to play in both verifying identities and granting access. First, let's explore how behavior analytics can help us verify identities.

It is easy to impersonate a user by stealing their password. It is difficult, but possible to defeat MFA methods. It is nearly impossible to be successful in an attack without deviating from a user's normal behavior patterns. Once an attacker is in an environment, they will behave very differently from an authorized user because their objective is different from an employee trying to do their job. As a result, using behavior analytics to trigger a password reset or step-up authentication makes an attacker's objective more difficult to accomplish. Implementing this capability would frustrate and deter all but the most sophisticated and motivated attackers. It would also highlight insider threats because most become malicious, and when they do, they change their pattern of behavior. Next, we will discuss how we can use behavior analytics to combat over-permissive accounts.

Over-permissive accounts are a major problem because most organizations do not know what resources a user actually needs to perform their job function. With behavior analytics, we can analyze how a user leverages the permissions they have been granted. You could even set a policy that says all permissions that have not been used in the last 90 days will automatically be removed and the user must request them again if access is needed. This will immediately solve the over-permissive account problem. In some organizations, a shorter time frame may be appropriate.

Example Case: US Navy Warship Data

The story of a husband and wife trying to sell United States Navy submarine propulsion secrets is entertaining because of the methods they used to try to smuggle the information to people they thought were foreign agents. However, the case itself is sobering. In 2021, the **Naval Criminal Investigations Service (NCIS)** arrested a 42-year-old engineer and his wife for stealing Navy secrets and attempting to sell them to a foreign government.

As part of his job, the engineer had access to some extremely sensitive secrets about how the US Navy built propulsion systems for its nuclear submarines. The engineer stole documents related to these secrets and sent a sample pack of the stolen information to at least one foreign government. In a poorly translated email, he made it clear that he had secrets and he was willing to share them in exchange for payment.

The engineer was sent a $10,000 good faith payment and an arrangement was made for a meeting. When the meeting took place, the engineer and his wife agreed to hide an SD card containing the documents in a peanut butter sandwich and drop it at a mutually agreed upon location. The information was encrypted, and the agreement was made to provide the decryption key in exchange for an additional $20,000 payment.

Aside from the entertaining nature of the smuggling method, and the curiously low price demanded for such sensitive information, there are some lessons to be learned from this case as it relates to behavior analytics. This engineer was not stealing information and selling it to foreign governments his entire career. Based on the amounts offered for information that would take billions of dollars of research to re-create, he was not an expert in espionage. At some point, he went from an engineer doing his job to a malicious insider seeking to profit from the theft of sensitive information he had access to. Behavior analytics capabilities help detect those changes. While it has not been disclosed, there is a good chance this type of technology helped the NCIS identify this activity and intercede before the engineer was successful in making contact with an adversarial government (Osborne, 2021).

Behavior analytics is becoming an increasingly attainable capability for most organizations. Historically, the capability has been cost-prohibitive, but now technology has advanced to the point where most organizations could deploy these capabilities in a cost-effective manner.

Next, we will discuss **securing endpoints**.

Securing endpoints

Securing endpoints is another intentionally vague term because endpoints have changed. In the early *2000s*, the only smartphone in wide use was the Blackberry, and that technology used a server that was controlled by the organization. Now, most employees have a smartphone that the organizations do not control or have visibility into. In most cases, that smartphone is at least as powerful as a laptop. An endpoint refers to any device that digitizes a user's intentions. This could be a desktop, laptop, tablet, mobile phone, video game controller, smart refrigerator, voice-activated personal assistant, and so on. As you can see from the brief list I was able to come up with off the top of my head, there are an exploding number of endpoints. Securing them has become exceedingly difficult. Further, most organizations do not own most of the endpoints in a user's life. This presents a major problem for security.

Traditional endpoint approaches are no longer a comprehensive control. There is no way for an organization to secure every endpoint a person will use to access their workloads or information. However, it is part of the organization's duty of care to secure the endpoints they issue to users, often using an **Endpoint Protection Platform** (**EPP**). Organizations can also exert control over cloud workloads to stipulate the security posture of any endpoint being used to access that environment. This type of control helps organizations secure the endpoint, which is a critical security capability. However, when organizations think about endpoint security, they must think beyond software controls and think creatively about what the rules should be with respect to endpoint security and what leverage points they may use to enforce those controls.

Summary

In this chapter, we have discussed frames of reference that you can use as a lens through which to view security that will help design controls regardless of how the world around you changes. You have learned about the core security disciplines of protecting information, securing networks and workloads, securing identities, granting access, and securing endpoints. You now have the tools necessary to create a security program to meet the challenges of the modern world and a prism through which to view the future as change inevitably comes. In the next chapter, we will turn our attention toward specific problems facing the modern enterprise, along with solutions to help meet those challenges.

Check your understanding

1. Choose a security triumvirate and explain it in your own words.
2. What are some of the challenges with the traditional information security model?
3. What is the information life cycle? What are its stages?
4. What is a workload?
5. What are the three major categories of cloud services?
6. How can human behavior analysis help secure identities and ensure only the proper access is granted?
7. What is an endpoint? Can you name at least five different types of endpoint?

Further reading

- AllCloud. (2020). 2020 Cloud Infrastructure Report.
- Hammond, A. (2020, January 2). The 20 Biggest Advances in Tech Over the Last 20 Years. Retrieved from FEE: `https://fee.org/articles/the-20-biggest-advances-in-tech-over-the-last-20-years/`
- Houcheime, W. (2021, February 3). Tesla Experiences Internal Breach, Leaking Valuable Company Data. Retrieved from Security Boulevard: `https://securityboulevard.com/2021/02/tesla-experiences-internal-breach-leaking-valuable-company-data/`
- Northrop Grumman. (2013, April 8). Developing a Framework To Improve Critical Infrastructure Cybersecurity. Retrieved from NIST: `https://www.nist.gov/system/files/documents/2017/06/02/040813_northrop_grumman_response_part2.pdf`

- Osborne, C. (2021, October 11). FBI arrests engineer for selling nuclear warship data hidden in peanut butter sandwich. Retrieved from ZDNet: `https://www.zdnet.com/article/fbi-arrests-engineer-for-flogging-nuclear-warship-data-hidden-in-peanut-butter-sandwich/`
- Temple-Raston, D. (2021, April 16). A 'Worst Nightmare' Cyberattack: The Untold Story Of The SolarWinds Hack. Retrieved from NPR: `https://www.npr.org/2021/04/16/985439655/a-worst-nightmare-cyberattack-the-untold-story-of-the-solarwinds-hack`
- VanDerWerff, E. a. (2015, June 3). The 2014 Sony hacks, explained. Retrieved from Vox: `https://www.vox.com/2015/1/20/18089084/sony-hack-north-korea`

Section 3 – Solutions to Common Problems

A common question I get from business executives is, "*If we continue to spend more on security every year, why do we continue to see more breaches?*" Part of the answer to the question is what was covered in the first chapter: the economics of cybercrime are not static and while the cost of cybercrime is rising, the benefit to the attacker is rising faster. Outside the pure economics of the situation though, there are several common challenges organizations face. Fortunately, there are solutions available for these problems. Furthermore, automation can play an important role in solving some key challenges and controlling long-term costs while building a maturing program. Finally, in this section, we will discuss how to keep yourself and your family safe at home.

This part of the book comprises the following chapters:

7

Difficulty Securing the Modern Enterprise (with Solutions!)

The first three chapters defined the problems facing information security teams. The second three chapters described strategic solutions at a high level. The last three chapters will focus on very specific solutions to very specific problems. A common question I get from business executives is *If we continue to spend more on security every year, why do we continue to see more breaches?* Part of the answer to the question is what was covered in the first chapter, the economics for the attacker are not static and while the cost of cybercrime is rising, the benefit to the attacker is rising faster. Outside the pure economics of the situation though, there are several common challenges organizations face.

In this chapter, we will identify some of the most pressing challenges along with solutions I have found to be effective in my career. One of the things that makes cybersecurity so interesting is the ability to solve novel problems in interesting ways. Therefore, this is not an exhaustive list and is not intended to stifle creativity. Rather, it is an example of solutions that exist that may help spark some ideas for how you could solve problems that have not yet been identified.

In this chapter, we will talk about the following problems, each with some solutions I have found to be successful through the course of my career:

- Cybersecurity talent shortage
- Too much technology with too little process
- What are we trying to accomplish?
- Lack of continuing education

Cybersecurity talent shortage

The cybersecurity talent shortage is massive and growing. Cybersecurity is one of the best career fields for young people to enter. It is not uncommon for entry-level cybersecurity specialists to get several raises in their first year and be making a six-figure income within 3 years. There are few, if any, career fields outside of cybersecurity that offer that level of advancement and income prospects. Yet, cybersecurity continues to fail to attract a talent pool that can keep up with the demand for professionals.

There are many potential underlying factors. Cybersecurity is still not as diverse as it should be. Cybersecurity teams rarely reflect the entirety of the community. Solving this problem will require cybersecurity as a discipline to appeal to more people. Part of that appeal is representation in leadership and outreach. Part of it is changing the public perception that cybersecurity is a technical field with only engineering roles.

There are many people who have been successful on my teams throughout my career who have no technical background whatsoever. After entering cybersecurity, some gained a more technical skillset, but some did not. You can be successful in cybersecurity without ever getting into technology. We need critical thinkers to become analysts. We need strategic thinkers to help us build processes and programs and help us stay ahead of the attackers. These roles can be exciting and challenging and can appeal to people who would have never considered a career in cybersecurity. If you are reading this because you are considering a career in cybersecurity, I encourage you to join us. Cybersecurity has been the best thing that happened to me personally and professionally. If you know someone who is trying to decide what they would like to do for their career, please tell them about cybersecurity. We need all the talent we can muster to meet the current and future challenges we will face. Defending our way of life by protecting information and systems is vitally important, and we need you.

With respect to the skills gap, we will first define the problem and talk about meaningful ways that some are trying to solve it.

Not enough people!

Attracting, training, and retaining cybersecurity talent is a critical part of any program. It can be very difficult to accomplish because there are far more cybersecurity jobs than there are qualified people to fill them. I generally hesitate to use statistics because they become outdated quickly. However, the statistics in this space are sobering. Here are some that help define the human resources crisis facing cybersecurity leadership:

- The **International Information System Security Certification Consortium (ISC2)** estimates that there are currently 2.8 million cybersecurity professionals employed in 11 major world economies. The same article estimates the gap at 4 million professionals. Put another way, the total need for cybersecurity professionals globally is 6.8 million, meaning we have fewer than half of the professionals we need. (HDI, 2020)
- 88% of chief information security officers report very high levels of job-related stress. Many of them cite physical and mental health issues as a result. Their average tenure is 26 months. (Cimpanu, 2020)
- The average tenure for an IT security specialist is less than a year. The average tenure of an information security analyst is 1–3 years. (National Cybersecurity Training Academy, 2021)

These numbers are staggering and getting worse. Think about it from the perspective of a CISO. You are facing a tremendous amount of pressure and job-related stress. You lose an analyst or a specialist and go into a market where less than half of the job openings can be filled. It understandably takes a long time to try to find a qualified candidate. The workload of the person who left does not disappear. Instead, it is passed onto the remaining team members. They become overworked and burn out and they start to quit. The cycle repeats itself and ultimately the CISO quits.

This is a macro problem and solving it will require big solutions and a partnership between the public sector and the private sector as well as a change in the way that we approach education. None of these solutions will make an immediate impact. In the next section, we will talk about services and how they can provide immediate relief but embracing them simply passes the problem to a service provider who can focus exclusively on it. Services alone will not solve the skills gap.

I have been fortunate in my career to build cybersecurity teams in several jurisdictions, and I have had opportunities to work with security teams around the world. There are some examples of programs that work as a public-private partnership. In fact, the United States has the fewest programs designed to help solve this problem of all the countries that I have operated in. In the United Kingdom, the government has sponsored programs where they will train and place professionals in our operations centers as apprentices. We have the ability to train them further and advance them through our organization. In Saipan, there is a similar government-sponsored training program to ensure we have a pipeline of qualified candidates. In the United States, we have similar programs, but we must source the entry-level talent ourselves. All these approaches, however, require the ability to take entry-level professionals and train them so they can advance. Most security teams cannot do that, they need skilled resources now, which don't exist in the quantity they are needed. Cybersecurity professionals with 3 years of experience have very little difficulty finding their next job. However, finding your first job can be very challenging. We need to solve that problem to help get more talent into the field gaining experience.

However, there is a bigger problem earlier in the pipeline. Too few kids are interested in cybersecurity. Cybersecurity is an exciting field that offers amazing career advancement and very good earnings potential. However, too few young people choose to get into the field. Diversity is a major problem.

According to the career analytics organization Zippia, the cybersecurity field is 77.9% male and 72.6% white (Zippia, 2021). We will not fill the cybersecurity talent gap with white males alone. Cybersecurity professionals and education institutions must do more to interest a more diverse set of candidates in the discipline. We need to partner with colleges and universities and their associated student groups to have conversations about the job prospects in a cybersecurity field. We need to talk to our kids about cybersecurity for many reasons. Not only can we help them live a safer life online, but we may be able to interest them in a lucrative career in a rapidly growing field.

The reality of the cybersecurity skills gap is that it is too large to close during the current generation. Even if you paired every skilled cybersecurity professional with an apprentice and had them train their apprentice in everything they knew, we would still not have enough professionals. Solving the cybersecurity skills gap requires an investment in the next generation and encouraging them to get interested in the field now so we will have newly trained skilled professionals in the next 20 years. For now, companies struggling with the skills gaps will need to look elsewhere for solutions.

If you are currently struggling with the cybersecurity skills gap, there are essentially three options. First, you could continue to try to compete on the open market for the few professionals that are available on the open market. You can expect to pay increasingly more to hire these people every year, and you can expect to spend a lot of energy and time training and retaining these people. Second, you could automate as much as possible. You should automate as much as you can, and we will talk about that in a subsequent section, but it is infeasible to automate all or even most of your operations using currently available technology. Third, you can turn to a service provider for help.

Services can help!

For those who do not want to participate in the escalating race for a diminishing supply of cybersecurity talent, there are solutions that can help. Good service providers, especially **Managed Security Service Providers (MSSPs)** take the burden of talent management on behalf of their customers. An MSSP is not immune to the cybersecurity skills gap or the lack of available talent, but they are focused on acquiring and retaining talent as their core business and therefore have an advantage over a team of cybersecurity professionals in an organization whose focus is elsewhere. Also, service providers can use resources more efficiently by leveraging their pools of talent across multiple customers and are more resilient when an employee leaves because of their scale in terms of security professionals. That scale also helps create the infrastructure to bring unskilled talent in at entry level and give them the skills necessary to be contributing team members.

From the perspective of a security professional, a service provider offers much better career advancement opportunities when compared to working for a business that is focused on something other than security. Also, those professionals are the star of the show at a service provider, whereas their entire department may be an afterthought in many organizations. As a result, in a market where professionals can choose what job they want, it is no surprise that many professionals prefer security services companies, especially early in their careers. As a result, service providers often train new security professionals and have the incumbent advantage in retaining the most talented among their staff. When professionals do choose to leave, it is often for senior leadership opportunities. The result is many security leaders have experience with service providers and are increasingly turning to these providers for help when they struggle to staff their teams. All these factors are leading to rapid growth in the services sector of the cybersecurity market. Many organizations that would have not considered an MSSP previously are increasingly turning to them to help solve the skills gap. Not all service providers are created equally though, and many customers have had a bad experience with a service provider in the past. It is important to thoroughly vet any services partner to ensure they have the specific expertise that is needed, and the terms of the service will meet your objectives. While hiring service providers is fundamentally different than hiring an employee, the process should be similar. A service provider will be solving problems that an employee may have solved if professionals were in sufficient supply. Many organizations do not have an effective process to define their needs and hire the appropriate service provider. They are more comfortable with hiring traditional employees. To solve staff shortage problems using services, you must develop a process for identifying your needs and selecting the right service provider to fill those needs.

There are several types of service providers, with different core expertise and different approaches. Following is my list of the types of service providers available. This list is based on my experience and helps me compartmentalize the offerings I see:

- *Managed Service Providers (MSPs) offering security services*: Often, broad MSPs offer additional services in the security space. Some have deep security expertise and offer high-quality services. Many have a small number of security professionals and the service levels associated with security are much less robust than their general information technology skillsets.

- *Managed Security Service Providers (MSSPs)*: MSSPs are a broad category of organizations. I have put some sub-categories, as follows, because it is difficult to generalize MSSPs in terms of capabilities. What they have in common is they all provide managed security services for customers:
    - *Product-neutral generalists*: Product-neutral generalists is my term for MSSPs that offer a broad range of services across multiple security disciplines and vendors. These are generally the largest MSSPs, and among the most challenging to evaluate. In many cases, they have core expertise in some products and disciplines, and shallow expertise in others. The challenge is it is difficult to distinguish which disciplines are core and which are ancillary.
    - *Product-specific generalists*: Product-specific generalists cover a broad range of security disciplines, but only for a specific vendor. These are generally large security vendors such as Cisco, Symantec/Broadcom, or Microsoft. The advantage to using them is they generally have a strong relationship and deep support from their partners. The disadvantage is if you choose to switch technologies, you also must switch service providers.
    - *Product-neutral specialists*: Product-neutral specialists support multiple technologies in a few security disciplines. For example, some may focus on cloud security or information protection. The advantage of working with these providers is they will generally have deep expertise in their discipline and the ability to recommend alternatives if you choose to switch providers in their core area of expertise. The disadvantage is if you plan to use service providers for your broad security strategy, you will end up having to coordinate across multiple providers.

Important Note

One strategy that helps make this more effective is to work with a generalist for broad capabilities and a specialist for the disciplines that are most important.

-
    - *Vendor-provided services*: This category could also be product-specific specialists, but in reality, these types of services are generally provided by the technology vendor. There is a growing number of technology companies that are offering customers a holistic solution inclusive of technology and services in a comprehensive package. Essentially, you can buy the entire outcome as a service.
- *Consulting firms*: Consulting firms often offer *managed services*. However, in many cases, they are offering full-time consultants that are essentially outsourced full-time employees. There is nothing wrong with this strategy, but it is different from a leveraged pool of resources like a traditional managed service, and it is important to know what you are getting as a customer.

All these service offerings can help take the pressure off teams that are struggling to find enough resources. However, embracing services will not solve the skills gap. The only near-term way to take pressure off the global security talent market is to automate as much as possible.

Automation

Automation is an important topic and has an important role to play in helping to relieve pressure on overburdened cybersecurity teams, both as part of security teams and as part of an MSSP. There are many types of automation that are being explored and built into technology products and service operations. When talking about automation, there are many misconceptions. For the purposes of this book, we will explore machine learning, which is being used effectively right now, and artificial intelligence, which offers amazing long-term opportunities, but will require a longer time horizon to mature. I will define categories of techniques and not specific technologies. The idea is to spark your imagination so you can apply what you have learned so far to imagine ways we can solve problems better using technology.

First, let's discuss techniques that are currently in use in many products you likely interact with every day, starting with machine learning.

Machine learning

Machine learning can be thought of as pattern recognition by machines. The idea is that you can feed a machine large datasets and the machine, without knowing much about the subject matter, can recognize similarities, differences, and patterns. There are two major categories of machine learning, supervised and unsupervised machine learning. First, we will discuss supervised machine learning.

Supervised machine learning

Supervised machine learning is a technique to use a human as a *teacher* to help a machine correctly identify a pattern. As an example, you could upload a set of information that you want the machine to recognize and a set of similar information that you want the machine to learn. You could then allow the machine to try to learn from the dataset and analyze the results. You could then adjust the dataset as necessary to change the profile. When you are happy with the profile, you can deploy the resulting algorithm and allow the machine to recognize the patterns you have trained it to identify. Supervised machine learning is the most predictable form of automation. You can think of supervised machine learning as a controlled scientific experiment. There is little opportunity for something wildly unexpected to happen. In some cases, this is preferable, but in others, it may limit the effectiveness of the technique.

For those who are looking for surprising breakthroughs and that have a higher risk tolerance, there is unsupervised machine learning.

Unsupervised machine learning

Unsupervised machine learning is a more hands-off approach than supervised machine learning. Essentially, unsupervised machine learning feeds a machine a large dataset and asks the machine to draw its own conclusions. A major warning is to remember that correlation does not equal causation. One example is criminal justice. If you were to feed an unsupervised machine learning model criminal statistics over the past 100 years in the United States, the machine may conclude that certain racial groups or genders are more predisposed to crime, ignoring sentencing disparities and unequal enforcement between groups. If that model was then used to make risk-based decisions, unfair prejudice may be built into the algorithm. In general, there are major ethical concerns with unsupervised machine learning algorithms as many datasets large enough to meaningfully train a system are inherently biased.

That said, unsupervised machine learning has the potential to yield novel insights that escape human perception. As a result, I would say unsupervised methods should not be abandoned, but you should exercise caution when deploying them to make consequential decisions. Like many potential technology innovations and novel applications of existing technology, it is important that people making decisions become well versed in the ethics of artificial intelligence and remember that with great power comes great responsibility.

Next, we will explore artificial intelligence techniques and try to separate truth from fiction.

Artificial intelligence

Artificial Intelligence (**AI**) is among the most overused terms in technology. It seems every marketing campaign for every new technology product uses AI as a buzzword. This is a shame because it makes it more difficult for people and companies dedicating resources towards making meaningful advancements in terms of AI to break through the noise. Most commercial technology products are not really using AI, but it is real, and it does exist.

AI is not a single technology, but actually a range of technologies that are designed to replace human beings in tasks they have been historically well-suited for. For example, before 1997, it was thought that human beings at the grandmaster level were uniquely suited to be very good at chess. The thought was a machine could never out-think a skilled chess player at the game. That perception was shattered when IBM's Deep Blue technology defeated world champion Garry Kasparov.

If you go on YouTube, you can see AI applications in militaries around the world that are reminiscent of the old Terminator movies starring Arnold Schwarzenegger. Many of us interact with chatbots and automated phone systems on a daily basis that are designed to replace human interaction. They are a form of AI As you can see, there is a major difference between a chatbot and a machine designed to emulate human behaviors and with the capacity to drive a car or fire a weapon. Therefore, defining AI into categories can be helpful to understand the space and find meaningful applications of the technology to solve the problems you are facing. We will define four broad categories of AI from the least sophisticated to the most sophisticated, starting with machines that are designed to react to set stimuli.

Reactive machines

Reactive machines are the simplest form of AI IBM's Deep Blue was a reactive machine. In 1997, this was considered advanced technology. By today's standards, it is rather unsophisticated. Deep Blue was created specifically to play chess. Every potential move was programmed into the computer along with the ideal reaction to that move. The result was a machine that could evaluate the quality of every potential move and mathematically select the one that led to the greatest chance of winning the game. The result was a machine that could not lose. Even the best chess players in the world could not defeat Deep Blue.

Reactive machines may seem basic, but they have real applications. For example, autonomous vehicles will be powered at least in part by reactive machines. Road conditions or traffic conditions become the inputs and the car will be programmed to respond in the way that is most advantageous. This brings up an ethical question though. Advantageous to whom? What if the best reaction in terms of the greater good would cause the death of the driver and no one else? What if the best alternative would cause the death of several other people but not the driver? The machine would likely be programmed to kill the driver, but the human driver would never make that choice. When life and death decisions are made by machines, there are significant ethical implications. Even though it is unlikely any of us would face that particular dilemma, handing over control of life and death decisions to a machine that would not value your life the same way you would is a difficult thing to do.

Reactive machines are the most basic form of AI because they have no memory and have little ability to evaluate context. They do not have the ability to learn and are explicitly programmed to respond to defined stimuli. If they encounter an input they have not been programmed to respond to, the program will fail. As a result, these types of techniques work best in environments where there are a defined set of potential stimuli. A chess game is a great example. They could be used in more expansive cases such as autonomous driving, but these applications would require exhaustive programming and thorough testing to ensure all sets of potential stimuli are accounted for.

In a security context, reactive machines can be used for automating first-level alert management, often known as triage. If the task is to confirm or deny that specific elements are present, it is a good application for a reactive machine. A simple example could be applied to vulnerability management. There are several types of vulnerability management alerts that are only applicable to certain operating systems. A reactive model could evaluate that report for false positives before passing it to a human for deeper analysis. The machine could have an inventory of the operating systems of the target systems and confirm only vulnerabilities that are applicable to the operating system in use.

Next, we will examine a form of machine learning that is one step above on the maturity scale, limited memory.

Limited memory

Limited memory AI builds upon the foundation of reactive machines. Limited memory allows the model to take historical information into account and learn. Many limited memory AI algorithms use unsupervised machine learning to draw parallels between input sets. In many cases, they are explicitly programmed for certain stimuli and then run in a simulated environment and allowed to learn. In some cases, they may be used to supervise others and learn from them. These applications have great potential. In some cases, people are very good at what they do but would struggle to teach another person how to do those things because much of what they do feels natural to them. However, through observation and learning, machines have the potential to deconstruct what the most talented people in a field do to master their craft. Deep learning is a form of limited memory AI, and most modern applications of AI are limited memory.

An example of how limited memory could be used in a security context would be an algorithm that can be programmed similarly to the reactive machine example to discard obvious false positives. The machine could then supervise a skilled analyst who is performing tier-two triage, looking for patterns the machine could learn. Theoretically, with a large enough dataset, the machine would eventually surpass the human ability to perform analysis since the human would make an occasional mistake. In some cases, this AI could be used to identify potential mistakes made by analysts, and eventually take over analysis tasks completely. Limited memory has great potential in tasks that are repetitive. In those cases, human error is increased as the task is repeated, and people pay less attention to the task at hand. Limited memory AI capabilities could retain sharp focus. Both reactive machines and limited memory AI are in use in several applications currently. The next AI category, **Theory of Mind**, is less widely deployed but is a critical capability for expanding the use of AI in society.

Theory of Mind

Theory of Mind is an interesting title for an important AI concept. Theory of Mind AI is in the conceptual phase, but it is an important advancement that makes widely deployed AI technology more feasible. Theory of Mind AI is designed to understand the emotions, thoughts, and beliefs of human parties it encounters. The idea is that much of an appropriate interaction between people is the emotions and beliefs they hold. Understanding the human mind more deeply will yield insights that allow machines to attempt to understand a person's state of mind and preconceived notions to communicate with people more effectively. There are differing opinions of how close we are to having Theory of Mind AI deployed.

Personally, I am skeptical. People who have dedicated their lives to studying the human brain are open about how little we understand about how our brains work. If our foremost experts cannot understand large portions of how our minds work, how could we program a machine with that understanding? The counterpoint to this argument is that Theory of Mind AI can be built by equipping AI that understands the part of the brain that is well understood with an unsupervised machine learning model that can learn the rest. I am skeptical that is possible.

However, Theory of Mind does not have to be an all-or-nothing proposition. While I think we are at least decades away from full Theory of Mind AI technology in wide use, I do think AI algorithms can understand parts of human behavior to try to determine intent. This is not full Theory of Mind technology, but still could be a meaningful advancement.

For example, with current behavior analytics techniques and existing AI technology, it is possible to distinguish intentional data theft from accidental exposure in many cases. Routing incidents to the proper response teams based on the intent of the user could be a useful way to reduce the burden on initial triage teams. If you could refer accidental exposure to a retraining algorithm that leverages appropriate learning content, you could retrain an end user. You could then refer true data theft incidents or potential data theft incidents to an incident response team and build an efficient security analytics capability that could cut the **Mean Time to Respond** (**MTTR**) to events from hours or days to seconds or minutes.

The next category of AI is the one that scares people most, self-aware AI.

Self-aware AI

Self-aware AI is the type of AI that is popular in science fiction. This is a theoretical concept currently and is likely decades or centuries away from becoming reality. Self-aware AI is AI that so closely mirrors the way the human mind works that it becomes aware of itself and thinks of itself as a sentient being. You can see how self-aware AI could accidentally be invented as we push Theory of Mind AI to its furthest possible extent. It is difficult to understand the implications for humanity if self-aware AI is created and it would challenge our perception of what is means to be human. It is unlikely that there are any applications for self-aware AI in cybersecurity. Limited memory AI is likely enough for most applications. In some cases, you can see how Theory of Mind AI could help in certain scenarios, especially when dealing with very sophisticated actors and complex schemes such as business email compromise.

In a security context, it is likely that Theory of Mind capabilities could be more useful to sophisticated attackers than it would be to cybersecurity teams. Hopefully, by this point, you have a better understanding of the different types of AI. Perhaps you can now view AI-driven claims from security vendors through a skeptical lens and not be swayed by the term. (Joshi, 2019) (Schellen, 2021)

Generally, infatuation with technology is a problem that affects many organizations, especially in security, and this is the topic of our next section.

Too much technology with too little process

I have worked with countless companies in my career, specifically helping them with their security strategy. The majority are overfocused on technology. I have never seen any that were overly focused on process. In *Chapter 6, Information Security for a Changing World*, we discussed security triumvirates, including the triumvirate of people, process, and technology. A triumvirate by definition should be equal in power. However, on average based on my experience, most security programs focus 60% of their effort and budget on technology, 30% on people, and 10% on process.

There are several theories on why this may be, but mine is that it is simply easier to select a technology than it is to define a process. In a world where people in cybersecurity teams are overloaded and stressed out, the easiest solution becomes the preferred solution. This technology proliferation and accompanying neglect of process design lead to a concept known as **shelfware**. Shelfware occurs when a technology is purchased but never deployed properly. As a result, it sits on the virtual shelf rather than providing any real value. This has become prevalent.

Example Case: Target

The data breach involving Target in 2014 was one of the most famous and largest data breaches in history. Much has been written about how adversaries compromised a third-party vendor, in Target's case a **Heating, Ventilation, and Air Conditioning** (**HVAC**) contractor, to gain access to sensitive systems involved in processing credit card transactions. This intrusion speaks to many of the concepts in this book, including timeless best practices such as the concept of least privilege. While it is likely that the vendor needed some access to Target's systems, it is unlikely that they needed access to Target's payment card systems. However, that is not the focus of this example case.

This example case is focused on the fact that Target was alerted to what was happening and failed to act. Prior to the attack, Target had implemented a type of cyber security alarm system made by FireEye. The software worked as intended and alerted the security team to the activities of the criminals. For some reason, the team failed to act on those warnings and the breach continued until Target was forced to report the compromise of over 40 million credit card numbers during the 2014 holiday shopping season. Target survived, but they suffered large financial losses and a significant loss of trust with their customers. It took years for Target to repair the company's reputation and likely cost the company billions of dollars in sales.

Target missed identified warning signs. The most likely reasons for that miss are either that the security team had too many alerts and therefore could not respond to them properly, or they implemented a powerful technology like FireEye without building the necessary process to help their team members respond appropriately. In either case, this massive data breach was caused by people and process failures, even though they had the proper technology in place to sound an alarm while the attack was happening. (Harris, 2014)

To explain why people like to implement technology over process another way, a technology choice is a multiple-choice question, whereas process solutions require free-form thinking. There is a defined market and customers can purchase the technology they think most closely matches their needs. Process design is an essay question. To define an effective process, you must talk to multiple people on disparate teams and think critically about the best way to implement something. While the aversion to process design is understandable, it leads to specific consequences that can be detrimental to a security program. The first is a concept I like to call console whiplash.

Console whiplash

Console whiplash occurs when a company has so many technologies that do not integrate with each other that the people responsible for managing the technology get virtual whiplash as they switch between the consoles. This is detrimental because it increases the likelihood that a person will make mistakes. Because of the skills shortage, most analysts cannot specialize in a single discipline. The result is teams that have a base-level understanding of many different technologies but lack deep expertise in any of them. The continued proliferation of technology makes console whiplash worse.

In many ways, console whiplash is the natural result of the **best-of-breed** strategy that many security teams have employed for many years. The best-of-breed strategy says that technologies should be selected for their individual merits, and if you have a different vendor for every capability, that's okay as long as you have the best tool. The best-of-breed strategy makes sense conceptually, but in practice requires many more people to effectively operate a program. We have established that cybersecurity talent is in short supply, which means a best-of-breed strategy without accompanying service assistance is nearly impossible to execute well in the current labor market.

The **pure platform** strategy is likely an overcorrection. A pure platform strategy says that we will select a single platform that can meet all our security needs. While there are broad platforms available, there are none that are best in class for every security discipline. They may have offerings in every category, but it would be hard to find any example of a company that was simultaneously delivering quality products in every security discipline. As a result, a pure platform strategy often results in an unacceptable compromise for critical security capabilities.

In my view, a better approach is the modified **pareto Principle**. The Pareto principle, often referred to as the 80/20 rule, says that 80% of the consequences come from 20% of the causes. In security, I would say that a pure platform strategy is likely sufficient for 80% of security use cases, but the most important 20% should use a best-of-breed strategy. This allows a security team to focus effort and budget on solving for the most important 20% of use cases while gaining efficiencies from the pure platform strategy for the remaining 80%. Of course, which 20% of the security use cases are most important varies between organizations but classifying the top 20% is an important exercise to help an organization focus. Applying the modified Pareto principle will help reduce the worst effects of console whiplash while protecting the ability to deploy advanced capabilities to protect the enterprise.

Another problem caused by too many technologies with too little process is siloed programs.

Siloed programs

A silo is a reference to grain silos in the physical world. Multiple grain silos are separate from each other. In a security program, a silo is a discipline that focuses only on its own view of security and does not effectively collaborate or share information with any other discipline. A security program made up of silos is inefficient and ineffective. Siloed programs are also a sign of poor security leadership.

Great leadership ensures people understand why they are doing what they are doing before focusing on what they are doing. Employees who understand the reasons behind their instructions will naturally collaborate with their peers to help further their mission. Employees who only understand what they are supposed to do are more likely to retreat to their own silos, especially when they become stressed out or overwhelmed.

When technology is disparate for each discipline and does not integrate in a meaningful way, it encourages silos to form. If technologies are tightly integrated and multiple teams are working with the same data or in the same tools, collaboration is often the default mode of operation. There are, of course, instances where companies with a best-of-breed strategy build collaborative security teams through great leadership or teams with a pure platform strategy still develop silos, but in general, there is a high correlation between best-of-breed technology strategies and siloed security programs.

The next issue related to an over-dependence on technology is a lack of business involvement in the security program.

Lack of business involvement

Most companies are not in business to do security, their core business is something else. This is obvious, but worth discussing. If business stakeholders are not involved in the security program, how could the security program be aligned with business objectives? Before working with a publicly traded company in the United States, I read the 10-K filing section 1A, titled *Risk Factors*. These are the risk factors for the business, but I read them looking for how the security program can help reduce these risks. It is rare to not find anything in the 10-K report that can be related to information security. Often, when I speak to security teams, they do not know what the business risks are, or how the security program relates to those business risks.

I recommend that a governance group be formed in every organization to steer the information security strategy. That governance group should include cross-functional leadership. The idea is that the business goals and security goals should remain aligned.

The next section is focused on making sure that everyone involved with the security program can answer a simple question. What are we trying to accomplish?

What are we trying to accomplish?

Many organizations do security for security's sake. There is a legitimate higher purpose for what they should be doing, but if no one on the team knows the higher purpose, does it matter? It is important to ensure security teams have clarity of purpose. If they can connect their day-to-day work to a higher purpose, they are more likely to do a great job in protecting the organization. If they are going through mundane tasks with little understanding of why, they are more likely to make mistakes.

There are some specific pieces of information that the security leadership should be aware of. First is the relationship between cyber risk and business risk.

Cyber risk is business risk

Cyber risk is business risk. The reason cyber security matters is because it is designed to protect the organization from harm. If a system is breached or information is stolen, the impact is a business impact. If a negligent employee discloses regulated information, the resulting fine is a business impact. It is important for everyone to know the connection between security risk and business risk and how their contribution to the security program protects their organization. In my opinion, each security team should spend time understanding why they are protecting what they are protecting and what could happen if they are unsuccessful.

Example Case: FlexMagic Consulting

When studying cybersecurity breaches, we often focus on large-scale breaches with very high costs, often launched against the world's largest and most recognizable companies. These case studies are useful because the target companies often have the resources to investigate the breach, providing us with valuable information about how it occurred that we can use to prevent similar future breaches. Also, those companies often continue to operate, which allows us to understand the long-term impacts of the security breach. This focus on large breaches involving large companies leads some to incorrectly assume that cybersecurity breaches do not affect small companies as much as their larger counterparts. This assumption could not be further from the truth.

Many small companies cannot survive a significant cybersecurity breach. To them, cyber risk is not only business risk, but also an existential threat. 3 of 5 companies that are hit by a cyber-attack go out of business. Most of them are small- to medium-sized enterprises, and many were successful prior to the cybersecurity event. Put another way, more companies go out of business after a cyber attack than those that can survive such an attack, even if the business is otherwise healthy. FlexMagic Consulting is one of these stories.

FlexMagic Consulting was a third-party consulting business with $2million in revenue and 9 employees. They were a well-respected business that had been operating in Colorado for over 30 years. As part of their benefits program, FlexMagic Consulting issued Flexible Spending Account cards, which could be used by employees for medical expenses.

In 2016, Russian attackers gained access to an administrator's password and used it to issue fraudulent Flexible Spending Account cards, with limits up to $5 million. These cards were used for procedures such as cosmetic surgery. When creditors demanded payment from FlexMagic consulting, they had to file for bankruptcy since they could not pay the claims. The attackers were caught and prosecuted, but the damage was done, and a business that had been successful for three decades was gone forever. With it, 9 people lost their jobs.

It is unlikely FlexMagic Consulting counted cybersecurity risks among catastrophic risks to their business. The events of 2016 showed that their cyber risk was an existential risk to their business. They should have defined the cyber risk as a business risk. If they had, they may have been more prepared to defend themselves against the fraudulent scheme that cost them their company. (Insure Trust, 2021) (ID Agent, 2021)

The next element that security leadership teams should understand is the entire cyber risk treatment plan.

Risk treatment planning

A **risk treatment plan** is a document that identifies risks to an organization in a register and defines how that risk will be treated. There are four categories of risk treatment:

- *Risk acceptance* is the default risk treatment. If an organization does nothing about a risk, they are accepting it. Sometimes risk acceptance happens intentionally, and sometimes risks are accepted because they are not known, or the organization fails to treat the risk in another way. It is important to note that risk acceptance is a legitimate treatment, but only if the risk is identified and intentionally accepted by someone with the proper level of authority to do so.
- *Risk avoidance* is a risk treatment that is applied when a company decides to stop engaging in a risky activity entirely. An example is if a company chose to avoid the risks associated with PCI compliance by ceasing to accept credit card payments. They no longer need to address the risk, but the impact on their business is in the form of lost revenue. True risk avoidance is rarely economically feasible for companies.
- *Risk Transference* is a treatment where a third party is paid to accept risk on your behalf. This sounds confusing, but there is a common example that everyone is familiar with, insurance policies. When you buy an insurance policy, you are transferring risk to the insurance company.
- *Risk Mitigation* is a treatment that seeks to reduce or eliminate the potential impact of a risk. Information security as a discipline is a risk mitigation strategy.

Risk treatment planning should create a risk register and assign a risk treatment to each identified risk along with the name and title of the person approving the risk treatment. This is especially important for risk acceptance. People get themselves in trouble when they accept risk that they do not have the proper level of authority to accept.

Next, we will discuss a method for how you may prioritize some risks over others, known as looking for material risk factors.

Looking for material risk factors

The number of risks related to information technology is nearly infinite. How can you build a risk register in such an environment? How do you keep the risks to a manageable level, and how do you know when your risk register is complete? The answers to these questions may vary between organizations, but often the first exercise is to define what constitutes a material risk.

Risk is often measured on a scale of likelihood and impact. To build a threshold for materiality, it is important to set a threshold of likelihood and impact. Risks that could have a catastrophic impact but are unlikely should probably be on the register. However, there is a limit. I have built the following chart to show how I would judge materiality on a three-level scale:

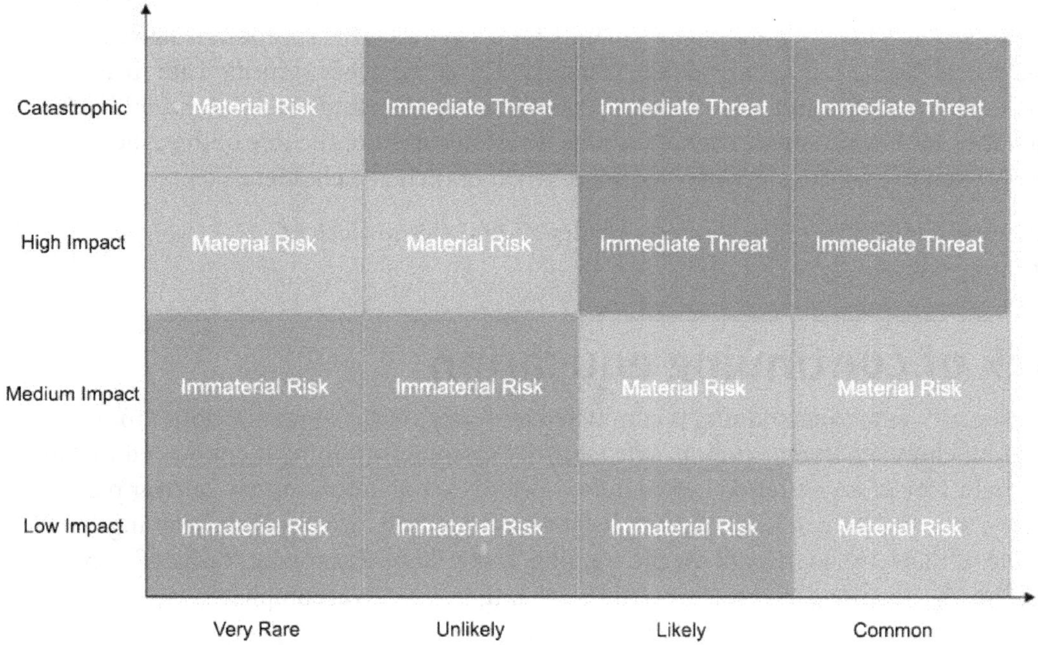

Figure 7.1 – Risk materiality matrix

Each organization can define impact and likelihood as they see fit. Also, the color-coding and materiality of each box is a suggestion. The idea is that decision makers set a framework for determining whether a risk is material and what that means. As an example, an organization could decide that immaterial risks are going to be accepted by default and not recorded on the register. All material risks must be recorded on the register and given a treatment that is reviewed annually. Any immediate threats must be put on the register with a mitigation plan that will be executed within 30 days, and that mitigation plan is to be reviewed quarterly.

The point is not that you must follow my prescription. Rather, the idea is that you have a framework for how your organization identifies and treats risk so a risk register and a risk treatment plan can be developed in a reasonable time frame. Many organizations have a risk office or even a chief risk officer that can help build risk treatment plans. Many organizations treat cyber risk entirely differently than other business risks because they don't understand the risks and the treatments for cyber risk. This approach is flawed. Cyber risk is business risk, and it is the responsibility of the cyber security team to act as subject matter experts and help business stakeholders understand the risks and mitigation capabilities so they can make sound business decisions. It is not the role of the cyber security team to make business decisions on behalf of their stakeholders.

Next, we will look at another common challenge, which is the lack of continuing education.

Lack of continuing education

Cybersecurity awareness training is conducted in nearly 100% of organizations around the world. However, in my opinion, cybersecurity awareness training is conducted *well* in fewer than 10% of organizations around the world. Few organizations have a clear plan for what the training is intended to accomplish or how they will measure if the training was effective. If there are no metrics for the training, it should be assumed it wasn't effective. Also, few organizations have a clear goal for what they hope to accomplish.

In *Chapter 5, Protecting against Common Attacks by Partnering with End Users*, we discussed the process for creating an effective training program along with best practices for how the training should be delivered and reinforced. We will not repeat that content. Instead, we will address issues that make it difficult to maintain relevant skillsets in the modern security landscape. While these challenges apply to all employees, leaders generally have a longer tenure and are more likely to struggle to keep their understanding of cybersecurity challenges current.

First, we address a common theme in the modern enterprise, the pace of change.

The pace of change

In *Chapter 6, Information Security for a Changing World*, we discussed the pace of change and some examples of how much the world has changed during the average executive's career. People who have 20 years of experience or more have seen a tremendous amount of change in the workplace. Even people who have a technical background lose touch with changing technology when they move into leadership roles and their daily responsibilities change.

Example Case: "Microsoft" Data Breach

In May of 2021, an analyst with security company UpGuard notified Microsoft of a security flaw that exposed sensitive information housed by 39 of Microsoft's customers. This data breach is often unfairly attributed to Microsoft. While Microsoft created their cloud tool suite known as Power Apps, complete with their **Open Data Protocols (OData)** API, the public exposure of the data was due to a misconfiguration on the part of the 39 customers, not a flaw in Microsoft's own technology.

The OData API is designed to allow customers to expose information from their Microsoft services to other applications or users. As is always the case, the customers are responsible for controlling identity, access, and data. It is Microsoft's responsibility as a provider to secure its infrastructure and provide access to tools. It is the responsibility of the customer to ensure those tools are used properly and access is not granted to unauthorized people. Microsoft fulfilled its responsibility in this case. Its customers did not.

It is likely these customers did not understand how to use the API, and how to enable the proper permissions to secure it. The rapid pace of change and proliferation of cloud services in many organizations require additional training for security teams so these types of misconfigurations cannot happen. Too often, teams are expected to secure changing environments without getting the necessary skill updates for them to be successful in their mission. (McKeon, 2021)

The result of the pace of change is the need to constantly refresh the skills that are relevant to a person's job. It is important to determine what is relevant. For example, most executives have no need to understand the latest threat actor groups and the specific malware payloads and tactics they use to move laterally in an environment and execute ransomware attacks. However, it is likely relevant for those executives to understand that ransomware is primarily delivered through email and often when users click on links. They also should be aware of business email compromises and how they can work with their staff to ensure only valid requests are acted upon. This training need not be technical but is vital.

Next, we will discuss the need to update certain skills.

Updating certain skills

Updating certain skills returns to the idea that an organization must develop the discipline to define what cybersecurity skills are necessary for a person's job so those skills can be kept up to date. One-size-fits-all cybersecurity awareness training is ineffective and can sometimes be counterproductive since important messages are lost in the noise. It is more effective to develop module-based training and deliver to each role the modules that are relevant for their role and job function. This will not only make training more efficient, but also easier to keep up to date over time. When something materially changes in the module, the user can re-take only that module to update their understanding.

It is important to give our people the necessary tools to succeed. Part of that success is everyone doing their part to protect information and systems in the modern enterprise. It is my belief that most people want to help support the security program. However, security teams have historically made it difficult for non-technical people to do so.

Example Case: Home Depot

In 2014, American home improvement retailer Home Depot suffered a large security breach estimated to have compromised 56 million payment cards across the United States. This remains one of the largest cyber security breaches in history. The fallout from the Home Depot breach included a consequential settlement reached with 46 of the 50 states and the District of Columbia for $17.5 million. The overall breach is estimated to have cost Home Depot $179 million and is still growing.

Obviously, the business impacts of the Home Depot breach are significant and highlight the fact that cyber security risk is business risk because if those risks are manifested, there is often a significant financial impact on the company. The plaintiffs claim Home Depot failed in its responsibility to protect sensitive consumer information and therefore caused individuals and states unnecessary distress and economic harm. The terms of the agreement Home Depot made do not explicitly highlight the failures that led to the breach, but they do mandate actions Home Depot must take in the future, which indicates that appropriate protocols in these areas were not in place and directly led to the breach.

The terms of the agreement require Home Depot to hire a qualified **Chief Information Security Officer (CISO)**, provide a robust security training program, and maintain a set of security policies designed to better protect sensitive information. It is unlikely that Home Depot did not have a CISO at all prior to the breach, so the agreement insinuates that the person was either unqualified for the position or, more likely, had not been provided with relevant training to update their skills. It is also likely that the training programs inside Home Depot were found to be inadequate. The strategies defined in this chapter could help the new CISO at Home Depot deliver more relevant and impactful training that would be helpful in preventing future security breaches. Finally, it is unlikely that Home Depot had no data security policies, but it is likely that the policies were found to be inadequate, outdated, or both.

At the heart of all these problems is people. Home Depot's focus should be to put the right people in place, allow security leadership to craft meaningful and effective policies, and to create an effective and ongoing security training program designed to ensure everyone responsible for protecting sensitive information entrusted to Home Depot has the training and skills necessary to be successful. (Starks, 2020)

Next, we will discuss another area that is important for employees to understand, especially leaders. I call it applying timeless concepts.

Applying timeless concepts

In *Chapter 4, Protecting People, Information, and Systems with Timeless Best Practices*, we defined the best practices in information security that have not changed although technology has changed significantly. It is important to ensure leaders across the organization understand these best practices. For example, if the CFO understands the concept of least privilege, they are more likely to request only the permissions necessary for the new accountant starting next week.

The timeless best practices are timeless because they are not tied to any specific technology. Therefore, everyone should be able to understand them, at least conceptually.

Summary

In this chapter, we discussed several challenges for the modern enterprise. We started by talking about the cybersecurity talent shortage, which is among the most significant challenges for securing the modern enterprise. We can and should be trying to inspire more people to join the cybersecurity profession, but we will be dealing with a talent shortfall for at least the next 10–20 years. As a result, automation will play a key role. You have learned about categories of machine learning and AI so you can apply the right technology solutions to the right problems. You have learned about the imbalance of technology and process in most security programs and the problems that imbalance can cause. You now understand how to identify and treat cyber risk as business risk and how to set up a continuing education program that ensures all team members, especially those in leadership, are equipped with the skills necessary to secure the modern enterprise. With what you have learned, you are ready to lead the cybersecurity function at your organization into the new world, and you have the context necessary to adapt to the next transformational change that will inevitably come. In the next chapter, we will look deeper into automation as part of our future, focusing on how we can identify and act upon automation opportunities.

Check your understanding

1. In your own words, describe the difference between machine learning and AI.
2. What are the four AI categories described in the chapter?
3. Why do you think organizations deploy technical solutions and not process solutions?
4. What are the four types of risk treatment? Provide a brief description and an example of each.
5. What is a material risk factor? How would you determine if a risk is material or not?

Further reading

- Cimpanu, C. (2020, February 12). Average tenure of a CISO is just 26 months due to high stress and burnout. Retrieved from ZD Net: `https://www.zdnet.com/article/average-tenure-of-a-ciso-is-just-26-months-due-to-high-stress-and-burnout/#:~:text=Average%20tenure%20of%20a%20CISO,high%20stress%20and%20burnout%20%7C%20ZDNet`
- Harris, E. A. (2014, March 13). Target Missed Signs of a Data Breach. Retrieved from The New York Times: `https://www.nytimes.com/2014/03/14/business/target-missed-signs-of-a-data-breach.html`
- HDI. (2020, December 16). The cybersecurity skills gap: 4 million professionals needed worldwide. Retrieved from HDI Global: `https://www.hdi.global/infocenter/insights/2020/cyber-skills-gap/`
- ID Agent. (2021, March 4). 60% of Companies Go Out of Business After a Cyberattack. Retrieved from ID Agent: `https://www.idagent.com/blog/60-percent-of-companies-go-out-of-business-after-a-cyberattack/`
- Insure Trust. (2021, November 11). Out of Business - Hackers Bankrupt Firm. Retrieved from Insure Trust: `https://insuretrust.com/out-of-business-hackers-bankrupt-firm/`
- Joshi, N. (2019, June 19). 7 Types Of Artificial Intelligence. Retrieved from Forbes: `https://www.forbes.com/sites/cognitiveworld/2019/06/19/7-types-of-artificial-intelligence/?sh=39b2e6fe233e`
- McKeon, J. (2021, August 24). Microsoft Data Breach Exposes 38M Records Containing PII. Retrieved from Health IT Security: `https://healthitsecurity.com/news/microsoft-data-breach-exposes-38m-records-containing-pii`
- Schellen, E. B. (2021, May 11). Robot Gaze Behavior Affects Honesty in Human-Robot Interaction. Retrieved from Frontiers in Artificial Intelligence: `https://www.frontiersin.org/articles/10.3389/frai.2021.663190/full`
- Starks, T. (2020, November 24). Home Depot to pay states $17.5 million over massive 2014 data breach. Retrieved from Cyber Scoop: `https://www.cyberscoop.com/home-depot-settlement-data-breach/`
- Zippia. (2021, November 5). CYBER SECURITY SPECIALIST Demographics And Statistics In The US. Retrieved from Zippia: `https://www.zippia.com/cyber-security-specialist-jobs/demographics/`

Further reading

8
Harnessing Automation Opportunities

The cybersecurity skills gap is real, and it is growing. Based on demographics, it is likely to continue to get worse. Unless the near future holds a historical influx of new security professionals, automation will become increasingly necessary to meet the information security challenges we will face. Further, attackers have access to the same technology as us, and if they make better use of emerging technologies than we do, they will have an advantage. Capabilities such as machine learning and **Artificial Intelligence** (**AI**) are already in use by bad actors to evade countermeasures and learn how to emulate the behavior of legitimate users. However, most organizations rely solely upon human analysis to review and classify potential incidents. As a result, the mean time to detect threats is months to years on average in most organizations. Modern technology enables large-scale data transfers in seconds and minutes. If there is this gap between the ability to move large volumes of data and the ability for our teams to respond, data breaches involving large quantities of data will remain common.

Human beings are not machines. They cannot work around the clock, and they generally need time to perform their functions. Machines are not humans. They lack the ability to understand the nuances of human emotions and behaviors and rely upon patterns to make decisions. However, combining the response time of a machine with the emotional context of a human offers an opportunity to build programs that are both responsive and nuanced. We will not automate the whole of the information security field in the foreseeable future, but machine-augmented teams are likely to become the standard for security programs around the world.

To meet current challenges in the short term, most organizations will need to either automate significant portions of their operations or turn to a **Managed Security Services Provider (MSSP)**, who is likely leveraging automation to maximize efficiency and profitability. In either case, security programs that do not leverage automation effectively have little chance of protecting their organizations from modern and evolving threats. This is due to both the shortcomings of currently available technologies in the AI space and the shortages of qualified security practitioners in the talent marketplace.

In this chapter, we will talk about the role of automation in security programs today, and opportunities to leverage automation technology in new ways as we approach the future. We will discuss the role of automation using the following sections:

- Defining automation opportunities
- Gathering data and applying context
- Testing the systems
- How attackers leverage automation

Defining automation opportunities

Automation offers the potential to lower operational costs while limiting human error and improving response times. However, not everything can be automated, and many organizations lack the processes necessary to identify automation opportunities. Too often, teams focus on solving large, complex problems rather than automating the mundane, repetitive tasks that are not only easier to automate, but also the most taxing on skilled resources. Human beings are very good at understanding context and behaviors. We are not good at consistently performing repetitive tasks with minimal errors and maximum efficiency. Machines are very good at recognizing patterns and performing repetitive tasks with minimal errors. Not everything a human being does is easily automated, but there are tasks that machines are better at than humans. These are ideal automation opportunities. The challenge with automation is finding the right problems to solve with the technology.

Example Case Study: Public Sector Automation

The public sector is rarely held up as a model of cost efficiency. However, when it comes to the average cost of a data breach, according to the *2020 Ponemon Cost of a Data Breach* study, the public sector had the lowest costs compared to other industries at $1.08 million per breach. That is compared to an average across all industries of $3.86 million, and the highest average cost belonging to the healthcare industry at nearly $10 million per breach. Why is the public sector able to control costs so much better than the private sector? Many factors could contribute but it is widely believed that automation plays a significant role.

According to recent research, the public sector is adopting automation faster than any other industry and is using automation and orchestration to help correlate data points across multiple systems and agencies. Automation is not being used to lower the number of staff, but to allow existing staff to focus on other priorities and vulnerabilities. This means that not only are agencies able to respond more quickly to attacks but they are also able to build countermeasures across a larger percentage of their attack surface.

Finding tasks that can be automated and focusing resources on tasks that cannot are key to building an effective security practice in the modern world. There simply aren't enough people and resources to continue to throw people alone at the problem.

Building an automation program is like building other types of information security programs. First, the program must define what it intends to accomplish and what problem it intends to solve. Then, it needs to define who is responsible for solving the problem and what role each individual or group will play. Finally, it must clearly define the processes necessary to achieve success. In the case of finding automation opportunities, this requires the discipline to identify automation opportunities and the resources to act on those opportunities (Ponemon Institute, 2020), (Kanowitz, 2020).

There is a long-term opportunity for automation to perform very complex tasks that humans are unable to perform efficiently or effectively. However, there is also an immediate-term opportunity to replace low-skilled human labor with technology that exists today.

Before we do so, we should have a brief discussion about financial concepts as they relate to automation.

A brief introduction to finance

It is my opinion that a basic education in business concepts is critical to success in information security. One of the most important disciplines is finance. While it is not necessary for information security professionals and leaders to be accountants or have finance degrees, it is important that they understand some basic concepts in order to make sound investment decisions, such as the decision of whether to automate a process or not.

It is important to understand that simply because a task can be automated does not mean it *should* be automated. In order to determine whether it should, we need to consider factors such as the cost of capital, the time value of money, and the difference between operational expenses and capital expenses.

Operational expenses are expenses that continue every month. Capital expenses are expenses that are paid upfront in one go, but whose benefits extend over a period of time. A common example is buying a software license and deploying it in your data centers, which is a capital-intensive strategy. Subscribing to a cloud service is an operational-intensive strategy. The primary difference is capital strategies require more money upfront and less over time, and operational expenses require little capital investment upfront, but more money to be spent on an ongoing basis. So which strategy is better? That depends primarily on the cost of capital and the time horizon.

When evaluating an operational strategy against a capital strategy, there will always be a break-even point. That is the point in time where the total investment of the operational strategy and the capital strategy cross, and the capital-intensive strategy becomes less expensive than the operational-intensive strategy. Because a capital-intensive strategy has higher upfront costs and lower ongoing costs, the lines plotting the total investment will always cross, the question is when. The amount of time it takes for the lines to cross is known as the payback period for the capital investment, which is a key determining factor for decision-makers when evaluating an investment.

You could calculate the payback period in nominal dollar terms, but that is only part of the story. Money has a *time value.* The time value of money is equal to the return of that money if it were to be invested elsewhere. Money now is worth more than money in the future because of the time value.

Another consideration is the cost of capital. In some cases, the capital investment may make sense, but you do not have the capital available. In those cases, the cost of acquiring capital, in terms of interest on debt or the value of equity that must be sold to fund a project must be considered.

It is infeasible to cover these concepts in detail in this book. However, if you don't understand these concepts, a finance course would be helpful to help you evaluate investment decisions, including the decision of whether or not to automate specific tasks.

Now that we understand some basic finance concepts, we can continue to identify automation opportunities. The first step is to map out tasks by cost basis.

Mapping a task by its cost basis

The discipline of mapping tasks by cost basis is not limited to cybersecurity but is a best practice for identifying and evaluating all automation opportunities. The first step is to define each cost basis available to you from the lowest to the highest cost basis. The lowest cost basis for the purpose of this exercise should be automation.

Automation is often a project with fixed capital expenses and limited operational expenses. Human labor has little capital expense and is mostly an ongoing operational expense. Therefore, automation is a way an organization can increase its operating leverage, which means it gains efficiency as it takes on more tasks. When someone says an operation has an ability to scale, they are speaking about its degree of operating leverage. While this is a financial term, it is relevant to a security operation as well. When a security team takes on additional capabilities or the organization they are supporting grows, they need to grow their team's capacity. Teams using automation well may be able to add additional value at one third of the additional cost of a team that is using limited automation. Therefore, automation is often an upfront investment in scale and growth. While most of us don't think about contraction, operational leverage has the opposite effect on shrinking teams with shrinking budgets. This means shrinking teams with high degrees of operating leverage become less efficient as their team gets smaller and there are less tasks for them to perform.

When mapping cost basis categories, it is not uncommon to have a result that looks like the following diagram. Often, skill sets will diverge as the cost basis gets higher. This is natural as higher-cost resources are generally more specialized and lower-cost resources are often generalized. The same could be said for service providers. Hiring a generalist firm that does everything is likely to yield mediocre results across the board. When a specific outcome is needed, a specialist firm is more likely to be able to deliver a superior outcome. The output of mapping the skill sets available by cost basis should yield a diagram. The following diagram is a simple example of what a Security Operations Center may yield:

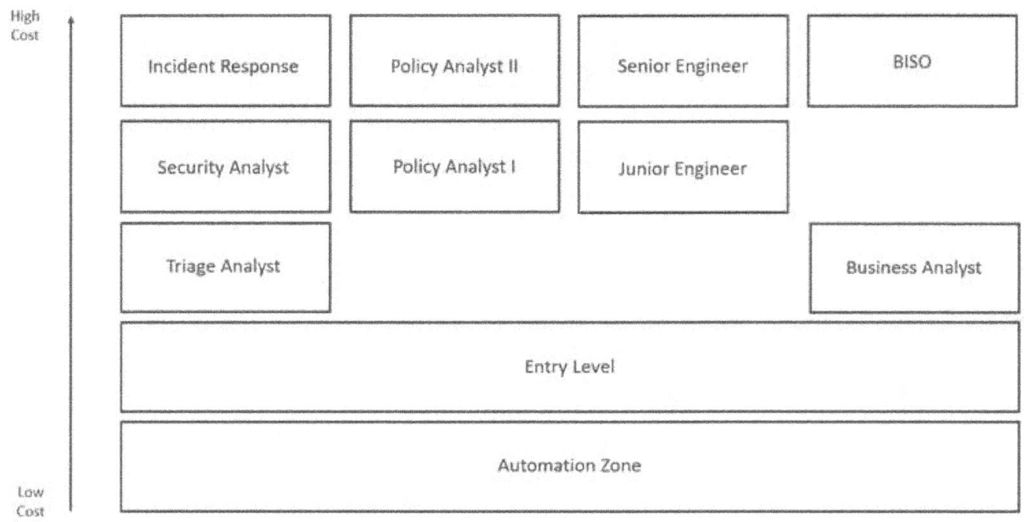

Figure 8.1 – Automation Opportunity Matrix – Stage 1

You may notice that there are gaps in this matrix. This is normal. There are often skill sets where even the most junior person is a relatively high-cost resource. The easiest tasks to automate are those that have a continuous path to the automation zone. However, it is possible to automate across gaps, it simply requires more planning and effort to automate those tasks.

Once the matrix is built, it is time to map tasks performed by each of those team members. In some organizations, the tasks each team member performs are well understood and documented. In others, this exercise may require a whiteboard session with cross-functional leadership. In either case, the output should be an understanding of the tasks each role performs. From my experience, even organizations that think they know the tasks each team member performs will gain valuable insight from the exercise of mapping it out with other stakeholders. Tasks that are taken for granted or are not well understood outside the team itself are often the best targets for automation.

The next step is to analyze the current costs of each of the tasks. To find the costs, you must understand the average hourly fully burdened cost for each skill set and the time spent per task in an average week. It is important to use fully burdened costs, which include not only the salary, but also benefits, paid time off, training, and bonuses. I see many organizations who use simple salary data to estimate costs or compare options and it is a skewed perspective. Often, the fully burdened cost of a resource is significantly more than their base salary. This discrepancy can be enough to change the outcome of an insourcing versus outsourcing decision, as well as the potential **Return on Investment** (**ROI**) of an automation opportunity. It is acceptable to estimate the time spent for operations that do not track time spent on tasks by role, but the more precise the data is, the better the team will be able to evaluate the ROI for automating the task.

The next step is to find the lowest logical cost basis for each task. There may be some tasks where automation is not appropriate. Others may be performed by higher cost resources due to necessity. Knowing the difference is valuable.

By the end of this exercise, you should be able to build a map of cost categories available, with a list of current tasks per cost basis in one color and a desired end cost basis in another color. The following diagram is a simplified version of what the end product will look like:

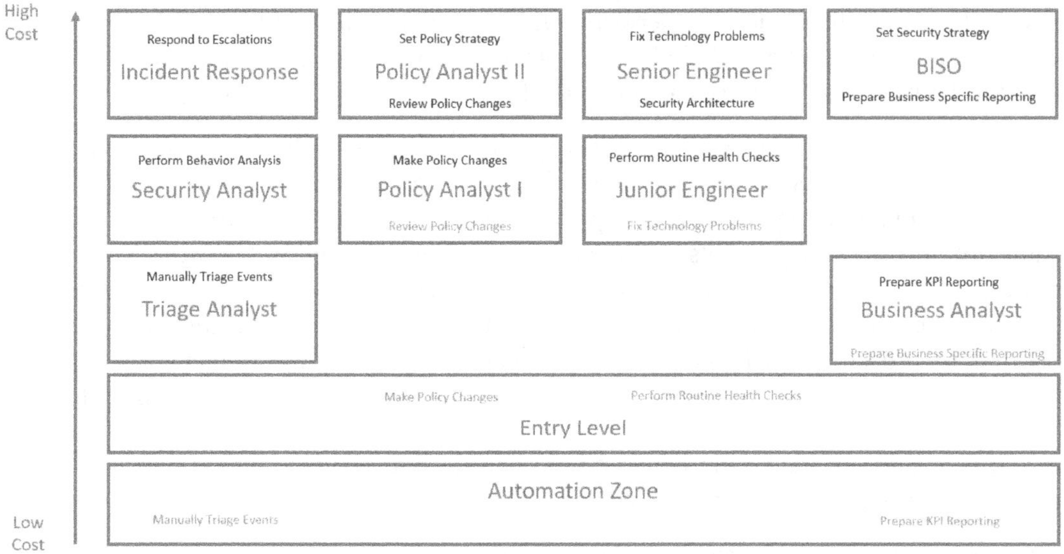

Figure 8.2 – Automation Opportunity Matrix – Stage 2

As you can see, not all tasks move down, and not all of those that do are candidates for automation. However, this matrix will highlight opportunities to drive tasks down to their lowest logical cost basis. The lowest possible cost basis is automation, and most tasks that can be taught to a true entry-level employee could be automated eventually. This is an important point. While cybersecurity is desperate for talent, there are few true entry-level jobs available. Addressing the talent shortage requires us to build entry-level opportunities for newly trained professionals. Assigning an entry-level person to test whether a process is ready for automation is a great learning opportunity for the employee, and an opportunity for the employer to save high-cost development resources who are trying to automate a process that is not yet well defined.

Once you have decided which tasks should be driven down the cost scale, you are ready for the next step in the process, which is documenting the processes in detail.

Documenting manual processes

Documenting a process allows you to consider whether the process could be accomplished on a lower cost basis. Some tasks are assigned to high-cost resources because they require certain skills and experience. Others are performed by high-cost resources because they are not well documented and require an unnecessary amount of judgment. Documenting those processes allows the organization to evaluate whether a lower cost resource is capable of performing the task. While not every task can be automated, most could be driven to a lower cost basis, which frees more senior resources to address more consequential problems for the organization. Also, the act of writing a process down often highlights gaps in the process or inefficiencies. Most processes in a security program are built by habit and few are intentionally designed. Intentionally designed processes are often more efficient and effective.

It should be highlighted that there are few automation techniques currently available that will allow a team to automate a process they don't understand. Techniques to allow AI to learn tasks that are not explicitly taught to it are rare. Therefore, if you hope to automate a process, the first step is to learn the task and document it to the point where a non-technical user could accomplish the task with consistent results. When the task can be reduced to a series of if-then statements in a decision matrix, the task is ready to be automated using commonly available techniques.

Once the process is well defined and documented, the next step is to automate the process.

Automating processes

Once the decision matrix has been built to the level that a person with no experience in the field could follow it to get the desired result, the task is ready to be automated. At that point, all that is necessary to automate the task is to code the decision matrix. This is a process that can be accomplished using coding languages, open source technology, and coding skills that are widely available. There are other possibilities for automation that require a deeper skill set and can solve a wider range of problems. However, most security operations can become more efficient without using advanced techniques.

In my experience, few information security teams have the necessary resources to perform complex automation operations. Complex automation techniques are likely to be the domain of security technology companies. When using automation through a security technology, understanding the **Total Cost of Ownership** (**TCO**) should take all costs into account including the cost of software, of hardware if applicable, and the fully burdened cost of the resources necessary to achieve the intended outcome. Comparing that TCO to the TCO of the current solution will allow for a cost comparison, which should be compared to a benefit comparison to do a proper cost-benefit analysis. One thing that should be clear by this point is that understanding business concepts is a critical skill for security leaders. Past generations of security leaders were often technical but not business savvy. Nowadays, the security leadership role is being redefined as a business role with an understanding of technology. This is the opposite of what was required from the role in the past, where security leaders were often security experts with a basic understanding of business. As security matures as a discipline, more business skills are required from the security team.

In my experience, when technology decisions go wrong, it is often due to underestimating the human resource costs. Technologies that are more expensive than their peers may have a favorable TCO if there are automation capabilities built into the product. Other companies offer services that may allow an organization to reduce the risks associated with underestimating their human resource costs.

Once the basic tasks have been identified and automated, it is time to build upon the automation foundation by gathering more data and applying context.

Gathering data and applying context

A general rule concerning machine learning specifically, and automation techniques generally, is that they require large amounts of data to be effective. More data will enable the machine to make better decisions and solve more complex problems. Part of the data that can be gathered will help the machines apply context to what they are seeing. Currently, algorithms struggle with qualitative analysis. Algorithms that can tell you *what happened* using a large dataset are commodities at this point. This is not to say these algorithms are not helpful, they are simply common. Some algorithms are also predictive. With enough historical data, some algorithms have become good at predicting *what will happen next*. This is largely based on pattern recognition and determining the next logical data point given the historical data. People should be very careful with predictive algorithms because incomplete datasets can lead to poor predictions. Also, machines have difficulty putting **black swan** events into perspective.

> **Black swan**
>
> A black swan is an event that cannot be predicted and changes everything. The COVID-19 pandemic which began in 2019, is not a true black swan event. It could be argued that a fast-spreading respiratory illness causing a global pandemic has been seen before and will likely occur again. However, assuming aspects of human life return to their patterns before the pandemic, most predictive algorithms would have difficulty making multi-year future predictions if data from 2020 and 2021 is in the dataset. True black swan events cause even more challenges.

What algorithms are currently most ineffective at is trying to determine *why* something happened. *Why* is an important question when dealing with security or law enforcement. Some machines attempt to answer why, but programming such algorithms leads to major ethical questions more often than yielding useful insights. Next, we will briefly introduce some of the ethical issues in AI.

Ethics in AI

AI offers exciting potential for a variety of applications. I am not an AI skeptic; in fact, I believe that we will need AI solutions to help us solve some of the problems we will face in the near future. However, there are some major issues with AI that we need to consider before the widespread use of AI in society can be ethical. It should be noted that this is not an exhaustive list. Ethics in AI is becoming a field in itself. This is simply an introduction to the top three ethics issues that I have seen arise when AI is used.

First, we will explore the challenges that arise when biased datasets are used, and their bias is built into automated systems.

Bias in datasets

AI systems need very large datasets to be effective. In many cases, those datasets go back for many years. The problem is that it is hard to find the necessary amount of unbiased data to create effective AI systems. As an example, I will use a hypothetical thought experiment. This is not a real example, but there have been enough examples of this thought experiment where it could be considered realistic, if not likely.

Let's imagine a city wants to deploy an AI algorithm to help predict crime rates in an area to help ensure police are close to where they are likely to be needed. The city has been struggling to staff its police force appropriately, which has led to rising crime rates and falling conviction rates. The city inputs all the historical data from the city from the previous 100 years into a large dataset. It then allows an AI algorithm to dispatch police cars based on the patterns it has observed. The system works. Police are now able to cut their response times to calls and their conviction rate increases significantly. *Proponents of the system argue the high arrest rates in places where police were deployed versus other places they were not is evidence the system is working.* Critics say the data is a self-fulfilling prophecy because police are making arrests where they happen to be.

Facing a wave of judge retirements, the city decides to extend the algorithm to make sentencing recommendations to the remaining judges within the statutory sentencing guidelines based on the likelihood that a person will re-offend. These suggestions help narrow sentencing guidelines and make the system more efficient. The system is expanded to parole boards to help make decisions on who should be released and reintegrated into society.

The **American Civil Liberties Union** (**ACLU**) is skeptical that the system is just. After an investigation, they find that minorities are more likely to be arrested. When arrested, they are more likely to be convicted and if they are convicted, they are more likely to receive a harsher sentence. Further, they are less likely to be released when they are eligible for parole. How could a seemingly unbiased algorithm create such inequity?

The answer is that there have been historical inequities in a variety of our institutions that have led to minorities being disproportionately impacted by the criminal justice system. With no way to understand that historical context, the algorithm incorrectly associated ethnicities and socio-economic factors to a higher propensity to commit a crime. Also, due to similar factors, the system determines minorities have a higher recidivism rate. These challenges are real, and we will see these debates expand in the coming decades as a decreasing labor force in many developed economies leads more organizations and jurisdictions to look for solutions in algorithms.

We are already seeing examples of bias in technology. There have been studies that show facial recognition technology is most effective for light-skinned faces and has diminishing accuracy rates when recognizing faces with a darker skin complexion. While it can be hurtful when Snapchat filters do not recognize a person's face, the consequences are more severe as facial recognition technology is used by police forces and customs and border patrol agents. A mistaken identity could lead a person to be wrongfully arrested. If juries are unduly confident in the technology and not aware of its imperfections, the bias could also lead to wrongful convictions.

Example Case Study: The Nijeer Parks Case

Challenges with bias in AI are concerning in the theoretical realm, but what many people don't realize is that immature AI algorithms are in use today. In some cases, like the case of Nijeer Parks, they are causing real-world negative consequences. In 2019, Woodbridge, New Jersey police arrested Mr. Parks for shoplifting candy and attempting to hit police officers with his car. He had been identified using facial recognition software. He was taken to jail and had to hire an attorney to defend himself before the case was eventually dismissed. The problem with the case? Mr. Parks was 30 miles away and the person in the surveillance video was not him, but another man with a similar complexion.

Facial recognition technology is seeing widespread use by law enforcement and conceptually it seems like a positive development. Over 200 cities in the United States use facial recognition technology to solve crimes. However, facial recognition software is prone to errors across the board, but the frequency of those errors increases for people with darker skin tones. When the tool is used appropriately to narrow a large list of potential suspects into a smaller list, it can make investigators' jobs less time-consuming, and the technology could be effective. However, too often the technology is being used as a basis to arrest people without meaningful human verification and mistakes are common.

This is a perfect example of a technology that should be used to aid humans rather than replace them. In fact, most automation technology will fall into that category for at least the next few decades as we continue to tune the models. However, the question of the proper use of technology is not the sole issue in this case.

There are civil rights implications associated with using technologies that have inherent bias when making decisions related to whether a person is arrested and charged with a crime. Many people have spent their lives fighting systemic injustices and to have those injustices written into algorithms that will form the basis of policing decisions in the future represents a major step backward for civil rights. It is important that we work to free our datasets and algorithms of bias, especially unconscious bias, or we risk transferring our worst historical impulses from ourselves to our machines (Hill, 2020).

Technology providers should not be expected to solve these problems themselves. It is expensive and time-consuming to collect large datasets. Inconsistent privacy regulations around the world make it more difficult than ever. I am an advocate for an open source data repository that can be used by anyone developing AI systems. The open source project could then gather large volumes of data and curate it in such a way where it had adequate representation from all ethnic groups and was free from inherent bias. This unbiased dataset would lead to higher-quality AI products that are less likely to have unintended negative consequences. Partnering with governments to create this dataset and make it available to companies in their country could help grow the tax base and thus their economies, giving them an incentive to cooperate. Making the data available to universities around the world will allow for deep tech research into better, fairer algorithms and will allow for the study of embedded biases and the improvement of the dataset overall. This dataset would be very important to fighting bias and improving the quality of AI.

Next, let's look at another ethical issue, which is privacy.

Protecting privacy

The Chinese government has hundreds of millions of cameras around the country using facial recognition technology to track citizens as they move. Based on where they go and what they do, an AI algorithm can match the movements to a personal profile. Based on surveillance of their communications, AI systems can gain an understanding of their thoughts and attitudes. In short, the Chinese government has created a system to predict who may become a problem so they can intervene before that happens.

During the COVID-19 pandemic, the government used this massive surveillance system coupled with an AI algorithm to assign risk to people before they boarded a train or entered a city. The system could just as easily be used to assess political risk. There is no doubt such a system could be helpful in reducing the spread of the coronavirus and may have other useful applications. However, it is also easy to imagine a scenario where such a system could be used in a way that is more controversial.

As we move into the future of technology, we need to think critically about what privacy means to us and how we should protect it. Regulations such as the European Union's GDPR are a good example of thoughtful legislation designed to get ahead of these problems. However, there have been countless other jurisdictions that have passed similar privacy legislation, and each one is slightly different. Since data does not respect terrestrial borders, it is very challenging to comply with this patchwork of legislation.

Example Case Study: Reading Between the Lines – The CCPA and Privacy in AI

On June 28, 2021, the California State Legislature passed the **California Consumer Privacy Act (CCPA)**. At first glance, the CCPA is another piece of legislation loosely based on the European Union's GDPR that adds to the problematic global patchwork of privacy legislation. However, upon closer inspection, you can see a window into the challenges society will face as more companies leverage AI platforms around the world.

While much of the CCPA looks like GDPR, there are some important differences in the scope of what is considered personal information. California is home to Silicon Valley, one of the world's most robust technology innovation centers. The California State Legislature is foreseeing some of the problems that the rest of the world will face and trying to give its citizens some control over the data that may soon be used to make decisions about them without their consent.

The CCPA calls out personal information such as identification numbers, phone numbers, addresses, and other common forms of **Personally Identifiable Information (PII)**. However, the CCPA also calls out things like a person's gait, or the way they walk, photos of a person, and other pieces of information often linked to visual media. Further, the CCPA covers inferences about a person going into an AI model and the derived data coming out of that AI model. This means that if an AI model uses information about you to derive some further piece of data, you own both the source data and the derived data as a data subject and you can exert your rights over the derived data as well as the source data. The CCPA also has a catch-all broad definition of personal data that allows the State of California to exert control over the use of new technologies, defining personal information as data that *is capable of being associated with, or could reasonably be linked, directly or indirectly, with a particular consumer or household.*

Is this approach going to solve problems with privacy and AI in California? It is difficult to predict, but the idea that we need to define who owns what information as we develop data-hungry technology capabilities is important. We need to consider what privacy means in the modern world, where governments can use technology to track our movements in the physical world and monitor everything we say in the digital world. There has never been a time in human history where surveillance was easier to conduct, nor a time where so much information about every individual exists. It is time for us to think critically about what the rules should be and how that data should be used (State of California, 2018).

It is easy to criticize the Chinese Communist Party for their use of surveillance and technology to create a police state. They are open about the fact that they do not believe in individual privacy rights. However, hundreds of cities in the United States are creating similar systems using facial recognition and AI to track citizens and their movements along with their online communications. Most cities are not notifying their citizens when they deploy these types of monitoring tools.

Some states have passed legislation similar to the **California Consumer Privacy Act (CCPA)**. The CCPA protects an individual's right to privacy and defines personal information to include a person's likeness and their movements. The challenge is that privacy legislation is not consistent even within the United States, let alone globally. This leads to organizations scrambling to understand the requirements they must comply with to do business in each jurisdiction.

In my opinion, we need national legislation that supersedes the state-by-state approaches to privacy to create an environment where companies can respect privacy in an efficient way. Where countries agree on certain elements of privacy legislation, international treaties should be formed to simplify the regulatory landscape. Modern technology systems are not designed to respect terrestrial borders. The more inconsistent regulation is across jurisdictions, the less likely it is to be followed and its objectives met.

Next, we will talk about another ethical debate, behavior modification.

Behavior modification

The idea that companies would like to modify our behavior is nothing new. In fact, the field of advertising can be seen as the art and science of behavior modification through persuasion. However, companies using technology have become very good at behavior modification. Social media companies have been under fire recently for creating algorithms designed to push people toward their darkest impulses to increase their engagement with the platform, thereby amplifying advertising revenue for the company. The more extreme a person's views become, the more alienated from wider society they will be, and the more they will be driven toward online communities. This has been shown to have wide-ranging impacts, and it could be argued the impacts it has on children are most detrimental.

Example Case Study: How Social Media Divides Us

Social media was originally invented to help people who already knew each other stay connected. As it matured as a technology and a business model, social media companies realized that they could increase engagement by creating communities of like-minded people. As the algorithms continued to gather data about engagement, they determined that the more polarized the group, the more time they would spend on their online communities. Since the algorithms are designed to create maximum engagement, strategies that create division between groups of people continued to proliferate.

The challenge with social media was people who were members of these groups were not only holding alternative opinions from those in other groups, but they were also shown alternate realities. Since confirmation bias in people is so strong, over time, when presented with information that did not confirm their worldview, they rejected the information without considering it. The effect on society has been profound as people with minor disagreements on policy have turned into extremely polarized groups who have trouble communicating. This is because there is no basis of shared facts or shared reality, with each group inhabiting a world that is unrecognizable to the other.

Hyper-customization allows each of us to live in an online world of our own creation. Our preferences allow algorithms to feed us more of what we prefer while blocking what we don't. Over time, some people start to believe the things they don't prefer don't actually exist. This becomes a major challenge. While print media was doomed as soon as online media was developed, there are some merits in everyone reading the same sets of facts. Even if two people draw different conclusions from what they have read, at least there is a common basis for debate.

Similarly, online retailers have become very good at using technology to find the sets of stimuli necessary to maximize the number of products a person purchases on each visit. Where will we draw the line between acceptable commercial behavior and an unacceptable detriment to society? When does advertising and persuasion cross the line into infringing upon a person's basic right to self-determination? At what age, if ever, is a person's brain sufficiently developed to have a chance to resist these techniques? I do not intend to provide an answer to these questions, but I think it is important we continue to ask them, especially as technology improves and becomes more intertwined with our daily lives. We are rapidly approaching a place in our technological evolution in many spaces where the question shifts from *What can we do?* to *What should we do?*

Next, we will discuss what we should do once we have identified an automation opportunity and put a solution in place that we think will be effective – testing the system.

Testing the system

When you automate a task, sometimes you will have a more efficient and more effective method of achieving a necessary goal and it will be an overwhelming success. Other times you will have an outcome that is neither efficient nor effective, and it will be clear that you should return to the previous way of doing things and try again. Often, it will be somewhere in the middle. How do you test a system you have built? What is an acceptable error rate? How do you measure it?

First, we will talk about a framework for measuring test results known as the confusion matrix.

The confusion matrix

For each task, there are four possible outcomes. These four outcomes are collectively known as the confusion matrix. The following diagram is a visual representation of this simple concept:

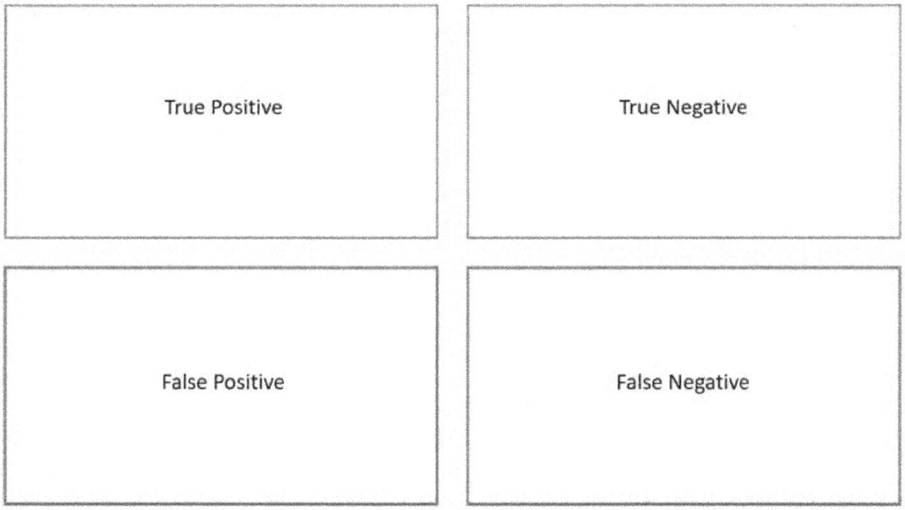

Figure 8.3 – Confusion matrix

When testing systems, each outcome will fall into one of these categories. Here is a brief description of each:

- True positive: Something the algorithm should have flagged and did
- True negative: Something the algorithm should not have flagged and did not
- False positive: Something the system should not have flagged but did
- False negative: Something the system should have flagged but did not

When defining acceptable parameters, tolerance for both false positives and false negatives should be considered. In some cases, some false positives are acceptable, but there is low tolerance for false negatives. In other cases, the opposite may be true. In most cases, a simple accuracy rate is insufficient.

Once someone has defined their test criteria and the expected results, the system can be tested. Automation, like most types of innovation, is unlikely to be perfect the first time. As a result, we often see hybrid implementations as the technology is improved. Further, my opinion of the future is that humans and algorithms will work together to perform most tasks. Therefore, hybrid implementations are likely to be the way most tasks are accomplished for the foreseeable future.

Hybrid implementations

The term hybrid implementation refers to implementations of automation technology that work alongside a human, doing the same job. For example, you may have a self-driving car algorithm running silently in a car. You can then record the actions the algorithm would've taken in any given scenario and compare that data with the actions the human driver did take. Also, you could layer in the positive and negative outcomes. Over time, you can compare how effective the machine is at a given task, in this case driving, against the human. In the case of driving, the acceptable error rate for an algorithm is much lower than it is for human drivers. We accept a certain number of annual car accidents due to human error. Any time an automated system causes an accident, it is national news.

Other uses, such as those in most security applications, are more benign. When we were first building our event triage automation technology at InteliSecure, it started as a quality assurance mechanism. Once we felt we had an effective algorithm, we would run it alongside a human analyst. When the machine and the human agreed, nothing happened. When they disagreed, the event was escalated to a senior analyst who could review the event and determine whether the analyst or the algorithm was incorrect. In the beginning, analysts outperformed the algorithms. After some time, we were able to find tasks that the algorithm was better suited to and achieved a far lower error rate. As it turns out, those were the tasks least desirable and intellectually stimulating for the analysts. We were able to improve outcomes, efficiency, and job satisfaction through a hybrid implementation.

Sometimes a hybrid implementation is a means to an end. The solution is implemented in a hybrid fashion until the algorithm can be improved to the point it is more effective than the human, at which time the algorithm takes over. However, there are some tasks that will be hybrid implementations for the foreseeable future. In those cases, machines may be more adept at portions of an outcome and humans may be more adept at others. In these cases, the human and the machine will work together. For example, think of a research scientist. In the future, an algorithm could parse through a very large dataset, highlighting all the correlations in the data. The human could then analyze them and determine which correlations are likely coincidental and which may have causal factors. After listing the causal factors, the machine could then parse through the dataset again to confirm or deny the researcher's hypothesis. Using this method, research that once took months or years could be completed in days or weeks.

Many people see automation in the workforce as an all-or-nothing scenario. Hybrid implementations are likely to become more common as the technology improves. This will allow people to do what they're best at while being assisted by machines built specifically to do things humans find difficult or boring. If you listen to people talk long enough about AI, you generally get the sense that it will either be the best or worst thing that happened to humanity. It is likely to be somewhere in between.

Next, we will discuss the other side of the equation – how attackers can leverage automation.

How attackers can leverage automation

Of course, attackers have access to the same technological capabilities as defenders. Like security professionals, attackers have experts creating technology for them, helping them with consulting and expertise on demand, and generally making their jobs easier. It is similar with automation. If AI algorithms are good at pattern recognition, this provides an opportunity for attackers to use those capabilities for nefarious purposes.

For example, could it be possible to train a machine learning algorithm on a list of best practices for incident response and teach a piece of malicious code to evade commonly deployed countermeasures? I couldn't imagine why not. Could attackers build self-healing worms that use multi-stage attacks to defeat commonly deployed security technologies? I think those types of sophisticated attacks are already happening.

The key point is to raise awareness that at its heart, security is about people attacking people. Just as with any other conflict in human history, there is an ever-escalating arms race in terms of technology and tactics. That is one of the things that is fascinating about security, but also one of the things that makes it so challenging. You can never rest on your laurels or declare yourself secure. Every day we must be improving our defenses and preparing to defend ourselves because one day we will be attacked, and our response could be the difference between the success and failure of our entire organization.

While it is impossible to predict every way attackers will use automation, it is safe to assume they will use it, and they will innovate ways to use it to defeat the defense mechanisms we build. Each time we build an effective countermeasure, we are likely to see a new form of attack.

Summary

Automation is a necessary capability that will help us meet the staffing challenges of the modern world. While we can and should grow the cybersecurity workforce, that is a long-term solution. We will require effective solutions to meet challenges in the interim.

In this chapter, you have learned how to identify automation opportunities, along with a practical methodology to act upon those opportunities. You have learned about datasets and context and the ethical challenges posed by AI solutions. You have also learned how to test your solutions to ensure they are effective, and you have been given a brief idea of how attackers could leverage similar technologies against you to become more efficient and effective at what they do.

At this point in our journey, we have covered a wide range of topics relevant to protecting modern organizations. You now have the necessary understanding to look at the landscape and hopefully identify an area that appeals to you. For our final chapter, we will discuss what steps we can all take to keep our loved ones safe at home in an increasingly dangerous digital world.

Check your understanding

1. What is the lowest cost basis for a cybersecurity task in any organization?
2. What types of questions are AI solutions well positioned to answer, and which do they struggle with?
3. What are some of the ethical challenges with AI systems?
4. What are the quadrants of the confusion matrix?
5. Which type of documentation of a manual process indicates that an automation opportunity is ready for coding?

Further reading

- Hill, K. (2020, December 29). *Another Arrest, and Jail Time, Due to a Bad Facial Recognition Match*. Retrieved from The New York Times: `https://www.nytimes.com/2020/12/29/technology/facial-recognition-misidentify-jail.html`.
- Kanowitz, S. (2020, February 12). *Government revs up IT security automation*. Retrieved from GCN: `https://gcn.com/articles/2020/02/12/it-security-automation-public-sector.aspx`.
- Ponemon Institute. (2020). *2020 Cost of a Data Breach Report*. Ponemon Institute.
- State of California. (2018, June). *California Consumer Privacy Act (CCPA)*. Retrieved from State of California Department of Justice: `https://oag.ca.gov/privacy/ccpa`.

9 Cybersecurity at Home

I have dedicated most of my career to helping organizations protect what matters most to them. I would be remiss if I did not include some best practices for protecting those that matter most to you, your family and friends. Our children live in a very different world than the one we grew up in. During their formative years when they are developing their emotional systems and prone to making mistakes, they inhabit a world where they are judged against an impossible standard driven by social media, and their mistakes can be publicized and live forever. We must be vigilant if we want to protect our children.

Similarly, our parents are coping with a world that is very different from the one they are accustomed to. There are countless scams targeted at senior citizens around the world. While we do not need to make our parents cybersecurity experts, there are some best practices we can share with them to help them stay safe in an unfamiliar environment.

Cybersecurity in an organization is different from cybersecurity at home. However, there are some best practices that can help you and your family stay safe online. The threats are different. Unless you have an ultra-high net worth person in your family, it is unlikely that they will be targeted by a sophisticated actor. Truthfully, they're unlikely to be targeted at all, but rather fall victim to broad attacks designed to fool whoever they can. The good news is basic best practices can protect against many of those attacks. In this chapter, I will share some simple suggestions you can give to your family members to help them protect themselves.

This chapter is designed for you to share with everyone in your life who may not understand how to protect themselves online. Read it with children, parents, or significant others. The objective is to make the digital world a little bit safer for the people who matter most to you. Some of the information from other chapters will be repeated to give the proper context to people who may not have read the entire book. However, the concepts will be presented in less detail than they were in the other sections of the book.

The topics we will cover in this brief guide are as follows:

- Protecting children and teaching them about online safety
- Password managers, how to use them, and why they are important
- Multifactor authentication
- Password complexity and why it matters
- Stop publishing your information!

Protecting children and teaching them about online safety

One of the topics I am most passionate about is protecting our children online. When I reflect on my childhood, I was able to come of age at a time where privacy still existed. I made mistakes as many children do, but my mistakes were not forever recorded on a social media server in a data center. The current generation of children does not have that luxury. Furthermore, they are subjected to unrealistic expectations of their appearance and accomplishments driven by social media, which can lead to them being bullied anonymously and constantly being reminded that they aren't good-looking enough or successful enough. Social media has connected people and done some good for society at large. However, there are few inventions in human history that have damaged the mental health of our children more than social media.

In my opinion, it is unlikely to be effective to forbid our children from using social media. Instead, we should equip them with the skills necessary to protect themselves from the dangers that lurk in cyberspace. It is difficult to impress upon children how long forever is and how the decisions they make now can negatively impact them in the future. It is also difficult to explain to them that what they see online is not real life, but rather a façade that the people they interact with want them to believe is real. Furthermore, it is difficult to bring ourselves to destroy our children's innocence by explaining to them that bad people exist and seek to exploit them. While each of these concepts is difficult, we cannot neglect our responsibility to educate our children. In the following sections, I will define each of these problems and provide some ideas for how parents can start the conversation. As always, it is important to ensure the message is age appropriate. However, in a world where toddlers have devices capable of connecting to the internet, it is never too early to start talking about online safety.

We will start with the permanence of social media.

The permanence of social media

There have been countless news stories that follow the same pattern:

1. A prominent person posts something offensive on Twitter.
2. A follower on Twitter takes a screenshot of the message.
3. The prominent person deletes the offensive post.
4. The screenshot is displayed on CNN or Fox News.
5. The prominent person resigns, is fired, is canceled, and so on.

Careers and lives have been destroyed by people exercising poor judgment on social media. All those examples should serve as a reminder that once something is publicly shared, you can never really delete it. Some services, such as Snapchat, have been successful with younger generations primarily because they market themselves as temporary messages that go away forever after a short period of time. Of course, that is not entirely true, and that marketing is dangerous. Children thinking their messages are temporary are further encouraged to say and do things they shouldn't on the platform. When they become adults, those messages can haunt them.

Example Case: Caitlin Davis

Caitlin Davis was a New England Patriots cheerleader. Many young girls dream of being on the cheer squad for a professional sports team, and the NFL is the pinnacle. She was removed from the squad after a photo from a college Halloween party surfaced from several years before, when she was 18 years old. The photo featured drawings on a classmate who was asleep at a party, some of which featured symbols that would be generally recognized as hate speech. As distasteful as the images were, it is important to note that Caitlin was featured in the picture. There is no evidence that she drew the offensive symbols. Regardless, the team did not want to be associated with the photo, and Caitlin lost her job, and likely a childhood dream.

The lesson here is one of social media. When a person experiences success, these types of images have a habit of surfacing at the worst possible time. Many people throughout the years have been at college Halloween parties. Many have had pictures taken at those parties that feature questionable content. However, if you were to post those pictures on social media, they can come back to haunt you. Most companies report that they have rejected candidates for a job based on their social media profiles. It is now common practice to look through publicly available information about a candidate before hiring them. Your online preferences can prevent you from getting a job or get you fired. It is important to ensure you are not saying things online or posting content online that you would not want a potential employer to read or see. Chances are they will see and read all of it. (Maivha, 2018) (The Manifest, 2020)

The digital world is a model of resilience. It is very difficult to destroy a piece of information entirely. Information is copied between servers effortlessly and is thoroughly backed up to the point where even when the owners of the servers and services want to fully delete a piece of information, they struggle to do so.

It should be assumed that everything posted online will last forever and be public. It should also be assumed that negative sentiments are more likely to go viral than positive sentiments. Furthermore, you have no idea when you post something whether it will be seen by a small group of friends or millions of people. Therefore, before you post anything online, ensure it is something you would be comfortable saying in real life, in front of a crowd, on video. If you would be comfortable in that scenario, you should post it proudly. If you would not, you should not.

Many people get into trouble on social media thinking they are speaking to a small circle of friends. While those people may see your post first, the mission of social media is to drive engagement. If your post will grab attention, whether for the right or wrong reasons, you should expect your post to be amplified. When you go to get your next job or get into a prestigious university, you should expect the hiring manager or admissions personnel will see that post.

Next, we will talk about the truth behind the façade of social media.

The truth behind the façade

Social media reminds me of Las Vegas. The first time I went to Las Vegas, I, like most people visiting it for the first time, was taken aback by the amazing buildings. However, when I went inside the buildings, I realized that they are standard buildings with a fancy façade. There is little difference in the actual architecture of the buildings; they have simply been decorated differently. As you spend more time in Las Vegas, especially away from the strip, you start to see more of the city that does not fit the image the entertainment capital of the world likes to project.

Social media is the same way. It is not real life. People post what they want you to see. Ironically, influencers, who people follow because they trust their opinion, are paid to position products and very rarely give real opinions that they are not compensated for. The result is entire online communities designed to appear real that are no more real than any Hollywood set or advertising campaign. The difference is people *believe* it's real life.

What many people post on social media platforms portrays a fantasy life people want you to believe they live. Some people go so far as to pay for photoshoots complete with props to make them look more successful. If you see someone sitting on the hood of an Italian supercar wearing fancy jewelry and designer clothes, it would be easy to think they own the car, the clothes, and the jewelry, and that's what they want you to think. However, it is more likely that they paid a studio to help them project that image of success. When people post their amazing pictures from vacation, you may be jealous that you are not able to afford such a lavish vacation to such an exotic locale. However, they don't post the other 51 weeks of the year they are not on vacation, or their credit card statements, which may show they couldn't really afford to take that vacation, either. There is nothing wrong with the platforms themselves, but the content can portray an unrealistic image that can be damaging, especially to children. When people view these platforms and use them to judge whether they are successful in their own life by comparing themselves to others they see on the platform, it becomes dangerous. *The most important thing to remember is most of it is not real.*

Other social media platforms are designed to drive engagement. These platforms can be dangerous in my opinion. Their goal is to get you engaged with the platform so they can sell your attention to advertisers who may want to target you. Because the platform knows so much about you, advertisers can target potential customers in a more granular fashion than any previous type of advertising. Social media is a genius invention as a marketing platform. However, what most people don't understand is the users of the service are the product. The platform only exists to create more users of the service so there is more product to sell to advertisers. This is what makes the platform dangerous. Engagement is all that matters. Positive or negative consequences are not built into the algorithms. The result is not only a commentary on social media but also a commentary on society. We engage more with negative content. We are more interested in argument than agreement, and we like to form groups of like-minded people. Over the years, the algorithms have learned to maximize this behavior in a way that maximizes profits. So, who is to blame, us or them? In the end, it doesn't matter. People are being hurt and social media platforms know it. They are now faced with a similar dilemma as tobacco companies in the past. *Evidence suggests they know their product causes harm, but their business model depends on the harm being caused.* Can they be trusted to self-regulate?

When I talk about this topic, people ask me about my social media choices. I am a former social media user, and I deleted most of my social media presence years ago. It is like any other addiction, it was difficult at first, but it got easier over time. Now I do not miss it, and I am happier and healthier than I was when I was an active user of social media. I maintain a presence on LinkedIn for professional connections, but I take great care to always speak on LinkedIn as I would in a business meeting. Ultimately, the choice is up to each individual. I understand the need for children to belong to a community. It was easier as an established adult to turn away from social media. I do believe that most children, teenagers, and young adults will have some social media presence. However, I am hopeful that they will be aware of what the platform is and why it exists and understand how to use it in a way that maximizes the benefits while avoiding the issues it can create.

Next, we will explore the dangers online that go beyond side effects and turn toward people who intentionally seek to hurt people online.

The danger lurking online

The internet has done wonders for people across all walks of life. It has made it easier to learn and connect. It has given us access to people and information that we would have never had otherwise. As much as it has done those things for all of us, it has done that and more for criminals and corporations that prey on people.

The internet allows people to communicate with others while pretending to be someone or something that they are not in ways that would be very difficult in the physical world. This ranges from companies profiting from harming our children to bullies who use online platforms to spread their negativity to a wider group than was previously possible, to traditional predators who now have the ability to lurk in new places and meet our children in ways that were previously impossible.

The digital world has all the same threats to our children and our families as the physical world, but just like the internet has helped bring multinational corporations or geographically dispersed families closer together, it has also helped bring predators closer to their victims. I talk a lot about children in this chapter because they are growing up in a world where they are so comfortable with technology that they trust things online more than they should. However, when it comes to predators, the warnings are as applicable to our parents as they are to our children. I talk about this simple fact with many of the companies I work with, but it is applicable to all of us. Never before in human history has someone with negative intent had more access to victims, a higher likelihood of success, and a lower likelihood of facing consequences than they do right now. Simply put, *it's never been easier to be a criminal*. Therefore, it is important that we all understand the dangers and how we can protect ourselves.

First, we will talk about how social media monetizes misery and how we can help our loved ones resist the gravitational pull of negativity in those platforms. Also, I will try to provide some advice on how parents can recognize this before it ends in tragedy.

Social media and monetizing misery

Social media platforms are designed to keep us engaged. Negative emotions drive our behavior more than positive ones. As a result, social media platforms can lead to toxic environments where people are mean to each other, and participants' mental health is impacted in a negative way. Some have accused social media platforms of monetizing misery. That is both true in one sense and unfair in another. Social media platforms are run by algorithms, not monitored by people. The algorithms don't have emotions and are not built to recognize emotions in us. They are built to drive engagement. They learn how to drive engagement by running micro-experiments over time. The way we react to different stimuli builds the algorithm and teaches it how to keep us engaged. Our increased engagement with negative content means the algorithms are more likely to show us that negative content. Social media platforms are not necessarily monetizing misery; they are monetizing engagement. We are engaging with content that makes us miserable.

Example Case: Molly Russell

In 2017, 14-year-old Molly Russell died of suicide days before her birthday. She was heavily engaged with social media, and among her other interests, she was exposed to graphic images of self-harm and suicide-promoting content. Molly's father accuses the social media companies of helping to kill his daughter. Based on the messages she left before her suicide, it was clear Molly was dealing with a mixture of mental health issues and common challenges for a teenage girl. She did not feel like she fit in and she was struggling with her place in the world. Many teens have dealt with these feelings throughout human history. Until now, they did not have access to content that showed them how to harm themselves or that normalized the idea of self-harm and suicide. It is impossible to know for sure whether Molly would be alive today if it were not for social media; however, it is impossible to imagine that the content she was shown on the platform did not contribute to her tragic death.

Molly's father has been outspoken about the role he believes social media played in his daughter's death. As a result, Instagram pledged to remove content depicting self-harm or encouraging suicide. One month later, similar content was found on the platform. It is easy in this case to demonize Instagram, but there is a math problem at work. Instagram has 450 employees, most of which are not involved in content moderation. It has 1.3 billion users on the platform. Any one of those 1.3 billion people can post content. Do we really expect the 450 employees to review all posts from the 1.3 billion users and remove everything that could be offensive or harmful? It isn't possible. Social media is designed to democratize content and allow anyone to post anything they'd like. You cannot have an open platform like that and expect it to be moderated.

Meanwhile, the family is exploring their legal options. As part of the case, thousands of images and pieces of content Molly was exposed to were shared with the legal team, who had difficulty viewing the images because they were so disturbing. The challenge facing us with social media is that there are no easy answers. It is impossible to expect the platforms to be policed by the companies themselves. They don't have enough employees to do that. Perhaps we could develop algorithms that promote positive content, but would we still use the service, or would it break the business model? We should do everything we can to prevent young people like Molly Russell from seeing things with such tragic consequences, but what can we do? I don't have the answers, but it must start with meaningful dialogue about the problem. (BBC News, 2020) (Hurynag, 2020)

Parenting in the information age is difficult. Parenting is always difficult, but it is more difficult than it has ever been right now. However, it is likely easier now than it ever will be again. This is the technology flywheel. With each passing day, there are more potential dangers emerging and more ways for children, especially teenagers, to engage with the world away from the watchful eyes of their parents. It is more important than it has ever been for parents to engage with their children to understand how they are feeling and what they are thinking.

It is difficult to raise children, and teenagers are especially difficult. I do not advocate trying to spy on your children, although some of my friends do and there are some great technologies that will allow a parent to do so. However, I do advocate trying to understand your children's emotional state and monitor for changes. If you see signs that your child is less happy or more absorbed in the digital world than you would like, you should intervene.

That intervention can be in any way you see fit. For example, you could try to limit screen time or introduce your child to alternatives that get them out of the house and off their phones. A friend of mine was concerned about his daughter and took her on a trip to a beach. Each day, they went snorkeling. While this was great bonding time, more importantly, his daughter couldn't use her phone while she was in the water. While she returned to social media when the trip was over, the break was enough to get her back in a positive frame of mind.

The type of intervention is up to the parent. My recommendation is to act. There are too many heartbreaking stories where parents saw warning signs and didn't act quickly. Everything happens faster in the digital world, including downward spirals that lead to tragic outcomes. Humans are naturally more affected by negative stimuli than positive stimuli. We see this in loss aversion. Studies have shown that people are far more upset when they lose something than they are happy when they gain something of equal value. We see the same pattern on the news, which also thrives on engagement. People wonder why the news shows more negative stories than positive ones. The reason is simple. We engage more with the negative than the positive. Social media algorithms have learned this tendency as well. The most important thing to remember is there is no part of a social media algorithm that is altruistic. It does not take into account whether its users are happy or sad, just whether they are engaged. We cannot trust the algorithms to care for our children. They won't.

Next, we are going to discuss the challenges associated with giving bullies a platform.

Cyberbullies

Bullies are not a new phenomenon; however, when they are given a platform as large as that offered by social media, it can feel to the victim as if the entire world has turned against them. Bullies are often insecure, attention-starved people and they bully others, so they feel better about themselves by making others feel lower than they are. Social media gives bullies a platform to accomplish their aims on a larger scale.

Cyberbullying often has real-world consequences. Victims of bullying often suffer significant mental health problems that are amplified when the bullying happens online. Next, we will discuss the issues that can occur when predators seek out their victims online.

Cyber predators

It is much easier to hide your true identity online than it is in the physical world. While most of us understand this intuitively, we may not consciously think about the fact that it has aided predators who would like to target our children online. Predators may lurk anywhere they can find their intended victims, including chat rooms and popular children's games. They can then use the relationships they've built with children online to target them in real life.

While it may be tempting to monitor everything your children do online, it is unrealistic to do so after a certain age. The United States Federal Bureau of Investigation advises parents to instead talk to their children about what is going on in their day-to-day life, including asking them about the friends they interact with online. While online communities have made it more difficult to control the sphere of people who may influence our children, it is still possible to use parenting best practices to try to keep our children safe.

Next, we will talk about scammers.

Scammers

Like other criminals, frauds, con artists, and scammers have moved online. There are several scams that target different groups of people. Many of them are laughable when you see them, but it is important to remember that scammers do not need a high success rate for their schemes to be lucrative. Often, the scams target the very old and the very young or the disabled. In short, scammers are targeting the most vulnerable people among us. Other scams are designed to prey on people who are desperate to believe the scam is real. Romance scams are a common type of scam that plays on a person's need to be loved. These scams involve someone pretending to be someone else. Sometimes called catfishing, romance scams often result in financial fraud.

Example Case: Nnamdi Marcellus MgBodile

In 2021, Nnamdi Marcellus MgBodile was convicted of multiple crimes, including various fraud charges, and sentenced to 13 years in prison for running romance scams that cost their victims over $5 million. MgBodile ran these romance scams, among other scams, with a group of other people. Essentially, a romance scam preys upon lonely people in an effort to siphon money from them or their families. In one of the scams involving a Virginia woman, the money was coming from a trust fund set up to take care of her children. MgBodile also ran other scams, including business email compromise scams designed to trick people into sending him money from their businesses.

Romance scams often follow familiar patterns to phishing schemes, but the romance element, especially for people who are desperate for companionship, obscures people's ability to think critically about what they're being asked to do. MgBodile was a prolific con man, but there are hundreds of examples of romance scams, and there is even a movie and a TV show dedicated to one specific type, known as catfishing.

While many people are able to find people to talk to or even romantic partners online, it is important to be able to separate what you know from what you think you know. If you are trying to meet someone in person or talk to them live on a phone call and they are resistant, that should be a red flag that they may not be who they claim they are. This does not mean you should meet everyone you communicate with online in person; that would be dangerous. It simply means that anyone you communicate with online should be treated with skepticism and suspicion. The old adage also remains true. If something seems too good to be true, it probably is. We need to educate our children and potentially our parents or other loved ones about romance scams and what types of things can happen when they trust people online. As was shown in the MgBodile case, the results can be devastating for victims. (Hollis, 2021)

Other types of scams prey upon people's innate desire to help others or to achieve some benefit for themselves. Think about how little you can verify about a person. If you have never spoken to them or met them, you know only what they tell you, and there is no guarantee that any of that information is real. Scammers love online communication because of the anonymity they are granted by default.

Next, we will shift gears to talk about how a person can practically avoid reusing passwords. Among the best tools available for this purpose are password managers.

Password managers

Most people do not understand the lessons you have learned in this book about reusing passwords and why it is so critical to have complex passwords. It is important for them to learn the importance of not reusing passwords and what can happen if they do. It is also important to familiarize them with the tools, such as password managers, that can help them. When I talk about complex passwords and using unique passwords for every site they visit, the reaction is always the same. *How will I remember all of those complex passwords?* Of course, the answer is you don't need to remember them; a password manager will remember them for you.

It is important to highlight the need to use a password manager that you trust. You are inputting all your passwords into a vault. If the vault itself is not secure, your passwords are also not safe. Choosing a password manager should be an intentional process with due diligence. You should look into the company that provides the password manager. There are some large, reputable companies that provide password manager technology. Many of them offer both free and paid versions.

This advice is valuable for evaluating all services, not just password managers. People don't create software without trying to generate some economic benefit. If you do not understand their model for how they monetize their software, that should give you pause. There is no such thing as a free service. Free social media services are gathering information about you that they can sell to advertisers. It's OK to use social media as long as you understand what you are trading for what you are receiving. Whenever you sign up for a *free* service, ask what you are trading. If you cannot answer that question, you should be wary of the service. Most legitimate password managers offer a free version, but the features are limited and there is a more feature-rich paid version. Even if you only use the free version, you know how the company makes its money.

Next, we will talk about multifactor authentication.

Multifactor authentication

Consumer multifactor authentication involves verifying your identity using a text message to your phone or a verification sent to a mobile application. While multifactor authentication can be a hassle at times, it will prevent most attacks against your account. The result is any application or service that will allow you to purchase something or log into other applications should be protected by multifactor authentication. While that seems like a small subset of services, most services in common use will do one or both of those things.

Most actors looking to compromise a consumer account will not go through the hassle of trying to defeat multifactor authentication. This is especially true when there are so many targets who do not have it enabled. In some cases, such as most consumer banking applications and websites, multifactor authentication is required. In other cases, it is optional. In most cases, it should be enabled when it is an option.

Next, we will discuss password complexity and the reason it is important.

Password complexity and why it matters

Password length and complexity are particularly effective against brute-force attacks and rainbow tables. A brute-force attack is where a system is used to try combinations of passwords until one works. This is where password length is supremely important. Each additional character increases the work factor of a brute-force attack exponentially. Using a baseline of 15 million key attempts per second, a brute-force system could crack a seven-character password in less than 10 minutes. A 13-character password using the same system would take well over 300,000 years. As computing power continues to improve, those time frames continue to come down, but longer passwords are exponentially better than shorter ones. Adding three characters to every password the next time you change it will significantly reduce the risk of a successful brute-force attack.

A rainbow table attack is an attack against commonly used passwords. Passwords are not stored as plain text; they are stored as hashes. A rainbow table is a database of common passwords that are converted to a hash. The attacker can then look for collisions and gain access to the system. Using password complexity to ensure your passwords are not common words will reduce your exposure to rainbow table attacks as well.

Of course, many passwords are compromised and if they are reused, no combination of length and complexity will protect you. However, length and password complexity can make it unlikely that you will fall victim to these types of techniques that do not rely upon compromise or social engineering.

Next, we will talk about one of my favorite topics. Many people who are concerned with their personal information being exposed in a breach are giving similar information away for free by answering surveys or posting on social media. The easiest way to protect your personal information is to stop voluntarily publishing it online.

Stop publishing your information!

Most people do not understand how valuable information about them can be. One of the practices that makes me cringe most is posts that say something to the effect of *Your rock star name is your favorite color and the street you grew up on*. When you post your *rock star name*, you have given away valuable information about yourself that may be used to steal your online identity. There are countless examples of surveys, quizzes, and similar posts that may be innocuous but could just as easily be used to harvest information about people on social media.

The reality is if you live in a developed nation there are many databases that contain information about you. Some are maintained by nation states such as China or Russia, and some are maintained by bad actors who will sell their aggregated data to the highest bidder on the dark web for a variety of purposes. While it is impossible to ensure you don't exist in these databases, you can take steps to make it more difficult for bad actors to create a comprehensive digital profile about you.

You may be thinking it is infeasible for an attacker to be reading social media posts and meticulously gathering information about everyone they encounter. That is correct, and that is not how it is done. Information is gathered in an automated fashion using a technique called scraping.

Scraping

Scraping is a method of using automated tools to gather and organize large volumes of publicly available information. Many times, aggregated data that results from scraping is mistakenly referred to as a data breach. It is not a data breach because all the information was publicly available. However, while the individual pieces of data often have little value, the aggregation of large volumes of data can be useful to bad actors. Scraping is common. There are technologies that help providers prevent others from using scraping tools on their websites, but there is little way for a consumer to know whether their favorite services use those tools and if so, whether they are effective. It should be assumed that anything you post online is visible to anyone and that they will have the ability to copy it to a data repository.

Example Case: LinkedIn "Breach"

In June 2021, reports of a large-scale data breach of over 700 million LinkedIn members were published. This was reported as a data leak of information belonging to over 90% of the LinkedIn membership. The *data breach* was made known when it was discovered that the information was available for sale on the dark web. However, none of the data was stolen; it was simply publicly available information that was scraped. The reality is this was not a data breach at all, but a highlight of the fact that anything that is posted online is public and anyone can scrape it and aggregate it for whatever purpose they choose. If someone wants access to a database of this information and is willing to pay for it, there is little to stop them from aggregating the data and putting it up for sale.

Once it was made known that no private information was stolen and the information was simply an aggregation of what was publicly available, most LinkedIn members reacted with a shrug. However, some people on social media are posting things online that they shouldn't, and these types of scraping could be damaging to them. It is important to pay attention to what you post online and assume it will live forever. (Morris, 2021) (LinkedIn, 2021)

I am certain that social media has done good in the world. Helping people connect with others or stay connected with distant family members or friends likely has a societal benefit. However, there are major dangers of social media, especially for young people.

Summary

The digital world is a dangerous place, but there are steps you can take to keep yourself and your loved ones safe online. In this chapter, you have learned about the permanence of what you post online, the façade of social media, and the dangers lurking online in the form of bullies, predators, and companies who will seek to profit off misery. You have learned about password managers, multifactor authentication, and password complexity, which are tools to help you keep your accounts safe and prevent you from falling into common security traps. Finally, you learned about the importance of keeping your personal information safe by not publishing it online.

This is the end of our journey. By this point, you are ready to make a difference in the field of cybersecurity. You understand more about the problem and ways to formulate solutions. It is my hope that reading this book has interested you in this field and that you will build on these ideas to make every organization and person you encounter in your career a little smarter, a little more cyber aware, and a little safer.

Check your understanding

1. What is a password manager? What problems does it help people solve?
2. What is multifactor authentication?
3. Explain why password length is important.
4. Explain why password complexity is important.
5. What is scraping?

Further reading

- BBC News. (2020, September 26). Molly Russell social media material 'too difficult to look at'. Retrieved from BBC News: `https://www.bbc.com/news/uk-england-london-54307976`
- Hollis, H. (2021, November 19). Marietta man who ran $5M romance scam gets 13-year prison sentence. Retrieved from The Atlanta Journal Constitution: `https://www.ajc.com/news/crime/marietta-man-who-ran-5m-romance-scam-gets-13-year-prison-sentence/OLBS6R4LVNBILJAAERHQ4IVC34/`
- Hurynag, A. (2020, January 17). Grieving dad of Molly Russell says tech giants must be forced to hand over data. Retrieved from Sky News: `https://news.sky.com/story/father-i-have-no-doubt-that-social-media-helped-kill-my-teen-daughter-11910407`
- LinkedIn. (2021, June 29). An update on report of scraped data. Retrieved from LinkedIn Press Room: `https://news.linkedin.com/2021/june/an-update-from-linkedin`
- Maivha, M. (2018, August 23). A woman loses her internship at NASA after swearing on social media. Retrieved from News 24: `https://www.news24.com/w24/work/jobs/10-people-who-lost-jobs-because-of-their-stupid-social-media-shares-20150512`

- Morris, C. (2021, June 30). Massive data leak exposes 700 million LinkedIn users' information. Retrieved from Fortune: `https://fortune.com/2021/06/30/linkedin-data-theft-700-million-users-personal-information-cybersecurity/`
- The Manifest. (2020, April 28). 79% of Businesses Have Rejected a Job Candidate Based on Social Media Content; Job Seekers Should Post Online Carefully. Retrieved from Cision: `https://www.prnewswire.com/news-releases/79-of-businesses-have-rejected-a-job-candidate-based-on-social-media-content-job-seekers-should-post-online-carefully-301048157.html`

Answers

Chapter 1

1. What makes cybercrime attractive for criminals?

   Cybercrime is a very profitable business model with relatively few risks for the attacker. The proceeds from cybercrime grow every year and it is uncommon that an attacker is caught and made to face consequences for their actions. (Section: *Why cybercrime is here to stay – a profitable business model*)

2. Why is cybercrime damaging to companies and the larger economy?

   Identity theft is a global problem costing the economy trillions of dollars per year. Intellectual property theft can be very damaging to individual companies as detailed in the American Semiconductor case. In some cases, such as the Colonial Pipeline attack, cybercrime can also cause outages in critical infrastructure. (Section: *The macro-economic cost of cybercrime*)

3. What are governments doing to convince organizations to harden their defenses?

   Regulations such as the GDPR in the European Union and the CCPA in California are examples of how governments are trying to convince organizations to better protect the information they are entrusted with. (Section: *The Role of Governments and Regulation*)

4. Choose a case study from the chapter and describe what happened in your own words.

   You may choose to describe the GozNym gang and how they stole $100 million, the Uber versus Waymo case study dealing with trade secret theft, the British Airways case study relating to a large GDPR fine, or the case related to Lennon Ray Brown and Citibank, which covered damage done to systems by a malicious insider.

5. What are the three foundational elements of cybersecurity?

   People, information, and systems. (Section: *The foundational elements of security*)

Chapter 2

1. Define well-meaning insiders and describe how security technology can support them.

   A well-meaning insider is someone who is trying to perform their job function but could make a mistake that exposes the organization to risk. Technology can be used to ensure that any mistakes they make do not cause irreparable harm to the organization. (Section: *The three types of insider threats*)

2. Describe some common social engineering techniques in your own words. Which is the most common?

   The types of social engineering techniques covered in the chapter were phishing, spear phishing, baiting, scareware, tailgating, shoulder surfing, and pretexting. Phishing is the most common. (Section: *People exploiting people*)

3. Describe some types of malicious software in your own words.

   The types of malicious software covered in the chapter were viruses, worms, trojans, ransomware, and spyware. (Section: *People exploiting people*)

4. What does lateral movement mean?

   Lateral movement refers to an attacker using access gained to one system to move to other systems on a network. Unsegmented or flat networks are most susceptible to lateral movement. (Section: *The three types of insider threats*)

5. What are some of the reasons a trusted insider may become malicious?

   In most cases, the insider becomes disenfranchised at some point, or they become motivated by potential financial gain. In either case, it is difficult to predict how or when an insider will become malicious. In every case, however, after the motivating event occurs, the insider's behavior will change. (Section: *The three types of insider threats*)

Chapter 3

1. Describe the major threat actor groups and how they differ from each other.

   The three major threat actor groups are organized criminals, primarily motivated by financial gain, state-sponsored actors, motivated to advance their national interest in some way, and hacktivists and terrorists, who use cyberattacks to advance their ideology. (Section: *Understanding the risk from targeted attacks*)

2. What are the stages of a ransomware attack?

   Gaining access to a target system, installing malicious software, spreading the infection, notifying the victim, and making demands. (Section: *Stages of an attack*)

3. How does an information theft attack differ from a ransomware attack?

   In an information theft attack, there is no need to notify the victim to monetize the attack, so it may be performed in a clandestine manner. (Section: *Stages of an attack*)

4. Which threat actor groups are likely to launch attacks with the intention of disrupting or destroying systems?

   Hacktivists and terrorists. (Section: *Understanding the risk from targeted attacks*)

5. How would an attacker use the dark web to launch a sophisticated attack?

   Attackers can find skills and resources available for sale or lease on dark web marketplaces. (Section: *Attackers for hire*)

Chapter 4

1. Describe business email compromise in your own words.

   Business email compromise is a type of malicious email message that does not have a payload but instead tries to deceive the recipient into acting against their own interests. (Section: *The most important threat vector*)

2. What is the *concept of least privilege*? What is *need to know*? How are they the same and how do they differ?

   The *concept of least privilege* refers to the idea that people should be given the minimum permissions necessary to accomplish their job function. *Need to know* states information should only be shared with those who need to know it. The primary difference between the two is that the *concept of least privilege* refers to access, while *need to know* refers to information sharing. (Section: *Time- honored best practices that could stop most breaches*)

3. What are the three factors of authentication?

   Something you know, something you are, and something you have. (Section: *Capabilities necessary in the remote world*)

4. Describe how human behavior analysis can be used to enhance your security program.

   Human behavior analysis can be used for authentication, detecting anomalies, and building adaptive security models. (Section: *The role of human behavior*)

5. In your own words, describe the challenges associated with granting users access to systems and information remotely.

   It is more difficult to verify that users are who they say they are when access is granted remotely. It is also more difficult to monitor and control how the access granted is used. (Section: *The everything, everywhere world*)

Chapter 5

1. What are the three elements of a framework for effective training?

   Frequency, or how often the messages are reinforced; content, or the messages themselves; and scope, which refers to making the training consumables. (Section: *A framework for effective training*)

2. Which are more effective, simulated exercises or informative presentations? Why?

   Simulated exercises are more effective because people often retain more information from exercises they participate in than they do from presentations they watch and listen to. (Section: *Making people your partners*)

3. Describe some of the elements of a message that could be a red flag indicating that the message is a phishing attempt.

   The phishing red flags mentioned in this chapter were the sender's address, the style and tone of the message, creating a sense of urgency, links in the message, unexpected attachments, and unusual requests. (Section: *Training people to protect against common hacking techniques*)

4. Describe some of the technologies designed to support end users in the event of a mistake.

   The technologies discussed in this chapter included URL rewriting, attachment sandboxing, browser isolation, reputation blocking, and emerging machine learning approaches. (Section: *Training people to protect against common hacking techniques*)

5. What is a tabletop exercise and why would one be valuable to an organization?

   A tabletop exercise is a simulated incident that allows a response team to practice their role in the response to an incident. It is valuable because it ensures everyone knows their role and it allows for improvements to be made in a low-stress environment. (Section: *Tabletop exercises*)

Chapter 6

1. Choose a security triumvirate and explain it in your own words.

   The three triumvirates discussed in this chapter were people, process, and technology; confidentiality, integrity, and availability; and people, data, and threats. (Section: *Security triumvirates*)

2. What are some of the challenges with the traditional information security model?

   Traditional security models often are techno-centric and do not use the security triumvirates discussed previously. Instead, they focus on the technology used and therefore are vulnerable to change. (Section: *Challenges with the traditional information security model*)

3. What is the information life cycle? What are its stages?

   The information life cycle defines the stages of the life of information in an environment. The stages are creation, storage, use, sharing, and destruction. (Section: *Protecting information*)

4. What is a workload?

   A workload is a program or application that runs on a computer somewhere. (Section: *Securing networks and workloads – past, present, and future*)

5. What are the three major categories of cloud services?

   Software as a Service (**SaaS**), **Platform as a Service** (**PaaS**), and **Infrastructure as a Service** (**IaaS**). (Section: *Securing networks and workloads – past, present, and future*)

6. How can human behavior analysis help secure identities and ensure only the appropriate access is granted?

   It is easy to impersonate a user by stealing their password. It is difficult, but possible, to defeat MFA methods. However, it is nearly impossible to be successful in an attack without deviating from a user's normal behavior patterns. (Section: *Securing identities and granting access*)

7. What is an endpoint? Can you name at least five different types of endpoint?

   An endpoint is a device that a person uses to access a network or workload. Examples include desktop computers, laptop computers, tablets, mobile phones, video game controllers, smart refrigerators, voice-activated personal assistants, and many others.

Chapter 7

1. In your own words, describe the difference between machine learning and artificial intelligence.

   Machine learning is a technique to help machines recognize patterns and automate tasks. Artificial intelligence is a broad term referring to any technique designed to allow a machine to perform a task once performed by humans. (Section: *Automation*)

2. What were the four artificial intelligence categories described in the chapter?

   Reactive machines, limited memory, theory of mind, and self-aware AI. (Section: *Automation*)

3. Why do you think organizations deploy technical solutions and not process solutions?

   Generally, technical solutions only require a person to choose from a list of options, whereas process solutions require more effort and thought. (Section: *Too much technology with too little process*)

4. What are the four types of risk treatment? Provide a brief description and an example of each.

   Risk acceptance (doing nothing), risk avoidance (stopping the risky activity), risk transference (insurance), and risk mitigation (information security). (Section: *What are we trying to accomplish?*)

5. What is a material risk factor? How would you determine whether a risk is material or not?

   A material risk factor is one that could cause irreparable harm to an organization. A risk materiality matrix is one way to determine whether a risk factor is material or not. (Section: *What are we trying to accomplish?*)

Chapter 8

1. What is the lowest cost basis for a cybersecurity task in any organization?

   Automation. (Section: *Defining automation opportunities*)

2. What types of questions are AI solutions well positioned to answer, and which do they struggle with?

   AI solutions are best positioned to automate mundane, repetitive tasks and struggle with making decisions that require context. (Section: *Defining automation opportunities*)

3. What are some of the ethical challenges with AI systems?

   The three ethical challenges identified in the chapter were bias in datasets, protecting privacy, and behavior modification. (Section: *Gathering data and applying context*)

4. What are the quadrants of the confusion matrix?

   False positive, false negative, true positive, and true negative. (Section: *Testing the systems*)

5. Which type of documentation of a manual process indicates that an automation opportunity is ready for coding?

   A decision matrix. (Section: *Defining automation opportunities*)

Chapter 9

1. What is a password manager? What problems does it help people solve?

   A password manager stores passwords for different services in an encrypted vault. It helps solve the problem of password reuse. (Section: *Password managers*)

2. What is multifactor authentication?

   Multifactor authentication refers to using two or more of the following categories to identify a user: something you know, something you have, and something you are. (Section: *Multifactor authentication*)

3. Explain why password length is important.

   Each additional character in a password raises the effort required to crack the password using brute-force methods exponentially. (Section: *Password complexity and why it matters*)

4. Explain why password complexity is important.

   Adding additional types of characters helps to increase the number of possibilities for the characters in a password, making it more difficult to crack using brute-force methods. (Section: *Password complexity and why it matters*)

5. What is scraping?

   Scraping is a technique that allows someone to aggregate information from a public website automatically. (Section: *Stop publishing your information!*)

Index

A

D

E

F

G

H

I

L

M

N

O

P

R

S

Packt

Packt.com

Subscribe to our online digital library for full access to over 7,000 books and videos, as well as industry leading tools to help you plan your personal development and advance your career. For more information, please visit our website.

Why subscribe?

- Spend less time learning and more time coding with practical eBooks and Videos from over 4,000 industry professionals
- Improve your learning with Skill Plans built especially for you
- Get a free eBook or video every month
- Fully searchable for easy access to vital information
- Copy and paste, print, and bookmark content

Did you know that Packt offers eBook versions of every book published, with PDF and ePub files available? You can upgrade to the eBook version at packt.com and as a print book customer, you are entitled to a discount on the eBook copy. Get in touch with us at customercare@packtpub.com for more details.

At www.packt.com, you can also read a collection of free technical articles, sign up for a range of free newsletters, and receive exclusive discounts and offers on Packt books and eBooks.

Other Books You May Enjoy

If you enjoyed this book, you may be interested in these other books by Packt:

Cybersecurity Leadership Demystified

Dr. Erdal Ozkaya

ISBN: 9781801819282

- Understand the key requirements to become a successful CISO
- Explore the cybersecurity landscape and get to grips with end-to-end security operations
- Assimilate compliance standards, governance, and security frameworks
- Find out how to hire the right talent and manage hiring procedures and budget
- Document the approaches and processes for HR, compliance, and related domains
- Familiarize yourself with incident response, disaster recovery, and business continuity
- Get the hang of tasks and skills other than hardcore security operations

Cyber Warfare – Truth, Tactics, and Strategies

Dr. Chase Cunningham

ISBN: 9781839216992

- Hacking at scale – how machine learning (ML) and artificial intelligence (AI) skew the battlefield
- Defending a boundaryless enterprise
- Using video and audio as weapons of influence
- Uncovering DeepFakes and their associated attack vectors
- Using voice augmentation for exploitation
- Defending when there is no perimeter
- Responding tactically to counter-campaign-based attacks

Packt is searching for authors like you

If you're interested in becoming an author for Packt, please visit `authors.packtpub.com` and apply today. We have worked with thousands of developers and tech professionals, just like you, to help them share their insight with the global tech community. You can make a general application, apply for a specific hot topic that we are recruiting an author for, or submit your own idea.

Share Your Thoughts

Now you've finished , we'd love to hear your thoughts! Scan the QR code below to go straight to the Amazon review page for this book and share your feedback or leave a review on the site that you purchased it from.

`https://packt.link/r/1803248637`

Your review is important to us and the tech community and will help us make sure we're delivering excellent quality content.

Printed in the USA
CPSIA information can be obtained
at www.ICGtesting.com
LVHW060336300823
756654LV00003B/187

9 781803 248639